Global Arms Race and Its Economic Impact

GLOBAL ARMS RACE and Its Economic Impact

Rajesh Kumar

PRASHANT PUBLISHING HOUSE
DELHI-110094

Published by :
Prashant Publishing House
C-34, 28 Foota Road, Gali-3,
West Karwal Nagar, Delhi-110094
Phone : 011-22963970, Mob. : 9810396373
e-mail.: prashantpublishinghouse@gmail.com

Global Arms Race and Its Economic Impact
Reserved
First Published 2016

ISBN 978-93-80565-68-2

PRINTED IN INDIA
Published by Mr. R.K. Jha M/s Prashant Publishing House and Published at H.S. Offset House Press, Delhi.

Contents

Preface

Global Arms race, a pattern of competitive acquisition of military capability between two or more countries. The term is often used quite loosely to refer to any military buildup or spending increases by a group of countries. This definition requires that there be a competitive nature to this buildup, often reflecting an adversarial relationship. The arms race concept is also used in other fields.

Expenditure for arms, like any public expenditure, is made at cost to other possible use. Notably, it is made at cost to private capital use. This proposition is accepted by economists. Indeed, it is central in the general thought of the economists of the present American administration. The freeing of revenues now used for public purposes is deemed vital for private capital improvement–for the revitalization of the American industrial plant. The point, however, is not stressed as regards our military outlays. Although we have occasionally heard reference to the way military expenditures draw resources from other public needs, we have heard much less–there has been something approaching a conspiracy of silence or neglect–of the way these expenditures have contributed to our industrial decline.

Global Arms Races are frequently regarded as negative occurrences in both economic and security terms. Large-scale arms acquisitions require considerable economic resources. If two countries spend large sums of money just to cancel out each other's efforts, the expenditure might well be seen as wasted.

The arms race consumed non-renewable natural resources. It contributed to environmental degradation, especially through radioactive pollution. In the long run, the arms race may have undermined individual standards of morality, the resolve to defend freedom and democracy, and the civilian character of our society. The arms race has been used to justify Soviet and American imperialistic tendencies, thereby indirectly killing untold millions of human beings and keeping billions in political, psychological, and economic chains. It may be that the arms race contributed to America's move during the past two decades towards a government of the rich, by the rich, for the rich.

The Global has given highest main concern to the reduction and eventual removal of the weapons of mass destruction. This book also reflects briefly on ongoing global arms race, arms trade and increasing military expenditures and defence budgets of global nations.

In today's global world maximum loss of all sorts is being caused by ongoing conventional wars, conventional weapon system, conventional arms race, small arms and light weapons.

—*Editor*

1

Introduction

MILITARY EXPENDITURE, DEBT AND DEVELOPMENT

In most developing countries government revenues are insufficiently elastic to be able to accommodate rising military expenditures. In this situation a government has three options; it can reallocate expenditures from other government expenditure headings such as health and education; it can borrow foreign exchange in the international financial markets; or it could do a combination of these. In all three situations there is an opportunity cost in terms of development. Opportunity costs can be defined as the benefits foregone by selecting one option at the expense of another or several others. In a world where resources are scarce, choice implies sacrificing something. The benefit that could have been derived from the alternative, not chosen, is the opportunity cost of the option actually selected.

The UNDP has for some time utilised opportunity cost analysis in an attempt to understand the effect of military expenditures on sustainable development. In its Human Development Report 1994 it argued that the allocation of scarce national resources to military expenditures had incurred a huge loss of potential spending on human development, observing that 'some of the poorest African countries now spend more on defence than they do on their populations' education and health.' Military expenditure influences growth and development in a number of direct and indirect ways. By redirecting government expenditures away from education and health it has an indirect effect on human capital formation. Excessive military expenditure affects the balance of payments situation and levels of infrastructural investment, while large purchases of military equipment from foreign suppliers can distort the balance of trade situation.

Current Military Expenditure Trends in Developing Countries

In general, measuring military expenditures in developing countries is difficult, and in some cases impossible, because of the general lack of transparency and accountability in government accounting procedures and the resistance of authoritarian regimes to revealing their military expenditure accounts. For instance in 1996 no African country reported its military expenditures to the UN under the Reporting Military Expenditures programme. The IMF's latest audit of government finances, published in late 1997, gave 1996 figures on the military budgets of only Burundi, Madagascar, Mauritius, Tunisia and Zambia.

Nevertheless, considerable effort has been made by organisations such as the International Institute for Strategic Studies (IISS) to provide some sort of statistical account of military expenditure trends within the developing world. According to the IISS Military Balance in 1997 Sub-Saharan African expenditure was $8.8bn, a slight increase over the 1996 level, and accounted for around 3.3% of regional GDP. In Southern Africa and East Africa military expenditure has been on the increase largely as a result of recent acquisitions of weapon systems. Botswana's 1998 security budget was $323m, accounting for 11.5% of government expenditure. The armed forces accounted for about two thirds of the budget, with the rest being allocated to policing expenditure. Namibia's 1998 military budget was N$443m ($89m), up from N$416m in 1997. Botswana and Namibia are involved in a border dispute over Kasikili-Sedudu and Sintungu islands in the Caprivi strip of the Linyanti-Chobe river, so their recent arms acquisitions have raised concern within the region.

The Angolan government had an estimated budget of $380m in 1998, about 10% of government spending, although final outlays will probably be higher due to the continuing conflict with UNITA.

Military and police spending in Mozambique continues to decline, although it still consumes 19.4% of government expenditure, down from about 38% of government expenditure during the height of the war in the 1980s. Zimbabwe's military expenditure of $456m in 1997/98 dramatically increased because of a one-off disbursement of $210m to war veterans, and is certain to increase because of its involvement in the Congo conflict.

Within the Southern African region, South Africa's military expenditure and budgets, at around R11bn ($1.9bn) for each of the years 1996 to 1999, dwarfs all other military budgets. Current plans to purchase $4.8bn worth of military equipment will reinforce its overwhelming balance of military power within the region and contribute to neighbouring countries' growing concerns over South Africa's hegemonic intentions. In East Africa, military expenditure continues to grow in Uganda, which is engaged in war with the Democratic Republic of Congo and is contending with guerrilla insurgency operations in the north of the country. The 1998 budget was $153m, 26% higher than in 1997. In Tanzania the combined military and police budget of $311m accounted for 23% of the government budget. In Sudan, where civil war wages on relentlessly, the military budget is thought to account for 80% of government expenditure.

In addition to the formal military expenditures, there is a high degree of off-budget funding of military activity in many sub-Saharan African countries, most notably in the procurement of military equipment and the funding and expenditures of armed opposition groups and mercenaries. In the Middle East and North Africa, regional military expenditures increased between 1996-1997 by some 5% in real terms despite declining oil revenues. At an average of 7%-8% of GDP, the region continues to spend significantly more than any other region of the developing world. Countries increasing their military expenditure include Algeria, which is engaged in a vicious civil war, Iran, where rising expenditure is covering a number of expensively produced indigenous weapon systems and Saudi Arabia, UAE and Qatar, which are all involved in importing expensive state of the art weapon systems. Israel has a military budget of $7bn, accounting for between 10%-12% of GDP, and is a major market for US weapon systems. The region remains the largest and most lucrative arms market in the world for sales of advanced weapon systems. Regional arms deliveries in 1997 were estimated at $17bn.

Military spending in Central and South Asia showed a growth of 3% in real terms in 1997, from $18.7bn in 1996 to $19.2bn in 1997. India and Pakistan account for over 80% of regional military expenditures. Military expenditure as a proportion of GDP was around 5% in 1997, higher than anywhere else except the Middle East. In East Asia and Australasia military expenditures have been significantly affected by the financial crisis and fell by about 5% in real terms in 1997, from $149bn in 1996 to $142bn in 1997 (1997 prices). The depreciation of East Asian currencies against the dollar increased the cost of foreign imports forcing some countries to cancel orders for expensive weapon systems.

High levels of state and non-state military expenditure and the purchase of arms have done little to enhance the security of the majority of citizens in the developing world. Since 1945 more than 20 million people have died in wars and internal conflicts, a large proportion of these in the developing world. The UNDP maintains that 'countries spending very little on defence and much more on human development have been much more successful at defending their national sovereignty than those spending heavily on arms'. By way of illustration it compares the relatively peaceful experiences of Botswana, Costa Rica and Mauritius with the conflicts afflicting Iraq, Myanmar and Somalia.

Arms Sales

The reliability of data on arms sales to the world's poorest countries is even less conclusive than the information on military expenditures. Since 1994, statistical records of most government to government transfers of major conventional weapons are recorded by the UN Register of Conventional Arms Transfers. Of the 44 countries in Sub-Saharan Africa only Ethiopia, Mauritius, Namibia, Seychelles, South Africa and Tanzania reported their arms transfers, military holdings and domestic procurement to the UN Register on Conventional Arms in 1997.

The figures below on the regional distribution of arms transfers to the developing world produced by the IISS should only be taken as trend indicators as much of the data available only provides a partial picture of the actual scale of transfers.

Table: Regional Distribution of International Arms Transfers 1987 and 1997

	1987 ($m)	*% of world market*	*1997 ($m)*	*% of world market*
Middle East/& N. Africa	33,232	37.5	15,629	33.7
East Asia	10,531	11.9	14,693	31.7
South Asia	6,534	7.4	1,669	3.6
Latin America	5,319	6.0	1,982	4.3
Sub-Saharan Africa	6,791	7.7	991	2.1

Source: IISS Military Balance 1999

Arms sales to Sub-Saharan Africa are particularly difficult to quantify as the majority of transfers go unreported, particularly as the categories of light weapons and ammunition, which constitute a significant proportion of arms procurement in the region, are not currently included in any of the existing data bases on arms transfers. Light weapons and ammunition are supplied by local industries as well as by international suppliers, but more significantly there is a large trade in recycled weaponry from past conflicts for personal use, as well as for use by statutory and non-statutory forces. This latter form of trade is particularly hard to track and thus to quantify. Under these conditions it is very difficult, if not impossible, to measure in any statistical way the scale of transfers into conflict zones in the developing world.

The main sources of supply for conventional arms are from a handful of industrialised states which comprise the Permanent Members of the UN Security Council-the US, France, UK, Russia, China. In addition there are a number of newly industrialising countries such as Israel, Brazil and South Africa which have become recent entrants into the international arms market. Since the end of the Cold War, a huge second hand market in weapon systems has also emerged with large supplies coming from former Warsaw

Pact countries. Developing countries continue to be the primary focus of foreign arms sales activity by the major weapons suppliers. According to Grimmett, during the years 1989-1996 the value of arms transfer agreements with developing nations comprised on average 67.5% of all such agreements worldwide. The value of all arms transfer agreements with developing nations in 1996 was some $19.4bn, which represented the first increase in arms sales since 1992. In 1996 the United States was the biggest exporter, having sales agreements worth $11.3bn, the UK with agreements worth $4.8 was in second place, and Russia with sales agreements worth $4.6bn ranked third.

The influence wielded by military industrial elites of the supplier states and their drive to export, created by the need to maintain employment in domestic military industries and generate returns from large outlays incurred on domestic weapons procurement projects, ensures that certain violent and repressive regimes such as Indonesia, Nigeria and Pakistan have been able to acquire weapons with relative ease. In part, these patterns of transfers derive from patronage relations established during the Cold War which have endured despite expectations of a new and positive world order.

Patronage not withstanding, a contradictory trend is discernible amongst those Northern states which support the principles of conflict prevention, development and good governance, yet place little if any unilateral restraint on the export of arms to developing countries. There are some signs that measures are being taken to rectify this anomaly in the international community's dealings with post-conflict and conflict-prone societies. The recent adoption of a 'security first' approach, for instance, is based on the notion that security should no longer be considered discrete and unrelated to other spheres of foreign policy, but should instead form part of an integrated approach by donors.

One cannot conceive of an effective conflict prevention policy that does not tackle the problem of arms supplies. At present no multilateral system for controlling sources of supply of major weapons systems exists, as there is for nuclear, chemical, biological and intercontinental ballistic missiles. Even less control exists for light weapons which have caused most of the casualties in war in the developing world since the end of the Cold War. Nevertheless there are a number of initiatives that are likely to come to fruition in the next few years that may rectify this hiatus.

Spurred on by the success of the global campaign to outlaw anti-personnel mines which resulted in the signing of the Ottawa Treaty in December 1997 by more than 120 states, a number of interesting initiatives have been advanced with a view to controlling the flow of light weapons.

Support has been gaining momentum for a convention on the prevention of the illegal use of light weapons, aimed principally at establishing strict criteria to govern the export, collection and destruction of surplus armaments and at promoting more transparent international co-operation.

In this spirit the UN Panel of Governmental Experts on Small Arms has recommended a number of practical measures to reduce the quantity of weapons in circulation and to curb future acquisitions of small arms, including establishing a regional information-sharing network: providing assistance for democratic internal security forces and assisting post-conflict initiatives related to disarming and demobilising regular and irregular forces.

In May 1998, a UK-government-sponsored conference entitled 'Developing Controls on Arms and Illicit Trafficking in Southern Africa' examined ways of developing a regional action plan for Southern Africa, aimed at controlling light weapons proliferation and diffusion. The programme is to be supported by the European Union (EU).

Other initiatives by the EU, including the establishment in 1997 of its Programme for preventing and combating illicit trafficking in conventional arms and the adoption of an EU Code of Conduct in June 1998, are a step in the right direction. But it is important to recognise that current initiatives remain inadequately developed and in need of sufficient resources and greater co-ordination at regional and international levels. In the coming decade the challenge will be to enhance and empower these initiatives so that they become the foundations of a new multilateral arms control regime.

Debt and Conflict

Sub-Saharan Africa may only account for a small share of the global arms market but nowhere else is the relationship between debt, development and the arms trade so stark. The profligate policies of military regimes and the widespread proliferation of conflict on the continent have contributed to a high incidence of HIPCs on the continent. In fact 31 of a total of 41 HIPCs are located on the African continent. Moreover, of the countries identified by the World Bank as HIPCs over half are involved in, or have recently emerged from, conflict situations. Those countries currently engaged in either interstate or intra-state conflicts include Angola, Central African Republic, Chad, Republic of Congo-Brazzaville, Democratic Republic of Congo, Ethiopia, Guinea-Bissau, Guinea, Liberia, Sierra Leone, Senegal, Somalia, Sudan and Uganda. Note that all of the above are located in sub-Saharan Africa.

Five countries-Burundi, Mozambique, Nicaragua, Rwanda, and Yemen-are undergoing the fragile process of transition from war to peace, while Vietnam and Lao are still suffering from the effects of conflict which ended over 20 years ago, not least because of the large presence of mines, which affects agricultural production and the return of displaced peoples. Other severely indebted countries such as Nigeria, Kenya and Myanmar are experiencing serious internal instability. In other words, 23 of the 41 HIPC countries, that is over half of the world's poorest, most indebted countries are, or have recently experienced conflict. Many HIPCs are currently ruled, or have been ruled in the recent past, by highly militarised, authoritarian regimes. These include Bolivia, Central African Republic, Chad, Democratic Republic of Congo (formerly Zaire), Kenya, Liberia, Mali, Myanmar, Uganda and Zambia. A report produced by Jubilee 2000, entitled Dictators and Debt, has drawn attention to the fact that one fifth of all developing country debt consists of loans that were given to compliant dictators.

The Cost of Conflict

The cost of conflict to development has been systematically analysed in recent years. The economic consequences of war are multiple and complex. They can be divided into immediate human costs and the longer-term development costs. This division is somewhat artificial because human costs such as the deterioration in nutrition and education, the loss of life and depletion of skills constitute development costs, while developmental costs such as destroyed infrastructure and negative growth are among the causes of human suffering and deprivation.

In Southern Africa the sustained costs incurred through the destabilisation campaign waged by apartheid South Africa on its neighbouring states has been estimated to total $115bn. With the end of the Cold War the Southern African region has witnessed the withdrawal of superpower intervention, the end of apartheid, the termination of conflict in Namibia and Mozambique, a thirty percent decline in regional military expenditure and the demobilisation of tens of thousands of soldiers. However, the debts and cost of destruction that accumulated during the Cold War will remain a burden for generations to come. Children not yet born will have to pay the price of debt for wars they did not fight, for ideas they do not hold, for a regional and global system that no longer exists and for decisions made by regional and world leaders no longer in power.

Conflict contributes to debt, but by the same token unsustainable debt poses an ongoing and insidious threat to the well-being and security of millions of people in the developing world. Scarce national resources are siphoned away from poverty alleviation to service debt, enriching the creditors of the affluent Western world. At least 20 of the most heavily indebted poor countries (HIPCs) transfer more than one-fifth of their revenues to creditors in the developed world. In 1995 Africa's external debt amounted to $328bn of which approximately 45% was owed to official bilateral sources, 30% to official multilateral sources, and 25% to commercial lenders. In order to service this debt fully, African countries paid Western governments and external commercial lenders more than 60% ($86.3bn) of the $142.3bn in revenues generated from their exports. In fact, African countries paid more than 17% ($25.4bn) of their total export earnings to these creditors, but this still left a total of $60.9bn in unpaid arrears.

UK POLICY TOWARDS THE ARMS TRADE, DEBT AND DEVELOPMENT

As a leading OECD economy with a strong presence in the UN Security Council, the G8, the Paris Club and the EU, the UK government is highly influential in setting the international climate on issues concerning debt, development and the arms trade. Although there have been many progressive reforms in certain aspects of the UK's foreign policies towards the developing world, as this section attempts to show, there is a lack of coherence in the Labour government's current policies towards debt, development and the arms trade.

Development Policy

In November 1997 the Department for International Development (DfID) published the first White Paper on Development to be produced by a UK government for 22 years. The White Paper defined DfID's central mission to support the internationally agreed target to halve the proportion of the world's population living in abject poverty by the year 2015. To achieve this goal, DfID quickly realised that it would have to address one of the major obstacles to development, namely conflict and the highly militarised regimes that dominate many of the world's poorest countries. The DfID Departmental Report 1999 states that 'A major obstacle to the eradication of poverty is the persistence of violent conflict, or its legacy, in many of the poorest countries. Reducing the incidence, duration and effect of armed conflict is essential. DfID's policy for conflict reduction seeks to strengthen political and social systems to enable disputes and grievances to be resolved without recourse to violence.'

As part of this programme DfID has identified security sector reform as a priority for its development agenda. Given the controversial policies of the ODA (DfID's former incarnation) in supplying aid to sweeten arms trade deals, Clare Short, the Secretary of State for International Development, has been emphatic that no UK development assistance should be used to reinforce the role of the military or support arms sales, 'There is obviously no question ...of development resources being used to strengthen the aggressive capability of military forces or being linked to arms sales. Our interest is in helping to secure a security sector of appropriate scale that is properly accountable to democratic, civilian authorities.' A central objective of security sector reform is to reallocate military resources to social need. In the words of Clare Short 'In too many countries, a bloated security sector soaks up resources that would be better used elsewhere. And resources spent on excessive procurement and perks for the military mean the denial of essential public services for the poor.'

In pursuit of these objectives Clare Short has emphasised the importance of co-ordinating DfID's efforts with other government programmes such as the Foreign and Commonwealth Office programme of Assistance to Support Stability with In-Service Training (ASSIST) and the Ministry of Defence's (MoD's) Defence Diplomacy Programme. She stressed that 'Co-operation is essential in this area of policy, as in others such as trade or debt, to ensure that our Government's influence is used coherently in international affairs.' A problem that DfID is likely to encounter, however, is that the coherence in international affairs so necessary to the success of security sector reform simply does not exist between or even within Whitehall departments.

The UK Government and its Debtors

The UK government has been at the forefront of arguing the need for reform of the HIPC Initiative, and it has initiated debt cancellation in a number of cases on a bilateral basis. Yet the UK government has a track record of providing financial support to facilitate arms sales to unsavoury regimes, and as yet this pattern does not appear to have been altered. More than one third of all debt owed to the UK government is owed by Nigeria, which amounts to £3bn. Loans were extended to Nigeria while it was under a military dictatorship. Sudan, which is fraught with conflict, is the UK's fourth largest debtor owing £382m. The military regime in Algeria owes the UK £166m which was lent by the UK after the results of the democratic election were annulled. The Democratic Republic of Congo with its history of authoritarianism, human rights violations, corruption and cronyism owes £134m to the UK government.

A large percentage of UK bilateral debts have been incurred through the Export Credits Guarantee Department (ECGD). The ECGD is an independent department under the responsibility of the Secretary of State for Trade and Industry. Its main function is to promote UK exports abroad by guaranteeing payment to UK exporters in the case of a default by foreign customers. It takes on risk that the private sector is not prepared to accept. For the exporter this is an insurance policy. If an importing country does not pay, then the ECGD pays the supplier. A significant percentage of ECGD credit is made available to underwrite UK arms exporters. Between 1994-97, 20% of UK export credits were allocated to cover arms sales.

Many of the existing loans to unsavoury dictators were made under the former Conservative administration whose foreign policy practices came under considerable public scrutiny towards the end of its term. On taking power Robin Cook, the Secretary of State for Foreign Affairs, announced a new mission statement for the Foreign and Commonwealth Office which stated that 'Our foreign policy must have an ethical dimension and must support the demands of other peoples for the democratic rights on which we insist for ourselves. The Labour Government will put human rights at the heart of our foreign policy'. Many areas of foreign policy are undergoing a process of reform to reflect this new ethical commitment, but in the area of the ECGD continuity rather than change appears to characterise current practices.

Some of the most controversial ECGD decisions to have been made under the Labour government are those to cover recent arms sales to the incumbent Indonesian regime, currently facing financial crisis. There are of course strong moral and ethical issues for not exporting arms to Indonesia, which have been elaborated elsewhere. But there are also strong reasons to question the sagacity of the Labour government's decision not to withdraw ECGD cover to Indonesia given the endemic corruption within the former Suharto regime and the Golkar Party which remains in power. A recent World Bank internal document revealed the corruption which resulted in the embezzlement of vast loans meant for Indonesian development since 1997. One third of the loans worth

$24bn, intended for infrastructure projects, disappeared into the pockets of the Suharto regime. By extending cover to the current regime the UK government confers a high degree of legitimacy on a regime with a track record of heavy-handed militarism, corruption and human rights abuse, and which does not conform to DfID's policies on conflict resolution, humanitarian assistance and development.

UK Arms Trade Policy

Nowhere is the contradiction between the UK government's development goals and foreign policy objectives more at odds than in its arms trade policy. In July 1997 Robin Cook committed the FCO to a 'responsible' arms trade policy. He pledged to introduce tougher restrictions on arms exports and to play a constructive and leading role in pressing for a European Code of Conduct on arms exports. In theory at least, the Labour government has committed itself to restricting the sale of weapons to regimes that might use them for internal repression or external aggression, and is attempting to increase accountability and transparency in decisions on export licences. In addition the government has undertaken to reform existing legislation on strategic export controls and was instrumental in setting up the EU Code of Conduct which includes a set of eight Common Criteria for Arms Exports that EU governments must take into consideration. One of these is 'the respect of human rights in the country of final destination'.

Complementing the Foreign Office's 'ethical policy' on the arms trade, DfID has adopted a policy which links the arms trade to development. In its 1999 Departmental Report it has categorically recognised the relationship between arms supplies and conflict: 'The supply of weapons, particularly small arms, continues to fan the flames of conflict. In parallel with the FCO's work on developing a Code of Conduct for Arms Exports, we have tried to help developing countries and regions deal with the problem of illicit trafficking. We have supported seminars in central and Southern Africa to agree measures for tackling arms proliferation'.

In reality, however, the improvements in the government's unilateral and multilateral approaches to arms control appear to have done little to stem the flow of weapons systems to developing countries. According to IISS estimates, the arms trade grew by some 12% in 1997, bringing real growth between 1995 and 1997 to some 36%. In 1994 the UK exported $5bn worth of arms, by 1997 this had increased to $8bn. This contrasts with the general decline in arms export values that were sustained from 1987 to the early 1990s. The UK was the second largest exporter of arms in 1997, accounting for 18.5% of the global market and has in no small way contributed to the growth in arms deliveries particularly to the developing world.

The surge in arms exports reflects deliveries to the Gulf States-particularly Saudi Arabia's $11bn military imports which included the delivery of 36 Tornados and 20 Hawk trainer aircraft built by British Aerospace. Arms deliveries to East Asia also peaked in 1997. Whether primarily pursuing geostrategic interests or propelled by the profit motive, as a supplier state the UK has indirectly supported highly militarised regimes such as the Suharto regime in Indonesia, the Saudi family in Saudi Arabia, the military dictatorship in Nigeria. All these countries have been condemned for human rights abuses by Human Rights Watch and Amnesty International. Apart from conferring a high degree of political legitimisation to these repressive regimes, UK arms sales encourage regimes to spend scarce national resources on weapon systems rather than on development objectives. In this way arms sales promoted by the Defence Export Services Organisation of the MoD undermine the development objectives of DfID. Detailed illustration of the contradiction in the government's policy towards arms transfers, debt and development are to be found in their policies towards to Sierra Leone, Kenya, Indonesia and South Africa.

INDIA ABSTAINS AND EXPOSES THE ARMS TRADE TREATY

Once again India has been forced to abstain from voting in favour of a discriminatory global Arms Trade Treaty (ATT) – after its unpleasant experience with the NPT and the CTBT in the past. The treaty, aimed at laying down common international standards and limiting the illicit sale of conventional arms, was passed by the UN General Assembly with an overwhelming majority of 154 votes on April 3, 2013. Iran, North Korea and Syria voted against the treaty while China, India and Russia abstained.

As the largest importer of arms in the world1, India objects to the ATT on several counts. First and foremost, India finds it difficult to accept that the treaty will enable arms exporting countries to impose unilateral conditions on the countries that import arms. The treaty has failed to address Indian concerns about the illegal transfer of arms to terrorist organisations, insurgent groups and other non-state actors who oppose democratically elected governments. The treaty also does not ensure a "balance of obligations" between arms exporting states and the importers of arms.

As a country with a pacifist strategic culture, India has traditionally abhorred the export of arms and itself refrained from doing so for several decades after independence. India has 39 Ordnance factories, which are wholly government owned, and eight Defence Public Sector Undertakings (DPSUs). India's defence exports are less than two per cent of the total production of weapons and equipment and were valued at USD 191 million (Rs 859.60 crore) in 2008-09. These are mainly indigenously produced surplus small arms and light weapons that have been supplied to some of India's neighbours as a goodwill gesture. However, the new Defence Procurement Policy (DPP) and the new Defence Production Policy (DPrP) are encouraging the formation of joint ventures with 26 per cent foreign direct investment (FDI). This is expected to go up to 49 per cent, gradually resulting in an increase in arms exports as MNCs will begin to use their Indian joint ventures as hubs for sourcing weapons and equipment components for their factories abroad.

India is likely to spend approximately USD 100 billion for the import of weapons and defence equipment over the next 10 years. The DPP stipulates an offsets commitment of 30 per cent of the total value of a contract if it exceeds USD 66 million (Rs 300.00 crore). In fact, the offsets obligation specified for the multi-mission, medium-range combat aircraft (MMRCA) is 50 per cent of the total value, which is estimated to exceed USD 12 billion. Assuming that 60 to 70 per cent of the import contracts will exceed USD 66 million, defence MNCs exporting to India will be required to procure items worth approximately USD 18 to 21 billion from Indian companies over the next 10 years by way of direct and indirect offsets. Even though the items that may be exported by these MNCs and joint ventures will be mainly components and not fully assembled weapons system, India needs to ensure that the stipulations of the ATT do not bar such exports.

South Asia is arguably the second most dangerous global hotspot after West Asia and radical extremism in the Af-Pak area is making the region further dangerous. One of the major reasons for this is the large-scale proliferation and easy availability of small arms and light weapons (SALW).

India has witnessed around 152 militant movements since independence, of which 65 are believed to be still active in one form or the other. Pakistan is still the primary source of small arms that are India bound.

It uses SALW as political and military tools against New Delhi and facilitates smuggling of SALW both through sea and land routes to ISI-supported terrorist organisations and sleeper cells across India. Funding for SALW proliferation can be accredited to money laundering and safe havens abroad organised through hawala channels. The transfer of small arms takes place mostly through clandestine routes and the grey market.

The Chinese angle to SALW proliferation in South Asia also cannot be ignored. Chinese weapons gained immense popularity among the insurgent groups in the region as they were competitively priced and low-level officials offered counter-trade agreements. The Chinese weapons pipeline soon permeated into Myanmar's underground markets along the Thai border. Beginning with the Type 56 rifle, China produced and offered for sale five different varieties of rifles (Type 56, 68, 79, 81 and 5.56 Type CQ), allied light machine guns and sub-machine guns. China also became the prime official supplier to Sri Lanka, Myanmar and Pakistan (including anti-aircraft and anti-tank weapons). Significantly, large numbers of weapons of Chinese origin have been seized in Cox's Bazaar in Bangladesh.

The Chinese supplied small arms to Indian insurgent groups in Manipur, Mizoram, Nagaland and Tripura for many years up to the late-1970s. In a statement with far reaching consequences, India's Home Secretary, G K Pillai, said on November 9, 2009, that the Maoists in India were receiving small arms from China, "Chinese are big suppliers of small arms…" Earlier, then Union Home Minister P Chidambaram had said in an interview in October 2009 that the Maoists were acquiring weapons through Bangladesh, Myanmar and possibly Nepal since the Indo-Nepal border is a porous border.

Since 1989-90, Indian security forces have seized huge stocks of arms and ammunition along the LoC in J&K alone. It has been documented that between 1990 and 2005, as many as 28,000 assault rifles of the AK-47 series; 1,300 machine guns; 2,000 rocket launchers; 365 sniper rifles; 10,000 assorted pistols; 63,000 hand grenades; seven million rounds of ammunition; 6,200 land mines and IEDs and 37,000 kg of explosives were recovered from various hideouts in J&K during counter-proxy war operations. Large-scale recoveries are still being made. Large numbers of illegal arms also comes into the country through the north-east and from the Khyber-Pakhtoonkhwa province (NWFP) on Pakistan's Afghan border. India finds itself at the centre of two major international weapons warehouses—the NWFP and the Southeast Asian arms market comprising Thailand, Cambodia and Myanmar, with approximately 13 identified gun-running routes close to India's north-eastern border areas and the Chittagong hill tracts.

Countries exporting arms have a responsibility to ensure that they do not provide weapons without strict end user verification or else SALW may be diverted to wage intra-state conflict by non-state actors. The ATT should have refrained from imposing new norms; it should have reinforced the existing obligations and responsibilities of all countries under international law and should have provided a mechanism for their effective application to the trade in SALW.

The present treaty is also deficient on monitoring and verification. While initially monitoring may have to rely on the good practices of the member states, viable technical means need to be developed over time. Subsequently, the treaty must make provisions for intrusive international monitoring of sources, means of transportation of weapons and, where possible, their end use based on formal complaints being launched by affected state parties. Such a system can only be implemented by constituting an international body like the IAEA.

India accords immense importance to compliance with arms control, non-proliferation and export control regimes, even though India is not a signatory to some of them. Hence, an initiative like the ATT, that seeks to establish a global benchmark, would under normal circumstances have been welcomed and supported, but the treaty has turned out to be discriminatory.

The government of India has instituted stringent controls for the export of arms, including the requirement of an end-user certificate from the country to which SALW are to be exported. Each request is thoroughly vetted before an arms export license is cleared by the government.

India ensures that no arms are exported to countries that are involved in conflict, or to non-state actors engaged in intra-state conflict. In fact, most arms exports out of India so far have been those of goodwill gestures towards friendly countries in India's neighbourhood. Despite repeated requests from Sri Lanka and at the risk of driving it into Chinese or Pakistani arms, India had steadfastly refused to supply offensive weapons when the Sir Lankan armed forces were engaged in fighting the LTTE. Only non-offensive equipment like air defence guns and radars were supplied.

Elaborating on the complexity of small arms proliferation, former UN Secretary General, Kofi Annan had stated perceptively, "Small arms proliferation is not merely a security issue; it is also an issue of human rights and of development." The moral argument for an ATT, one that underpins human security, social and economic development is overwhelming. However, if it is viewed through the prism of disarmament or arms control instrument, it will not find much support. While India has not voted in favour of the ATT, it will undoubtedly adhere to all its provisions, much as it has done in respect of the NPT and the CTBT.

UN ARMS TREATY: A SORE SPOT FOR INDIA'S MILITARY

On April 2, a landmark treaty regulating the U.S. $70 billion conventional weapons trade was approved by the 193-member United Nations General Assembly in New York. Besides regulating business in conventional arms, the UN Arms Trade Treaty – which received 154 votes – aims to link sales of arms to a country's human rights record. The treaty also prohibits states from exporting conventional weapons in violation of arms embargoes, or weapons that would be used for acts of genocide, crimes against humanity, war crimes or terrorism.

No wonder then, that chronic human rights abusers Syria, Iran and North Korea became the only three countries voting against the treaty. However, several key powers abstained from voting, including Russia, China and India – taking the gloss off what was otherwise a historic vote.

While India's abstention disappointed many who were hoping to see the world's largest democracy sign on to an important normative framework to regulate the global arms trade, it is fair to say that it was borne out of hard-nosed realism.

As the world's largest conventional arms importer in 2012, representing 12 percent of all global imports, New Delhi is a significant stakeholder in the global arms trade. At the heart of India's abstention were concerns that its military – which relies heavily on foreign arms imports – could be affected adversely by unilateral decisions by arms exporters.

Explaining India's position, its chief negotiator Sujata Mehta said, "India cannot accept that the Treaty be used as an instrument in the hands of exporting states to take unilateral force majeure measures against importing states without consequences."

India's worry stems from the concern that once the treaty comes into effect, the nation's bilateral defense agreements could come under the treaty's purview. Article 7 of the resolution gives broad powers to the exporting country to make arms supply contingent upon an "export assessment" that could be abused to halt supplies. Without adequate safeguards, New Delhi deems the treaty to be skewed in favor of exporting nations.

More importantly, India's abstention highlights its over-dependence on foreign arms amid a failure on its part to meet its own defense needs via domestic production. Currently, India buys over 70 percent of its arms requirements from the international market and is expected to spend U.S. $100 billion over the next decade on arms purchases.

This over-reliance on foreign arms amid a number of high-profile cases of corruption in defense purchases have slowed and even threatened the modernization of India's military, prompting India's Defense Minister A.K. Antony to call for increased indigenous defense production in February.

By contrast, other major arms importers like China have made impressive strides in increasing domestic production. A report released by the Stockholm International Peace Research Institute (SIPRI) in March notes that China has replaced the United Kingdom to become the fifth largest arms exporter in the world, boosting its share of world arms exports from 2 percent to 5 percent between 2008-2012, an increase of 162 percent.

Indeed, China's massive military modernization drive has been matched by progress in the development of its military industry. However, India has failed to create a viable domestic arms manufacturing base, despite increasing its military spending in recent years. Part of the problem stems from its failure to create a strong policy environment that would allow the private sector to play a larger role in the defense industry. This problem has been compounded by vociferous opposition from public-sector unions. Pending reforms, defense manufacturing in India remains under the purview of state-owned firms such as the Defense Research Development Organization (DRDO), which have been a byword for chronic inefficiency. DRDO's major projects, including a program to build light combat aircraft as well as airborne early warning systems, are behind schedule by up to 13 years.

If anything, the approval of the arms trade treaty and India's reservations about it should serve as a wake-up call for New Delhi to make concerted efforts to overhaul its domestic defense industry. This means allowing private players to play a leading role in research and development, driving innovation in the sector.

THE MILITARY-INDUSTRIAL COMPLEX IS RUINING THE ECONOMY

Everyone knows that the too big too fails and their dishonest and footsy-playing regulators and politicians are largely responsible for trashing the economy. But the military-industrial complex shares much of the blame. Nobel prize winning economist Joseph Stiglitz says that the Iraq war will cost $3-5 trillion dollars.

Sure, experts say that the Iraq war has *increased* the threat of terrorism. See this, this, this, this, this, this and this. And we launched the Iraq war based on the false linkage of Saddam and 9/11, and knowingly false claims that Saddam had WMDs. And top British officials, former CIA director George Tenet, former Treasury Secretary Paul O'Neill and many others say that the Iraq war was planned *before* 9/11. But this essay is about dollars and cents. America is also spending a pretty penny in Afghanistan. The U.S. admits there are only a small handful of Al Qaeda in Afghanistan. As ABC notes: U.S. intelligence officials have concluded there are only about 100 al Qaeda fighters in the entire country.

With 100,000 troops in Afghanistan at an estimated yearly cost of $30 billion, it means that for every one al Qaeda fighter, the U.S. will commit 1,000 troops and $300 million a year. Sure, the government apparently planned the Afghanistan war *before 9/11*. And the Taliban offered to turn over Bin Laden. And we could have easily killed Bin Laden in 2001 and again in 2007, but chose not to, even though that would have saved the U.S. hundreds of billions of dollars in costs in prosecuting the Afghanistan war. But this essay is about dollars and cents.

The methods of awarding contracts for research and development reflect an even sharper departure from regular business practices. Again, some of the basic ideas may have been produced by cooperation between the prospective contractor and the scientific branches of the armed forces in which such requests originate. However, eventually the job is put out for proposals (which are major engineering tasks in themselves). The need to produce proposals has had a profound effect on the employment structures of military contractors. Technical proposals must be quite detailed. In them the prospective contracting firm gives an overview of its understanding of the job, describes the methods it would use to solve the problems, and tries to impress the government with an elaborate presentation of previous experience. That kind of exercise resembles the proposals that universities submit as part of grantsmanship more than any normal kind of business negotiation. In any case, the details of facilities and managerial organization that bidders must include in proposals of this sort go far beyond what a business would normally submit in contracting privately. (The government's power over the firm's internal affairs affects not only what is made but also methods and quantities as well, as will be explained later.)

A good technical proposal alone, however, is not all there is to winning a contract. To be considered eligible to submit a bid, a firm must be on the list of approved bidders. Inclusion in a list depends upon various considerations; one factor appears to be that certain firms are thought of as "belonging" to a particular unit of the armed services. For one of these regular bidders, it might be considered real diversification to supply a different command within the Air Force, or perhaps the Navy rather than the Army. In practice, each firm functions as an unofficial division of the Pentagon conglomerate or one of its parts.

The relationship between a contractor and its military sponsor is a peculiar one. For the company, having once won a military contract puts it in a position tantamount to engagement, or at least going steady. Once a unit of a company has become dependent upon military orders, its military controllers view with disfavor any efforts to diversify into commercial areas. The company is supposed to stay true to its military benefactor and grateful for a glance of favour. This outlook epitomizes the usual negative reaction of military industrial contractors to the subject of possible conversion or diversification away from dependence on the military.

How to Make It

The control of the "state management" over methods of production is at least as pervasive as its control over products. The ASPR takes four pages to list the areas over which the government exercises direct control. More than just technical surveillance of the item is concerned; one would expect technical standards to be imposed for any specialized, technically oriented equipment. Machine firms, for example, are certainly used to having customers' inspectors on the premises to see how the job is progressing. Engineering firms doing work on contract have customers' representatives among them to keep track of the design and procurement. Technical specifications often go into considerable detail on materials to be used and standards for quality, inspection, and performance.

However, the government control over military contractors goes much further than that. Not only are technical aspects covered in minute detail, but aspects of the operation of the firm (such as wage structure, insurance, benefits) are also fair game for the government to evaluate and inspect. (These considerations affect quantity of output required as well.) To some degree, this watchfulness on the part of the government could be attributed to the fact that the contracts are on a cost-plus basis. But the functional controls appear to go beyond even that. The subcontractors are all subject to similar rules, varied according to the nature of their work. The controls may apply only to the prime contractor if the item being supplied by the subcontractors is a standard one, similar to their usual commercial product. The control structure is so marvellously pervasive that it is worth studying carefully. Many a firm made up of many divisions would consider such a centrally determined and controlled list of characteristics an extremely onerous form of centralization of the kind that has been heavily criticized in textbooks on management. Be that as it may, this control is certainly unparalleled elsewhere in the American economy.

How Much to Build

Concerning the quantity of items to be manufactured for the military, three considerations diverge radically from determinants in the commercial sector. As mentioned, the functions of research and production are kept separate. This means that regardless of what organization did the research, another may eventually be responsible for production. This separation is conducive to inefficiency, wasted lead-time, and even outright flaws of production. Costs and quantities may be disproportionate to effort, and accurate projections of amounts are out of the question.

The government gains further control as it prescribes precisely how much of each item is to be produced. Normally, private management jealously guards the prerogative of deciding the quantity to be produced. The decision is reached by assessing such factors as the needs of the market to be served and its prospects for expanding, or the likelihood of new markets or market segments opening. The most important single variable in making the decision is the physical scale of manufacture.

In military procurement, however, the firm enjoys no such discretion. Unless the government alters its requirements, there is no way of changing the quantities. Although it may at times be possible for a firm to alter specifications slightly, there is no way of changing the size of the market except by political process. A limited market thus sets limits on production.

But perhaps most important, in a military setting the quantity to be procured cannot be determined rationally. The quantity depends upon a great many extrapolations, particularly in a time when (as government leaders are constantly assuring us) the product is designed solely to deter something or other, rather than to be used. Such overkill as has been endemic to military procurement for more than 25 years precludes using market saturation as an overall limit, so items are ordered to some extent just to maintain the industrial base. Some of that reasoning appears to hark back to the dear dead days of Rosie the Riveter in World War II, when a major war could be won on the production lines of America. Here, of course, enters the military predilection for refighting an old war. The Department of Defence cannot and should not assume the responsibility for creating a level of demand adequate to keep the economy healthy and growing. Nor should it, in developing its programs, depart from the strictest standards of military need and operating efficiency in order to aid an economically distressed company or community. This principle is, of course, violated continually; at any rate, whenever a weapon is proposed, its proponents invariably contend that it will produce jobs, and politicians present it as a plum for their constituents, even though most other activities are well known to produce more jobs for a given investment. Keynesianism is evidently alive and well at the Pentagon, whatever stern supply-side or monetarist precepts are in favour elsewhere.

At What Monetary Value

One of the tiresome cliches of recent times is, "If they can send a man to the moon, why can't they... ?" It makes its way into all kinds of discussions of industrial change, and even into advertising copy. It was used for the original promotion of Brim, the decaffeinated coffee, with the reassuring voice-over, "Consider it done."

The principal fallacy in this comparison, of course, is that there is no way of determining ahead of time how much a trip to the moon ought to cost, whereas other technically oriented developments (such as techniques of desalinating seawater) require precise economic parameters if they are to compete. In the case of weapons, as with lunar flight, no such assessment is possible in a rational way, even though it is obvious that there is some limit to the resources that can be devoted to military purposes. The price that society is willing to pay for progress is thus essentially a political decision. It simply is not an economic decision that can be based on needs and demand; decision makers, whether managers of enterprises or individual citizens, cannot verify possible results in advance.

Even if competition were fully feasible, however, the fact is that for many years, some 80 percent of all contracts have been negotiated rather than being put out for competitive bidding. Even with bidding, the specifications for the job (especially in research contracts, but also in manufacturing) are often written after the buying agency has consulted with a favoured prospective bidder. Any other firm whose proposal is solicited is thus trying hopelessly to guess the punchline of an incompletely told joke.

Such a firm, referred to as playing second fiddle in a one-man band, has no real chance, but must nevertheless bear the very real costs of competing. The different form of pricing of military economics is imposed upon society mainly through the system of using cost-plus-fixed-fee contracts, customary in military procurement.

In settling a price for a negotiated contract, the prospective contractor and the contracting officers have a mandate to base their final agreement on reasonable costs plus a standard fixed fee for profit. During World War II, contracts based on cost plus a fixed percentage led to considerable abuse; such contracts have Long been illegal.

However, now considerable leeway is allowed for engineering changes; these are the main cause of cost overruns. Once a large amount of money has been expended on a project that falls short of expectations, it becomes difficult and embarrassing to simply abandon it. Instead, more and more money is pumped into it by way of engineering changes—which in many cases include a provision for additional profit. The job thus seems to continue, in Jonathan Swift's apt phrase, "driven on equally by hope and despair."

All of these special considerations have had the effect of starkly distinguishing the military industrial firm from the conventional private enterprise. The latter is, broadly speaking, a cost-minimizing and profit-maximizing entity, regardless of long-range and short-range effects. By contrast, the military industrial firm maximizes sales or subsidy. The contract structure itself is a disincentive for cost saving. Occasionally the government has made attempts to provide incentives for performing on time and within budget. For some contractors this has meant juggling costs between various accounts so that as many accounts as possible could qualify for the incentive payments. This finagling is of great concern to the government auditors (who, consistent with the general head-office-versus-division arrangement, are a strong presence among the major military contractors). The emphasis in such firms on maximizing subsidization is the reason that they stockpile engineering talent. As long as it can reasonably be charged to a job in house, the stockpiling costs nothing extra—and having the resources available may help in securing a new contract. Overemployment is thus endemic in the military industrial firm.

2

Global Arms Trade

Unsurprisingly, the West dominates the world arms market in terms of sales. Over the last six or so years, the US has towered over the other countries in weapons sales, clocking up $49,271 million worth of sales (at 1990 prices) between 1996 and 2000. Its nearest competitor, Russia, made $15,690 million worth in the same period, but a large majority of these were of second hand weapons.

According to SIPRI, just under half of all transfers (movements) of major conventional weapons between 1996 and 2000 came from the US, Russia and France each accounted for 10 per cent, and Britain and Germany each accounted for between five and 10 per cent. The seven following biggest sellers-the Netherlands, Ukraine, Italy, China, Belarus, Spain and Israel-accounted for around 15 per cent of the world total transfers between them.

So it is clear that the global arms market is controlled by just a few players. The six biggest arms selling countries-four of whom, ironically, are permanent members of the UN Security Council-accounted for almost 85 per cent of all arms transfers I over the last six years.

The top 7 largest arms companies, in terms of military sales. The figures in italics represent the percentage of arms in total sales for each company. Figures for arms sales are in US $ billions at constant (1998) prices and exchange rates. Selection of top arms-purchasing countries between 1996 and 2000. Figures are trend-indicator' values expressed in US $ millions, at constant (1990) prices.

THE GLOBAL SMALL ARMS MARKET

Small arms require a special mention in any assessment of the global trade in armaments, simply because they are so prolific, the trade in them is so difficult to control and the devastation caused by them is so severe. Taking the definition of the UN panel of government experts on small arms, the category includes all of the following military, police and domestic weapons: revolvers and self-loading pistols, rifles and carbines, assault rifles, sub-machine guns and light machine guns, heavy machine guns, hand-held under-barrel and mounted grenade launchers, portable anti-tank and anti-aircraft guns, recoilless rifles, portable launchers of anti-tank and antiaircraft systems, and mortars of less than 100 mm caliber. So there are plenty of them, and they are everywhere. They are used by police and security patrols, by national armies and by guerrilla and revolutionary groups, they are carried by civilians legally in a number of countries, for sport in many more, and illegally in every country. They feature in practically every armed conflict between nation-states, in internal and civil wars, in gang fighting and as status symbols.

They are so prolific because they are small and relatively cheap, easy to pass on, smuggle, hide, steal, capture from an enemy or buy over the counter. But, they are ubiquitous because of the sheer numbers they are produced in: millions of them, every day, all over the world. It is a myth that the trade in small arms is only one of recycling second-and third-hand weapons. New production merely creates more second-and third-hand guns. In 1999, 45 different countries reported to the UN that firearms, components and ammunition were legally produced in their territories for domestic or export markets. Many more countries didn't respond to the requests for information. The main producers of these little killers are China, Russia and the US. Another 20 or so countries, mainly in Europe and Asia, produce most of the rest of the world's supply. A further 29 countries produce nominal quantities mainly to meet their domestic never be accurate data on which countries have the most of them. Even if there were, accurate figures for exactly which of these were legal, illegal, military or civilian would be impossible to determine.

'The total number and global distribution of small arms remains one of the greatest enigmas in the field of international peace and security', says the Small Arms Survey. The Survey is a project of the Graduate Institute of International Studies in Geneva, which has attempted to profile and estimate the proliferation of firearms (hand-held guns and rifles, rather than hand-held missile launchers and the like), based on rough estimates and incomplete reporting by countries.

Their research estimates that there are at least 550 million legally-held firearms in the world today-at least one gun for every 11 of the world's people. Over half of all of these are privately owned. The group was unable, not surprisingly, to estimate the number of illegally-held arms in the world. The 20th century was the most violent one in human history. Not only did it witness two world wars, and 30 years of major arms-fuelled tension between the world's superpowers, it also featured hundreds of localized conflicts, armed border disputes, civil wars, military coups and counter coups, revolutionary struggles and armed invasions.

According to the Armed Conflicts Report 2000 and the State of the World Report 1999, there were 40 armed conflicts underway in 36 different countries as the 21st century was born. Even in the short time since the millennium, the world has witnessed a new 'war on terror' waged by the US and its allies against Afghanistan, with the threat of extension to Somalia, and the possibility of intensified attacks on Iraq. Earth is a planet at war, and to a large extent this is a consequence of the legal and illicit sale of arms. In crude but plain terms, without weaponry, combat would be more limited in scale. In most conflict zones in the world, war is a way of life. Waging war is a means of generating money, exerting political power, and providing employment. In some areas of the developing world, children grow up knowing nothing else but bloodshed, dead, injured or maimed relatives, the daily risk of landmines; even bearing arms themselves. If they survive long enough to procreate, their own children will know only the same.

War today

Despite tension between India and Pakistan, the future stability of the world is probably now less at risk from an all-out nuclear catastrophe-as was thought during the Cold War era-than from a slow, insidious, systematic proliferation of small wars and local strife in mainly smaller nations, many of them in Africa. In 1998, Africa suffered 11 major armed conflicts. It is now the most war-torn region in the world. Those small wars are created and sustained in a constant battle to control territory, plunder resources and wield power. William Hartung, of the World Policy Institute, illustrates the problem. When the current Liberian president Charles Taylor invaded Liberia on Christmas Eve in 1989, he did so with just 100 irregular soldiers, armed with AK47 rifles. Within months they had seized mineral and timber resources and used the profits to purchase more light weapons: the first few turns in an ongoing vicious cycle.

According to Hartung: 'This pattern of war as plunder has been repeated with local variations in Sierra Leone, where the Liberian-backed Revolutionary United Front (RUF) has used diamond sales to fuel its campaign of terror; in Colombia, where government forces, right-wing paramilitaries and anti-government rebels have skimmed off profits, fees and bribes from the cocaine trade; in Angola, where UNITA rebel forces have raised billions of dollars through diamond sales and the Angolan Government has countered by stocking its arsenal with revenues drawn from its large offshore oil deposits."

The seizure or trafficking of drugs, diamonds and other valuable commodities produces profits for warring factions. Profits are spent not on peace, reconciliation or education, but on more weapons-bought on the illicit market, and through more 'legitimate' channels. The weapons suppliers to the perpetrators of the 1994 genocide in Rwanda included brokers and shippers in Britain, South Africa and France, working with collaborators in Albania, Belgium, Bulgaria, Egypt, Italy, the Seychelles and the former Zaire (now DR Congo/DRC). Arms and military training are also supplied to warring or revolutionary factions, both openly and secretly, by Western nations to serve their own political ambitions.

Bigger picture

But the arms trade also has a role in sustaining larger, more 'official' tensions and conflicts between states. The deadly dealing increases strains and thereby fuels wars between established nations. Here are some examples. From 1989 to 1998, the US provided over $227 million in weapons and training to African military forces. Of this, over $111 million went to governments that have been directly or indirectly involved in the war in the Democratic Republic of Congo (DRC): Angola, Burundi, Chad Namibia, Rwanda, Sudan, Uganda and Zimbabwe. The big seven arms-selling countries in the world-the US, France, Germany, Britain, Russia, China and Italy have all sold arms to states currently involved in conflict including Sri Lanka, Indonesia, Israel, China, Taiwan, India and Pakistan. And they usually show their deadly wares at arms fairs.

Military training

Military training Military training is an aspect of the industry often overlooked by campaigners and politicians working towards arms control. Yet the provision of training to foreign armies, or warring factions, is commonplace and was clearly illustrated with the allied forces' training and assistance given to the Afghan United Front forces during their reclaiming of Afghanistan at the end of 2001. Just as with the hardware, military training is used by governments to further their strategic and political objectives, as well as being a tool in international relations. But like arms sales, military training of foreign fighters can also bounce back. Since the US armed forces are among the most highly trained and best financially supported in the world, it is no surprise that the US is a major provider of military training. Here's an example. Towards the end of his presidency, Bill Clinton took a special interest in Africa. His proposed 'new partnership' was not to supply aid or help build civil society as was hoped, but apparently to establish a wide program of troop training. In 1998, the US provided $45.8 million in international military education training (IMET) for over 400 African soldiers.

ARMS EXPORTERS

One of the most marked aspects of major arms transfers over time is the stable composition of the list of the five biggest suppliers, with only slight changes in the ordering. For the period 1980–

1984, when global arms transfers were at the highest, the Soviet Union, the United States, France, the United Kingdom and Germany accounted for 84 per cent of all exports. The five largest suppliers of major conventional weapons for the period 2004– 2008 were the USA, Russia, Germany, France and the UK. These suppliers accounted for 78 per cent of world exports for this period, compared with 81 per cent for the period 1999–2003. The USA and Russia remain by far the largest exporters. More than a third (37 per cent) of US deliveries of major convention weapons for the period 2004–2008 went to the Middle East, including around 207 combat aircraft and over 5000 guided bombs. Several major new deals were under discussion in 2008, including the sale of Patriot Advanced Capability-3 (PAC-3) and Terminal High Altitude Area Defence (THAAD) antiballistic missile (ABM) surface-to-air missile systems to the United Arab Emirates (UAE).

Russia's arms exports were 14 per cent higher in 2004–2008 than in 1999– 2003, although its overall share of the global market remained roughly the same. Around 71 per cent of Russian arms were exported to the Asia–Pacific region for 2004–2008, with deliveries of advanced combat aircraft and naval vessels to China and India accounting for a considerable share. At the same time, deliveries to Africa and Latin America have increased by around 200 per cent and 900 per cent, respectively. The majority of these transfers went to Algeria and Venezuela.

The volume of Germany's arms exports increased by 70 per cent between 1999–2003 and 2004–2008, and its share of the global market rose from 7 per cent to 10 per cent. Much of this increase was due to exports to European destinations, which grew by 123 per cent. Greece and Turkey accounted for nearly a third of German exports. In recent years, both countries have received Leopard-2A4 tanks and licensed produced Type-214 submarines. For the period 2004–2008, 40 per cent of France's arms exports went to states in the Middle East. For the second year in a row, there were no outstanding orders for newly built French combat aircraft. However, France was reported to be in advance negotiations for deals with Libya and the UAE. The UK's largest customers in recent years have been the USA and India, which accounted for 21 per cent and 14 per cent, respectively, of British transfers for the period 2004–2008. India is in the process of receiving 66 Hawk-100 trainer aircraft and 20 Jaguar-S combat aircraft from the UK. In 2009 the UK began the delivery of 72 Typhoon combat aircraft to Saudi Arabia, which will help to cement its position among the top five suppliers.

While countries in other parts of the world may lack modern defence industries, they can still provide surplus or second-hand equipment, or newly produced but less technologically advanced weapon systems such as SALW and their related ammunition.

Arms importers

In contrast to the largest suppliers, the group of the largest recipients of major conventional weapons has varied more over the years. In addition, relative to the largest suppliers, the largest recipients account for a smaller share of the total market due to the large number of minor recipients. For the period 1980–1984 the five largest recipients of military equipment—Iraq, India, Libya, Syria and Egypt—accounted for 26 per cent of total imports. For the period 2004–2008 the top 5—China, India, the UAE, South Korea and Greece—accounted for 35 per cent of all imports. This change illustrates a shift in the major arms import markets over the past 30 years from the Middle East to Asia. However, recent data indicates that this process may be reversing, with the Middle East again emerging as a major destination for military equipment. Nonetheless, in recent years the composition of the list of largest recipients has remained relatively stable. China and India were the world's two largest arms importers for both 1999–2003 and 2004–2008. The most significant change in the composition of the five largest arms importers in recent years has been the entry of the UAE, which rose from being the 16th largest importer in the period 1999–2003 to being the third largest for the period 2004–2008.

Africa

African states accounted for 7 per cent of international imports of major conventional weapons over the period 2004–2008, compared with 6 per cent for 1999–2003. During the period 2004–2008, Algeria and South Africa were the two largest arms importers in Africa, accounting for 35 per cent and 27 per cent, respectively, of the continent's imports. The third largest recipient of major conventional weapons was Sudan, which accounted for 8 per cent of Africa's imports. Excluding South Africa, arms transfers to countries in sub-Saharan Africa accounted for only 2 per cent of the world total for the period 2004–2008. However, even small volumes of transfers of major conventional weapons can have a significant impact on conflict dynamics in the region. Deliveries to Algeria in 2008 included the last of 180 T-90 tanks and an estimated 18 of a total of 28 Su-30MK combat aircraft, both purchased from Russia. Two Project 636 Kilo Class submarines and a significant number of air defence systems are also on order from Russia. Morocco, Algeria's neighbour and long-term rival, embarked on a significant military modernization programme in 2008, ordering 24 F-16C combat aircraft from the USA, large FREMM frigate from France and 3 smaller SIGMA-90 frigates from the Netherlands.

Chad's arms imports were five times higher over the period 2004–2008 than in 1999–2003, although globally it remains a minor recipient. Weapons delivered to Chad in 2008 included the first of 6 Su-25 ground-attack aircraft from Ukraine and the last of approximately 82 armoured vehicles from Belgium. Sudan, which has tense relations with Chad, took delivery of an estimated 10 Su-25 aircraft from Belarus.

During 2007 and 2008 Ukraine delivered an estimated 110 T-72 tanks and 11 BM-21 multiple rocket launchers to Kenya. In September 2008 a consignment of 33 T-72 tanks and 6 BM-21 launchers en route from Ukraine to Kenya was hijacked by Somali pirates. The cargo was held for four months, during which time there was much speculation that its final destination was intended to be the government of Southern Sudan, rather than Kenya, despite Kenyan and Ukrainian protestations.

The Americas

States in the Americas accounted for 11 per cent of imports of major conventional weapons over the period 2004–2008, compared with 8 per cent for 1999–2003. Transfers to South America were 94 per cent higher in 2004– 2008 than in 1999–2003. The USA was the largest importer of conventional weapons in the Americas for the period 2004–2008, and the seventh largest in the world, up from 14th place for 1999–2003. Chile was the largest importer of conventional weapons in South America for the period 2004–2008 and the 11th largest in the world, up from 36th for 1999–2003. Several states in South America are undergoing force modernization programmes, indicating that the volume of transfers to the region will remain high. Most significantly, in December 2008 Brazil signed an •8.6 billion ($11.3 billion) agreement with France for the licensed production of 50 EC-725 helicopters, 4 conventional submarines and 1 nuclear-powered submarine.

For the period 2004–2008 Venezuela was the world's 18th largest recipient of military equipment, up from 55th place for 1999–2003. In 2008 the final delivery took place of many weapons that had been ordered from Russia in 2006 and 2007, including the last of 24 Su-30MK combat aircraft. During 2008 there was considerable speculation regarding follow-on deals with Russia, but no new contract was signed.

Almost half of US imports for the period 2004–2008 came from EU member states. Nominally, European products have been favoured over rival US products in several recent high-profile competitions, including for EC-145 helicopters and C-27J transport aircraft. However, most of the actual production under these contracts will take place in the USA.

Asia

Asian states received 37 per cent of all transfers of major conventional weapons in the period 2004–2008, compared with 40 per cent for 1999–2003. Transfers to East Asia (including South East Asia) accounted for 67 per cent of transfers to Asia in 2004–2008, those to South Asia for 25 per cent, to Oceania for 7 per cent and to Central Asia for only 1 per cent. Three of the four largest importers for 2004–2008 globally are Asian states: China, India and South Korea. Transfers of major conventional weapon systems to China in 2007 and 2008 were less than half their average annual volume in 2002–2006. The volume of deliveries to Taiwan has also fallen, dropping by 44 per cent between 1999–2003 and 2004–2008. However, in late 2008 the USA agreed to a long-discussed weapon package for Taiwan. The volume of deliveries to Pakistan has increased significantly in recent years. Forty-one per cent of all transfers to Pakistan over the past 5 years took place in 2008. Over the period 2004–2008, 40 per cent of Pakistan's imports of major conventional weapons came from the USA. Significant deliveries in 2008 included M-109A5 155-mm artillery systems, P-3CUP Orion maritime patrol aircraft and F-16A combat aircraft. South Korean imports of major conventional weapons were 61 per cent higher in 2004–2008 than in 1999–2003. In 2007 and 2008 South Korea was the world's largest importer of major conventional weapons. The USA accounted for 73 per cent of arms transfers to South Korea for the period 2004–2008, including long-range F-15K combat aircraft along with engines and other components for South Korean-designed aircraft and ships.

Europe

European states received 24 per cent of all transfers of major conventional weapons for the period 2004–2008, compared with 26 per cent for 1999– 2003. EU member states accounted for 19 per cent of global arms imports over the period 2004–2008 and 17 per cent over the period 1999–2003. The largest importer of major conventional weapons in Europe in recent years has been Greece. However, it has fallen from being the third largest recipient of major conventional weapons for the period 1999–2003 to fifth place for 2004–2008. Turkey has fallen from being the fourth largest recipient of major conventional weapons for the period 1999–2003 to eighth place for 2004–2008. Turkey signed a number of significant deals in 2008, including those for 6 Type-214 submarines from Germany and 51 A-129 combat helicopters from Italy, which will be produced under licence in Turkey.

Arms transfers to Georgia received a significant amount of media attention in the run-up to the conflict over South Ossetia in August 2008. Georgian arms imports were nearly four times higher over the period 2004–2008 than for 1999–2003. The largest supplier of arms to Georgia was Ukraine, which accounted for 65 per cent of transfers over the period 2004–2008. During 2004–2008 states in Europe imported an estimated 211 combat and ground-attack aircraft, compared with total world imports of over 1300.

During 2008 there were at least 10 European states with ongoing competitions for combat aircraft acquisitions. However, a number of these deals may be delayed, downsized or cancelled as a result of the global financial crisis.

The Middle East

Middle Eastern states received 18 per cent of international transfers of major conventional weapons for the period 2004–2008. Transfers to the region were 38 per cent higher in 2004–2008 than in 1999–2003. During 2004– 2008, 34 per cent of all transfers to the Middle East went to the UAE, while Israel received 22 per cent and Egypt 14 per cent. Despite significant speculation about Iran's arms import plans, it accounted for only 5 per cent of transfers to the Middle East for the period 2004–2008 and was the 27th largest recipient of major conventional weapons worldwide.

During the period 2004–2008 the UAE was the largest recipient of major conventional weapons in the region and the third largest in the world. Imports in this period included around 80 F-16E combat aircraft from the USA and around 50 Mirage-2000-9 combat aircraft from France. The UAE placed a number of significant orders in 2008 and looks set to remain a significant importer in the coming years.

During the period 2004–2008 Iraq was the world's 28th largest recipient of major conventional weapons, with 40 per cent of its imports coming from the USA. In 2008 Iraq ordered 140 M1A1 tanks from the USA and announced plans to obtain advanced combat aircraft and additional armoured vehicles. Israel's arms imports in 2004–2008 consisted primarily of 102 F-16I combat aircraft and related air-to-air and air-to-surface weapons. The vast majority of weapon systems ordered by or transferred to Israel during this period came from the USA, mostly in the form of military aid. Israel also imported components for its weapon systems from a variety of countries, including EU member states.

CAMPAIGN AGAINST ARMS TRADE

Campaign Against Arms Trade (CAAT) is a UK-based NGO and campaigning organisation working towards the abolition of the international arms trade. Founded in 1974 by a broad coalition of peace groups, CAAT is united in opposition to the military industrial complex and the growth of the private military industry. It argues that these organisations reinforce global militarism whilst undermining attempts by civil society and the United Nations to resolve disputes peacefully. CAAT's main focus is to end the influence of arms companies over the UK government, and works together with similar organisations in other countries to the same end. CAAT has grown in stature in recent years as a result of several high profile campaigns, particularly its legal challenge against the Serious Fraud Office's decision to suspend a corruption investigation into BAE Systems in 2007.

Current Issues

BAE Systems and Saudi Arabia Corruption Inquiry

BAE Systems formerly British Aerospace, is the world's third largest weapons trader. In September 1985 BAE was a signatory to the UK's largest ever arms deal, the Al Yamamah contract to provide military planes as well as servicing provisions to the government of Saudi Arabia. This ongoing contact has evolved through several phases to the present day and has thus made the company £43 billion pounds.

Shortly after the contract was signed however, corruption allegations began to surface concerning bribes paid to Saudi officials through a £60 million pound slush fund. On 12 September 2003 the Serious Fraud Office began an investigation into possible corruption. BAE are also the subject of four active SFO investigations for its dealings in Romania, the Czech Republic, South Africa and Tanzania, calling into question the general operating conduct of its agents. However on the 14th December 2006 the Government discontinued the Al Yamamah probe on the grounds that its conclusions may embarrass the Kingdom of Saudi Arabia and threaten Britain's national security.

CAAT in conjunction with the Corner House, an anti-corruption NGO, mounted a legal challenge to this decision, to assess if in curtailing the Serious Fraud Office's investigation the Government had acted illegally. Thus on 9 November 2007 the

High Court in London granted a request for a judicial review of the decision. Subsequently, on the 10 April the conclusion of this review stated that the Government had indeed acted illegally in stopping the corruption investigation. Lord Justice Moses and Mr Justice Sullivan ruled that the Government had capitulated under intimidation from the government of Saudi Arabia and that "no-one whether within this country or outside, is entitled to interfere with the course of justice." BAE Systems continue to deny any impropriety stating the court had failed "to distinguish between a commission and a bribe."

Subsequently the SFO launched an appeal that was heard before the Appellate committee of the House of Lords on 7 and 8 July 2008. On the 30th July the House of Lords overturned the High Courts' ruling, and decreed that the SFO had acted lawfully in the interest of national security.

Senior Peer Lord Bingham of Cornwall stated that "the director's decision was one he was lawfully entitled to make" but the ruling incited a chorus of condemnation from Nick Clegg in the House of Commons. The leader of the Liberal Democrats characterised the verdict as "a legal licence for international blackmail." The ruling also provoked considerable ire among anti-corruption campaigners and a string of NGO's. CAAT spokesman Symon Hill commented "BAE and the government will be quickly disappointed if they think that this ruling will bring an end to public criticism. Throughout this case we have been overwhelmed with support from people in all walks of life. There has been a sharp rise in opposition to BAE's influence in the corridors of power. Fewer people are now taken in by exaggerated claims about British jobs dependent on the arms trade. The government has been judged in the court of public opinion."

In response to the judicial review the Government has drafted a controversial clause of the Constitutional Reform Bill. This will grant the attorney-general the power to quash any further such investigations with immunity from judicial interference. CAAT and the Corner House have both condemned any such legislation as a perversion of justice which will erode the accountability of the executive and threaten the rule of law.

Closure of DESO

The Defence Export Services Organisation was an adjunct of the Ministry of Defence concerned with procuring contracts for private military companies to export arms to foreign governments. The closure of DESO had been a core campaigning aim of CAAT since its inception in 1974, and was their main focus in 2006. CAAT brought considerable pressure on the government concerning the ethics of some such trading, given that in 2004, UK arms export licenses were granted to 13 of the 20 'major countries of concern' identified by the Foreign and Commonwealth Office in its 2005 Human Rights Annual Report. CAAT also alleged that DESO unfairly privileged the interests of the arms companies and helped facilitate bribes to foreign officials. In response to this on 25 July 2007 Gordon Brown announced that DESO would indeed be shut down.

Chief Executive of BAE Systems Mike Turner condemned the decision by citing the damage it would do to Britain's export trade. CAAT argued that the closure of DESO is a step forward in transparency for the government. As a result it will be less hamstrung by lobbyists seeking to manipulate its human rights and budgetary policies.

In future export promotion will be the responsibility of UK Trade and Investment, the body that supports all UK exports. On 1 April 2008 the UKTI Defence and Security Organisation, which will be responsible for some of DESO's previous functions, was formed. The current head of UKTI DSO is Richard Paniguian CBE, a former BP executive. CAAT has pledged to monitor UKTI to make sure that military exports, (less than 2% of total UK exports in 2004), do not monopolise a disproportionate amount of its resources.

DSEi: Reed Elsevier Campaign

Defence Systems and Equipment International is one of the largest arms fairs in the world which takes place in London bi-annually, the last occurring in September 2007. From 2003 to May 2008 the DSEi was organised by Reed Elsevier, a publishing and information company, who acquired the previous organisers

Spearhead in 2003. As CAAT is opposed to the existence of arms fairs, it campaigned to encourage Reed Elsevier to extricate itself from the arms industry. There followed a sustained and concerted effort from academics, doctors and writers that use the company's products, who demanded they end their involvement with arms fairs on ethical grounds. This culminated in Reed's decision to sell its arms fairs to Clarion Events in June2007, a sale which was completed in May 2008

However, CAAT intends to continue campaigning for the overall closure of DSEi and other arms fairs.

Clean Investment Campaign

From universities to local authorities CAAT has consistently sought to highlight areas where public bodies hold shares in companies trading in arms. On 9 July CAAT released research that 75 local authorities in the UK held such investments through their pension funds.

It has argued that many council employees reject the notion that they should help to prop up such companies and continues to advocate a more ethical investment strategy. The long standing Clean Investment campaign has had many successes in the past, one of the most significant occurring in 2001. In response to pressure from the CAAT Christian Network the Church of England redefined its investment criteria and confirmed it will no longer invest in arms companies. Despite excluding arms company holdings, the Church remained, in 2005, the second best performer of more than 1,000 funds over the previous decade.

Furthermore, from 2005 the CAAT Universities Network has met with considerable success in its campaign to advocate ethical investment across the UK. A report entitled 'Study War No More' has highlighted military funding and involvement within 26 British universities. CAAT facilitates research into the details of university investment portfolios which has helped students to mount their own campaigns for clean investment. This has resulted in many universities divesting their shares in the arms industry, whilst many more campuses continue to campaign for similar action to be taken.

Private military companies

Since the invasion of Iraq in March 2003, the use of 'private military companies' has become standard practice for countries such as the UK and the US. CAAT considers these contractors to be modern-day mercenaries.

The Geneva Convention may classify as a mercenary a civilian contractor who is "motivated to take part in the hostilities essentially by the desire for private gain and, in fact, is promised, by or on behalf of a party to the conflict, material compensation substantially in excess of that promised or paid to combatants of similar ranks and functions in the armed forces of that Party". Private military companies have become big business, with an estimated turnover world wide of $100 billion, and their use is set to rise.

The UK Government's Green Paper of 2002 on Private Military Companies prompted a debate on the privatisation of a whole range of military services which has been taking place with little comment, high profile cases such as Sandline in Sierra Leone notwithstanding. CAAT seeks an end to all mercenary activities. If this cannot be achieved at this point, the following controls are its minimum immediate requirements:

- a ban on all combat activities
- all dealings between Government departments and agencies and the military companies, other than operational details, to be in the public domain
- any contract entered into between a military company and a foreign government to stipulate a cash fee and no other benefit. No other business sharing directors or offices with the providers of security should be allowed to have any dealings with the foreign government concerned for a period of, say, five years. The ownership of the military companies should be made transparent.
- companies to be made responsible under UK law for any breaches of human rights or the laws of war that may be committed by their employees

CAAT is also committed to publishing research on the issue

in order to raise public awareness of the ever increasing role mercenaries play in modern conflict zones.

Structure and Funding Network

CAAT has no formal membership structure. Individuals and affiliated groups (local branches of peace organisations, trade unions, churches, etc.), donate whatever they can afford towards the cost of running the campaign and receiving *CAAT News*, a bi-monthly magazine. There are also sponsoring groups who either took part in founding CAAT or have taken a major supporting role since. However 80% of CAAT's funding comes from individual donations.

CAAT is made up of grass-roots groups who come together to campaign for a variety of causes and issues surrounding its overall aims. In addition to local groups, CAAT also has a Christian Network, which looks at arms trade issues involving churches and mobilises Christians against the arms trade, (although CAAT as a whole includes members from many diverse faiths and those of no faiths). CAAT also has a Universities Network which involves students and university staff in campus-based campaigning. Potentially, other new networks can be formed at any time.

GATHERING THE FACTS ON THE SMALL ARMS TRADE

In late 1997, following the Oslo conference that drafted the treaty against anti-personnel landmines, many NGOs and governments began pressing for more public attention to the devastation wrought by the worldwide sale and distribution of light arms–weapons that can be carried by a person–such as assault rifles, mortars, and grenades. Such arms are believed to be responsible for the vast majority of combat deaths, including many tens of thousands of civilian deaths annually. Even after conflicts end, demobilization and reconciliation efforts are frustrated by the over-supply of these inexpensive weapons, which often flow into criminal hands.

Among the governmental and non-governmental initiatives at the time, in late December 1997, on the first anniversary of the murder of Red Cross/Red Crescent workers in Chechnya, PRIO and three other organizations in Oslo–Norwegian Red Cross, Norwegian Church Aid and the Norwegian Institute of International Affairs–banded together to form the Norwegian Initiative on Small Arms Transfers (NISAT). The database proposal here is a central part of NISAT's activities.

Need for the Project

In the past few years, the European Union, OSCE, Organization of American States, Organization of African Unity, Economic Community of West African States, and the South African Development Community all took up some aspect of small arms control. Almost every part of the UN engaged the topic, including—increasingly—the Security Council. Modeled on a 1997 OAS treaty, the UN in Vienna began negotiation of a global protocol against firearms trafficking in 1999. In addition, the UN General Assembly voted in 1999 to hold a United Nations conference in 2001 on the illicit arms trade "in all its dimensions."

Despite this high level of engagement by governments and NGOs, the knowledge base on which these efforts rest is extremely thin. There are enormous gaps in the factual record on arms production and transfers. The lack of focused research in this area leaves open fundamental questions such as whether the legal or the illegal arms trade is the leading source of supply, and which states are the largest legal exporters of small arms.

Approximately 70 states produce small arms and/or ammunition. Some production enterprises are state-owned (usually military armories), and some are private companies. From the existing reference works,

- it is not difficult to know what types of small arms the major producer states manufacture;
- it is much harder to determine production quantities; and
- it is nearly impossible to know where weapons are being exported.

The standard sources of data on the international arms trade–SIPRI, the UN Register of Conventional Arms, *World Military Expenditures and Arms Transfers*–do not include information on small arms shipments. Few governments provide information to their parliaments on major weapons exports they have approved, and even fewer on their small arms trade. An exception to the prevailing pattern of secrecy is the US government. Since 1997, the United States openly reports in a highly specific manner all of its small arms shipments and export license approvals (with the notable exception of covert government-run arms supply, like the Iran-contra operation). Other states that have recently begun to provide more detailed public reports on their arms exports (including small arms shipments) are Belgium, Canada, the Netherlands, Norway, South Africa, Sweden and the United Kingdom. These are the eight leaders in transparency, on which the database will first concentrate in 2000-2001.

Despite this improvement in transparency, there is a need to organize the newly available data. In the above eight and other countries, the relevant information is scattered across many agencies and departments–in shipping documents at customs offices, judicial records, police records, and documents in the foreign, defense and trade ministries. No one is currently pulling this information together systematically, translating it, or presenting it to the international community in a readily useable format. That is what the database project will do.

The Need for Transparency

The information included in the database will serve as a template for the kind of governmental transparency that we will encourage the Norwegian Foreign Ministry to press for through its diplomatic contacts and on the international stage. In addition, we hope the database itself will encourage greater openness on the part of some governments, when they see the amount and types of information that the United States and – to a lesser degree – some others already make public without adverse effect.

Increased transparency and organization of the available data will also improve the ability of governments to verify the appropriate end-uses and end-users of weapons exports they are authorizing. It will allow the non-governmental community, as well as national legislatures, to play an important role in aiding governments' efforts to curb diversion of these arms by providing oversight through research, questioning and reporting. Such information is also important for the safety of aid and relief workers operating in a region where a sudden influx of guns has occurred or is anticipated.

Increased openness about weapons shipments could serve as a confidence building measure among forces within a state, or states in a region, potentially heading off some purchases spurred by 'fear of the unknown'. Finally, such information will greatly facilitate formal disarmament activities, by providing some baseline information about arms stocks and supply in the state or region.

How the Project Addresses These Needs

The centerpiece of this proposal is an on-line database of small arms production and transfers. The database addresses the need for better information on three levels:

- it provides a composite picture of the small arms trade by collecting, translating and organizing the hard-to-find data;
- it interlinks policy-relevant information so as to provide both governments and activist organizations a stronger base for argumentation, strategy and agreement on common norms; and
- it demonstrates the positive aspects of transparency.

The database will eventually contain information on virtually every country of the world. It will be a public resource, accessible to all Internet users.

We believe that the database will yield substantial results within one year of full funding, and if so we are committed to further developing and sustaining the initiative for as long as small arms control measures are required. As more governments provide public information about their light weapons shipments, the resource will grow in value (in terms of providing a fuller picture of the dynamics of the arms market).

CONTENT AND STRUCTURE OF THE DATABASE

The information will be layered and arranged in a graphically attractive manner. It will be hyperlinked to relevant external sources of information on the Internet. However, only the PRIO/NISAT project will be able to post information, thus ensuring that quality control remains our responsibility.

The database will be built to allow easy on-line searches using several types of variables. For example, someone using the database should be able to retrieve a list of all enterprises around the world manufacturing M16 (or AK-47) assault rifles.

American English is the working language of the database, although links to web sites and government documents in the native language are included as well. Monetary values are converted into US dollars for the relevant year, to allow for comparison in the magnitude of exports and imports by various states.

For each country, the database will provide a concise overview of the "small arms issues" for that particular country. The main page of each country will five types of information:

Small Arms Production The information focuses on military small arms producers, including location of production plants and output quantities (when possible). Links are provided to the web pages of the military small arms manufacturers in order to help investigators research the various weapons. Also included are one-page profiles of the various weapons, written in plain English (as opposed to gun jargon).

Small Arms Export Laws and Policies This section contains links to the laws and regulations in force in each state concerning small arms production, imports or exports. The texts of recent official speeches or pronouncements on small arms control and disarmament are posted, as well as a survey of the existing data sources for the particular country.

Authorized Small Arms Imports For each country, links are provided to all its sources of small arms supply, going back to 1996. Authorized Small Arms Exports For each country, the database shows the destination, value and quantity of small arms sent to other countries through legal arms export procedures. These data go back to 1996.

Unauthorized (Illegal) Small Arms Imports and Exports This section links to news clips on illegal imports intercepted and other incidents of arms trafficking reported in the press, in court documents, or through national investigations.

The database's many internal hyperlinks allow a user to assemble the fullest picture possible of arms flows to a particular country.

For example, data on the US page showing arms shipped to Israel will be linked to Israel's arms import page, where all known imports by Israel show up.

Each country page will also be linked to other data sources that focus on related information on a country-by-country basis, for example SaferNet (on domestic firearm casualty rates); Amnesty International (on the human rights situation); and relevant chronologies of small arms use (generally focusing on massacres) maintained by the Monterey Institute for International Studies.

To obtain *all* of the above information for *all* countries is of course impossible, as most governments do not release any information to the public domain. But we are certain that for every country of the world, we could today provide *some* information.

Development, Testing and Audience to Date

As of June 2000, with seed money from NISAT partner organizations and from the Norwegian Foreign Ministry, we have developed an initial database template.

This prototype already displays a significant quantity of organized information, including some 3,000 articles and reports describing black market gun trafficking incidents, organized by country.

In addition, four country profiles are completed and several others are nearing completion, with official trade data entered, as well as summaries of laws, policies and small arms production. The information here has also been cross-linked to external sources, as described above. Entering this initial data has allowed us to refine the design and search functions to make the database more useful and the interface more user-friendly.

The database already attracts a few hundred verified readers per week, accounting for about 5000 'hits' in the same time period. Slightly more than one half of the readers are currently from North America, 10 percent are from Norway and the rest are distributed among various Western countries.

Focus of Efforts in 2000-2001

PRIO's project team will concentrate its efforts in several areas, in the following priority:

1) Researching, developing and entering more country profiles into the database.
2) Identifying and contracting researchers to provide high quality information for profiles on their country or region.
3) Developing and implementing a marketing strategy to ensure that the universe of interested government policy makers, journalists, non-governmental activists and academics are aware of our resource.
4) Continuing to archive incidents into the black market file collection.
5) Continually evaluating, extending and improving the usability and information value of the database structure and interface.

The data-collection methodology is summarized in detail in the appendix.

Project Output

The on-line database is the main product of this project. It will facilitate the preparation of many research products by many analysts in various countries around the world. Three other, published outputs are planned. A Policy Memo on Transparency This memo is intended to assist and encourage the Norwegian Foreign Ministry in pressing for greater transparency about state-sanctioned small arms transfers through its bilateral contacts and through multilateral fora. The study will address obstacles raised by governments to greater transparency and provide rebuttal. It will also survey which governments currently make their exports transparent, and which do not.

Finally, it will assess the various proposals that have been made for greater transparency (for instance, inclusion of information on small arms in the UN Register of Conventional Arms, or within the Wassenaar Arrangement) and make realistic recommendations for an inter-governmental as well as a public transparency agenda.

Project Coordinator Lora Lumpe and Researcher Stig Aga Aandstad are scheduled to complete this manuscript by July 2001. It will be distributed widely to governments and activist NGOs at the UN conference on arms trafficking in July 2001.

Edited Book on the Black Market The UN began negotiation of a global protocol on illicit arms trafficking in January 1999. This treaty is slated to be finalized in late 2000. In addition, the United Nations will host a global conference on the illegal arms trade in June/July 2001. Lora Lumpe has just completed editing a book on today's black market in arms, based on commissioned papers and a round-table workshop for the authors and other experts. The volume will be published by Zed Books in summer 2000. We are not seeking funding for this work, but we mention it to note that the project is taking a holistic approach–focusing on both legal and illegal small arms proliferation, between which there are many linkages.

Campaign Materials : As the database evolves, project staff will also produce conference papers, magazine articles and op-eds and campaign materials derived from its information. These products will be posted on the web page, as well as distributed at conferences, on e-mail list servers and in newspapers. Among the topics of fact sheets which might be derived from the database are:

- sources of supply: who manufactures what?
- country-specific surveys (e.g., where do Colombian combatants get their arms?)
- transparency: which governments refuse to make available information about their exports?

These publications serve a dual purpose: presenting information on small arms via another medium and to a variety of audiences, but also advertising the existence of the database.

3

Global Arms Sales

CURRENT MILITARY SPENDING AND ARMS SALES

Despite their being locked into this poverty trap, poorer nations are still regarded as legitimate and profitable arms customers for Western states which helped create their situation. According to a report for the US congress, arms sales to developing countries together far outweigh arms sales to developed countries. According to their definition, countries of the South accounted for 66 per cent of the value of all international arms deliveries in 2000.

Social impacts of conflict

The servicing of debt for arms sales obviously affects health and education, and has other social impacts in the developing world. Money spent on arms, or money spent servicing debts, means less money is spent in social and developmental programs within the country. Countries are prevented by international trade rules from unfairly supporting their own industries above the industries of other nations. Caribbean countries are not allowed to give financial aid to their banana industry on which the region depends, because it is unfair competition for the American-owned banana industry in Central and South America. The Global Agreement on Trade and Services (GATS), which is currently being pushed through the WTO, intends to extend these kinds of rules to other areas such as water, healthcare and education provision.

But at the WTO, and in all other global agreements, the military is specifically excluded from the rules governing global trade. The main WTO governing document, the General Agreement on Tariffs and Trade (GATT), states that a country cannot be prevented from taking any action 'it considers necessary for the protection of its essential security interests... relating to the traffic in arms, ammunition and implements of war and such traffic in other goods and materials as is carried on directly for the purpose of supplying a military establishment.'

In other words, the WTO GATT and other trade agreements do not apply to the arms trade. There are no international restrictions on what munitions a country can buy or sell, how much these should cost, how much a country can spend, who they buy weapons from or to what extent they subsidize their own arms industry. This process has contributed to the pattern of rich countries becoming richer, and poorer nations staying poor, or becoming poorer. Western nations are not prevented by WTO rules from subsidizing their own arms industries, and so are able to acquire military equipment at artificially low knock-down prices, while keeping the finance within the country. Moreover, the exclusion from WTO regulations means they can buy arms domestically, even when other countries are offering better products more cheaply.

Developing nations rarely have established arms industries and so buy their weaponry from abroad at a cost often way above what the equipment is worth, draining yet more money out of the country. Even when there is a local arms industry, this is usually so small that buying abroad remains cheaper. Developing nations pump cash into their own arms industries too, in attempts to improve their economies, because it is the only industry they can legally support in this way.

When seeing how trade rules benefit the rich countries, especially in the arms arena, it is not surprising that airplane and arms manufacturer Boeing was the prime sponsor of the WTO meeting in Seattle in 1999. Global agreements to break down barriers to trade are having the effect of preventing developing and middle income countries from exploiting the resources they do have to trade on the world market, keeping those countries financially subordinate to the rich West.

The argument that the arms trade creates or sustains jobs, or brings money into the national economy, is one of the most difficult arguments campaigners face. These arguments have strong political currency-people don't vote for governments that threaten their livelihood-but they are based on a fallacy which is only now becoming fully apparent.

The arms trade is an immoral business that cause death, maiming, human rights abuses and suffering around the world. It is also a business that does not bring huge economic or employment benefits to the biggest arms-exporting countries. In many cases, high government subsidies, tax breaks, insurance schemes and promotion for arms manufacturers cost governments more money than weapons producers generate for them. Countries are artificially propping up their arms industries while refusing to explore fully the potential for diversification into areas that are not only more productive and socially positive but also economically viable.

The extent of government subsidies

Governments subsidize their arms sector in a number of ways. The difficult job for campaigners and academics is to show by how much, and why it is a bad thing. Information, such as how much a government spends on its own armed forces, what procurement decisions it makes, how much it spends on military research and development and how much export credit insurance it provides for arms companies, is usually secret or difficult to obtain.

Strong, well-informed estimates based on obtainable information are usually the best that campaigners can muster before issuing the challenge to governments: if we are wrong, it falls to you to prove how wrong. After all, if arms exports are big earners for state economies, wouldn't politicians be shouting it from the roof tops?

With that proviso in mind, valiant attempts to look at this issue have been made. In the US, the defence and foreign aid budgets are the largest single source of federal funding to private corporations. According to the World Policy Institute, more than half of all US weapons sales are financed by taxpayers instead of by foreign arms purchasers. During the fiscal year of 1996 (the last year for which figures were available) the US Government spent more than $7.9 billion to help companies secure just over $12 billion in agreements for new international arms sales.

Direct subsidies

Governments' direct financial support for their arms exports can be roughly placed into a few distinct categories. Each of these subsidies results in taxpayers' money being spent, or risked, helping foreign governments to buy arms.

Export promotion-The major arms-exporting countries each year spend huge amounts of money all over the world promoting and marketing their domestic arms companies' products. Export promotion ranges from diplomatic visits by politicians to the provision of advice and support for companies marketing their systems, to regular attendance and promotion at arms exhibitions and conferences.

At the US Pentagon, nearly 6,000 people were employed in 1996 to promote, broker, administer and finance arms sales abroad, at a cost of $378.2 million. In the State Department a further 75 personnel were employed, part of a defence export promotion budget of $3.7 million. And the US commerce department also plays a role, publishing 'defence market assessments' such as How to do business in Indonesia, and mounting US presence at foreign arms exhibitions. During 1996, the US Government sent equipment and personnel to 19 overseas weapons shows, at a cost of more than $5.1 million.

Export credits-Government insurance schemes to compensate arms companies when their foreign clients default on payment generally make up the bulk of the government direct subsidies. They also provide financing support for deals. Governments then attempt to recoup the cost from the defaulting nations, with usually only limited success. Often the companies insist on some kind of insurance or guarantee from their home government before embarking on large weaponry export deals. Arms sales make up, large proportions of the export credits extended in many major arms exporting countries. The US Export-Import Credit Bank, which could be seen as the equivalent of an export credit organization, is usually prohibited from guaranteeing arms deals (though not always-Congress occasionally makes exceptions). However the US more than makes up for it in other loans and funding programs which subsidize US arms exporters.

The US Foreign Military Financing Program (FMF) received $3.35 billion in 1999 to support grants and loans for the provision of US military equipment and services to more than 24 countries. Recipients of FMF grants in recent years have included Egypt, Israel, Jordan, Turkey and the Ukraine. More funds were allocated for Africa. Another $16 million of subsidy is granted through the US Defence Export Loan Guarantee fund.

Spending distortions-governments also artificially support their arms industries by distorting their own spending on domestic military purchases. They buy more arms from domestic suppliers than really needed, they pay more than these ought to cost, and they choose domestic arms suppliers even if foreign-made equipment is cheaper and better. In any other industry, World Trade Organization rules and other free-trade legislation would prevent such spending distortions as unfair competition. But as we have seen earlier, the military is exempt from international agreements on trade. In a report by the World Policy Institute, William Hartung decries this kind of spending in the US, which he calls 'defence pork'. He argues that politicians add unnecessary and expensive military equipment purchases to the Pentagon's budget in order to please arms companies, secure or create jobs and so gain campaign donations and votes. In 1998, $3.8 billion was added by senators and officials to the amount that the Pentagon had said it needed to meet its own defence plans. While most 'defence pork' is US-bought-so not an arms export subsidy-the example shows how political pressure distorts procurement decisions.

Other subsidies

The above are just three direct financial subsidies which governments provide for their arms industries. But there are many different ways that governments indirectly financially support their arms industries, and while it is more difficult to quantify this kind of support in concrete terms, the benefits to arms companies can be quite considerable.

Research and development (R&D)-Governments spend large portions of their defence budgets on research and development of new weapons systems, which they contract arms companies to carry out on their behalf. In 1998/99, the three big US weapons manufacturers received over $8 billion in R&D funding. Commissions and bribes-According to one World l Bank estimate, the sums distributed worldwide each year as pay-offs and bribes total $80 billion. Campaign group Transparency International (TI) has surveyed attitudes to corruption in business, and found that arms and construction companies were perceived to be the most likely to pay bribes.

Jobs in the arms industry

Off-set deals and joint procurement aside, a further argument-that the weapons business is a thriving employer-is also false.... the global arms industry has been gradually shrinking since the end of the Cold War. Linked to this, the number of people employed in the sector has also fallen.

Moreover, the argument that a government should spend huge amounts of money propping up an industry to safeguard a relatively small number jobs is one that only has so much credibility. Governments should no more subsidize their arms business than any other industry to safeguard jobs. Sir Samuel Brittan, the British economist and journalist, has written extensively on the weakness of the employment argument.

He says the argument is based on the myth that there is a 'lump of labour' that is engaged in making specific products, that cannot be deployed elsewhere. If defence orders are lost, those people become unemployed and unemployable, runs the line.

Brittan points out that millions of people change jobs, find jobs or leave jobs every year. 'Indeed, it is almost certainly easier for arms workers, many of whom have a wide range of valued skills, to find new jobs... Where will the new jobs come from to replace those lost in exporting weapons? Other jobs, on a much greater scale, arose to take the place of handloom weavers [and] drivers of horse-drawn carts. A report by the British Ministry of Defence and York University, published in 2001, revealed that 40,000 arms export jobs would be replaced by 67,000 civilian posts if arms exports were cut in half, albeit at a lower average salary per job.

Mercenaries: the dogs of war

Selling arms is one side; purchasing people to use them is another. The use of privately hired might is nothing new. The Romans used mercenaries, and the practice probably went back even before them. Italian merchants in the 16th century hired muscle to protect their assets and control trade routes. Colonial explorers were accompanied by hired fighters. From the mid-20th century, Western firms setting up mines and oil exploration in Africa, Asia and Latin America protected their assets by hiring armed heavies.

Mercenaries come under a number of guises, but all include the provision of military might or advice for a profit. Under the guise of 'security' for example, private military companies, consultants, advisors or training outfits, all manner of services to both governments and companies are supplied, including full participation in conflicts, the provision of arms, and armed protection of royal families and industrial plants.

Former members of security services often run modern mercenary companies, exploiting their contacts in the arms and political world. They hire disaffected, unemployed former soldiers wherever they win contracts, and source second-hand weapons and equipment for them to fight with. They will often provide whatever services are required, in exchange for hard currency or interests in mining and oil exploration. UN Special Rapporteur Bernales Ballesteros was appointed by the UN General Assembly in 1996 to report on 'the use of mercenaries as a means of violating human rights and impeding the exercise of the rights of peoples to self-determination'.

Child soldiers

At least mercenaries can usually make their own l choices; it is different for children. There are more than half a million children (under 18s) serving in armed forces, in more than 87 countries. At least 300,000 children are actively fighting in 41 countries, including Colombia, Sri Lanka, Sierra Leone, Uganda and Chechnya.; In some countries, very young children are used as messengers, spies and equipment carriers, but by the age of 10 they are given rifles, or rapid repeating machine-guns and set to fight in conflicts they cannot possibly understand.

As members of armed forces, children become lawful targets for attack, but the use of child soldiers also increases the danger faced by civilian children who come under suspicion from warring parties. Within armed forces, children are often treated brutally, suffering physical, emotional and even sexual abuse. But it is not only faraway nations mired in internal conflicts that use child soldiers. The US is the country most opposed to setting 18 as the minimum age limit for recruiting and participation in armed forces. One in every 200 of its armed personnel is 17, while many more become temporary members as part of youth military training programs.

The UK continues to recruit 16-year-olds leaving school, and the recruitment process begins even while they are still at school. British soldiers under the age of 18 fought-and died-in both the Falklands/Malvinas conflict and the Gulf War. Other countries that recruit under-18s to the armed forces, via conscription or voluntary enlistment include: Australia, Bangladesh, Belgium, Brazil, Burundi, Canada, Chile, Croatia, Cuba, Denmark, El Salvador, Estonia, Finland, France, Germany, Honduras, India, Indonesia, Iran, Iraq, Ireland, Israel, Italy, Japan, Jordan, Libya, Luxembourg, Mexico, Namibia, Netherlands, Aotearoa/New Zealand, Norway, Pakistan, Peru, Portugal, Republic of Korea, Sudan, Switzerland, Uganda and Yugoslavia.

A number of factors lead to the use of children as soldiers. Technological advances have made semi-automatic rifles light enough to be used and simple enough to be operated by a child, while rabid proliferation has made them cheap and easily obtainable. The longer a conflict goes on, the more likely children are to be 'recruited' as manpower becomes short-both young girls and boys are recruited-and new soldiers are needed to replaced the killed and injured.

Children are perceived to make obedient soldiers, they are cheap and are easy to manipulate. Children 'volunteer' or are coerced to join-up in order to survive, to prove their 'adulthood' or because it is a natural step in a culture of violence. In the Revolutionary United Front in Sierra Leone, children are held and trained for two or three months, threatened with death if they disobey orders or attempt to escape. In the Kamajors militias, they are initiated into secret societies and told they will gain magical powers and be immune to bullets if they join military forces.

Prevailing international law at the United Nations sets 15 as the minimum age for military recruitment and participation in armed conflict, though there is widespread agreement that this age is too low. The Coalition to Stop the Use of Child Soldiers is an international movement of organizations seeking the adoption and implementation of an Optional Protocol to the Convention on the Rights of the Child (CRC) setting the minimum age for all forms of military recruitment and use in hostilities at 18 years of age.

By the end of 2001, a total of 92 countries had signed or ratified the Optional Protocol, but implementation will take many years and a great deal of effort. Programs to prevent child recruitment, including monitoring, providing alternatives, and establishing proper procedures, as well as programs to ensure safe demobilization and integration of former child soldiers are particularly needed.

Landmines: the legacy

Children, whether child soldiers or not, are often the main victims of landmines, perhaps the most vicious weapons brokered by the arms dealers. In the words of the International Campaign to Ban landmines, Put simply, anything that landmines can do to an enemy's army, they can do to a civilian population. What they cannot do is discriminate between the soldier and the civilian. Their impact cannot be confined to the duration of the battle. Thus, under the laws of war, they are an illegal weapon.'

More than any other weapon of war, landmines have received much public and legislative attention over recent decades. They are horrific because their effects on civilian communities, after battles have ended, are so long-term and devastating. Under internationally recognized definitions, landmines fall into two broad categories:

* Anti-personnel (AP) landmine-'A mine designed to be exploded by the presence, proximity or contact of a person and that will incapacitate, injure or kill one or more persons'.
* Anti-tank (AT) landmine-A device designed to detonate by more than 100 kilograms of pressure.

Whether anti-tank or anti-personnel, the effect of landmines on civilian communities is the same. They kill and maim indiscriminately, taking children just as easily as heads of households.

Families are devastated not only because of the loss of a loved one, but also because their means of income or a future generation is destroyed. In the same way, those who are not killed when a landmine explodes are maimed or permanently disabled, becoming a long-term financial and emotional burden on families. Some landmines are designed to scatter thousands of shards of metal up to 50 meters, specifically to injure rather than kill.

Landmines also have devastating effects when they don't kill or maim, rendering thousands of acres of land unusable for farming or livestock. Families are forced to make a terrible choice between starvation or risking their lives on mined fields. In Cambodia alone there are over 35,000 amputees as a result of landmines, and they are just the survivors. Mine deaths and injuries in the past few decades amount to hundreds of thousands. They are a daily threat in Afghanistan, Angola, Bosnia, Cambodia, Chechnya, Croatia, Iraq, Mozambique, Nicaragua, Somalia and dozens of other countries. In December 1997, following decades of pressure from campaigners, a total of 122 governments signed the Ottawa convention, officially titled 'The Convention on the Prohibition of the Use, Stockpiling, Production and Transfer of AntiPersonnel Mines and on their Destruction'. Less than one year later the treaty became international law when Burkina Faso became the 40th country to ratify.

It is the most comprehensive international treaty of its kind, and became law quicker than any other treaty of its kind in history. But despite worldwide support, and condemnation of the use, sale and stockpiling of anti-personnel landmines, a total of 53 countries still refuse to sign including China, Egypt, Finland, India, Israel, Pakistan, Russia and the US. The US's refusal has a devastating political influence, giving credence to other countries' refusal. The campaign continues to demand that these countries drop their opposition to the treaty, and to expand it to cover anti-tank mines and other 'area denial weapons'-a euphemism meaning they blow you up if you stray where you 'should not'-like cluster munitions and unexploded ordnance.

The 'trade' in landmines, as traditionally defined at least, is all but non-existent. Cuba, the United States, Russia, Egypt, Iran, Iraq, Burma, China, India, North Korea, South Korea, Pakistan, Singapore and Vietnam are still classified as producers of the weapons by the International Campaign to Ban Landmines, though some of them have only failed to prove written attestation to the contrary. Military monitor Jane's Mines and Mine Clearance 2000-2001 revealed there has been a 'virtual absence of mines-legitimate or otherwise-at arms shows and military equipment exhibitions this year'. Thirty-four countries are known to have exported anti-personnel landmines in the past. All but Iraq have attested that they no longer do so. The trade in anti-personnel landmines has been confirmed to exist only in a relatively small amount of illicit trafficking.

For a book on the arms trade, it could be argued the issue should stop there-the trade in anti-personnel landmines no longer exists, and the manufacture is nominal. Unfortunately, the step is not so easily taken. The Ottawa treaty covers only certain types of antipersonnel landmines, leaving vast loopholes where area denial weapons, including anti-tank weapons, remain available and traded.

The campaign against landmines concentrates now on encouraging the states who have so far failed to sign and ratify the Ottawa treaty to do so, but it has also broadened its outlook to the new and next generations of landmines and weapons that are landmines by any other name. The weapon causing most concern for campaigners is the cluster bomb. Usually dropped from a plane, it explodes just above the ground, scattering hundreds of miniature 'bomblets' over a wide area. Many of these bomblets fail to explode, remaining in the ground, just like anti-personnel landmines, until disturbed.

Like landmines, unexploded ordnance (UXO) poses a serious threat to lives and livelihoods. Between 1964 and 1973 the US dropped a huge number of cluster bombs over Laos. It is estimated that millions of unexploded bomblets remain. Cluster munitions were used in Kosovo and Vietnam, during the Gulf War, in the Falklands/Malvinas conflict, and during the recent attacks on Afghanistan. NATO admits to a failure rate of between 8 and 12 per cent in Kosovo, leaving as many as 35,000 live bomblets on the ground. The campaign against landmines is far from won. Many countries, having signed Ottawa, pour money and research into mine clearance programs-an expensive and time-consuming business. But while taking mines away with one hand, the landmines of the future are being created and delivered across war zones all over the world. The arms companies which are earning millions from developing mine clearance equipment are also at the forefront of developing new generations of weapons, laying the foundation of devastation in the future. The International Campaign to Ban Landmines is calling for a moratorium, banning the use of cluster weapons because of their devastating and long-lasting effects.... government ministers, advisers and senior members of the armed forces frequently move into the employment of arms companies and vice versa. The supposed wall between government and the industry has a huge gaping hole in it, in which a constantly revolving door has been established.

In Frank Vogl's Earth Times article on bribery and I corruption in the arms trade, he outlines how the George W Bush regime in the US takes 'this game of political pressure to an unprecedented new level'. 'Rarely before has US business taken such total charge of the Pentagon. Not only does the Secretary of Defence [Donald Rumsfeld] come from big business, but so too do the new heads of the Army, Navy and Air Force... President Bush has nominated

James Roche a vice president at military aircraft seller Northrop Grumman, to become Secretary of the Air Force; Gordon England from arms and naval vessel manufacturer General Dynamics to become Secretary of the Navy.

For good measure, US Vice President Dick Cheney's wife, Lynne, serves on Lockheed Martin's board, a company which is a major contractor to the US Government and its allies.

Purchasing power

Donations from private companies to political parties and candidates are nothing new, and have been the foundation of many scandals for governments across the Western world. Not surprisingly, because there are lucrative domestic contracts to be won, and restrictive legislation to be challenged, the arms business is a major player in the cash-for-influence money-go-round. As Lumpe and Donarski note in The Arms Trade Revealed, 'Whenever and wherever arms export policy is being made, financially self-interested representatives of the arms corporations are present. Generous campaign contributions from the weaponeer's political action committees (PACs) open doors, providing access and influence on the policy making process. According to the World Policy Institute, the 25 leading weapons-exporting companies contributed a record $10.8 million during the 1995-96 general election cycle in the US. Of this, $6.6 million came in regulated PAC donations and $4.2 million in unregulated 'soft' money-donations theoretically targeted for party-building activities, but often used to benefit specific candidates. Lockheed Martin was the leading arms corporate donor during this time. The Republican Party, more military-minded than the Democrats, received the bulk of donations.

A US Code of Conduct?

Although the US has relatively strict legislation governing the involvement of its citizens in arms brokering the world's largest arms-exporting country has comprehensively stalled on drawing up its own code of conduct on arms exports. Progressive Congress representatives have been attempting for nearly a decade to introduce a Code of Conduct on arms exports into US legislation.

In 1995 International Relations Committee member Cynthia McKinney (Democrat) introduced the 'Code of Conduct on Arms Transfers Act' into the 104th Congress.

Campaign for an International Code I Finally, the US President has now been instructed by Congress to pursue multilateral steps for controlling and monitoring the arms trade. There is a real possibility that within a generation, perhaps even before, an International Code of Conduct on Arms Transfers could be introduced, building on the EU Code. In 2000 the US and the EU signed a declaration to work towards a common vision on the question of arms export controls. In May 1997, 14 Nobel Laureates met in New York to launch their own International Code as a first step to persuade arms exporting countries to adopt standards: 'Today, we speak as one to voice our common concern regarding the destructive effects of the unregulated arms trade. Together, we have written an International Code of Conduct on Arms Transfers, which, once adopted by all arms-selling nations, will benefit all humanity, nationalities, ethnicity, and religions.

Their proposed Code requires that arms transfers are only granted if transfer would complement and comply with international human rights standards, international humanitarian law, respect for international arms embargoes and military sanctions, promotes peace, security and stability, promotes human development and opposes terrorism. It calls too for public accounting of the Code's implementation, and transparent international co-operation through the UN and other bodies to improve and adjust the code as appropriate. While the proposal needs updating to account for recent changes in the international arms trade, it is a bold attempt to set in motion some international moves to curb the arms export business. It is perhaps the best tool arms trade campaigners currently have to effect change on a global scale.

A broader view of campaigning

From Seattle onwards, politicians and executives of the biggest and richest transnational corporations realized that wherever they went, and whatever they did, an inspired, passionate group of united people was watching, criticizing and acting for social justice and equality. Also for the first time, campaigners on widely diverse issues, from gay rights to third-world poverty, from peace and nuclear disarmament to environmental activists, joined together. They realized their concerns overlapped in many different and complex ways. They discovered that united campaigning, using the concerns they shared as a foundation, was more effective than disparate, isolationist campaigns along strictly issue-based lines.

The campaign against arms trading cannot, and should not, be considered in isolation from other concerns of social justice, except perhaps for convenience' sake. In almost every area of global injustice, the arms trade plays its deadly role. It was revealed how the trade exacerbates conflict, promotes human rights abuses and worsens poverty in developing countries. The trade is also intimately connected to environmental destruction, inequality, immigration and asylum, gender and cultural rights, privatization and worker exploitation-in fact, most of the world's evils have their roots in the fighters, tanks, mines, guns and bullets that corrupt individuals and destroy lives.

SMALL ARMS

The problem, however, is not confined to officially supported exports of high technology equipment such as aircraft and missiles. It is most often small arms that have been used for domestic repression in armed conflict in the last decade – the vast majority of them civilians and most of them killed by small arms. Clare Short's 2000 White Paper on International Development stated: 'Of the 40 poorest countries in the world, 24 are either in the midst of armed conflict or have only recently emerged from it. This problem is particularly acute in Africa... An estimated five million people have died.' Sophisticated defenders of arms sales agree that there is a case for banning exports of small arms altogether except for the armed forces of western democratic states. For instance Philip Towle argues that the profits Britain makes from this trade are very small despite the benefits to some specialised manufacturers.

The Scott Report of 1996 advocated legislation to put control on arms exports and arms brokering on a permanent non-emergency basis. In the spring of 2001 the Labour government undertook to introduce such legislation in the next parliament and published a draft bill with explanatory memoranda.

This will introduce a licensing requirement for trafficking and brokering in arms between overseas countries. It will also introduce licensing requirements for export of military technology by electronic means. Nevertheless the government is still likely to be inhibited by two factors: its reluctance to move too far ahead of competitor countries and its belief that small arms can legitimately be sent to official governments as distinct from so called rebels.

Al Yammamah

There is a further category which is not overtly a subsidy, but is certainly a special arrangement. This is the obscure Al Yammamah deal with Saudi Arabia under which weapons were exchanged for oil. Full details have never been published, but a great deal of information has been collected in *The Arabian Connection*, published by the Campaign against the Arms Trade, which is a useful source even for those who might not agree with all the objectives of the Campaign.

The first Yammamah deal was negotiated in the middle to late 1980s and has its origin in the reluctance of the US Congress to sanction weapons exports to Saudi Arabia. American policies have fluctuated since then; but a second Yammamah agreement was negotiated in the late 1980s; and despite may difficulties it became operational in the early 1990s. Its biggest 'achievement' was to produce a market for the Tornado aircraft, which was said at one time to have saved 19,000 jobs.

The Blair government shows no sign of wanting to banish this kind of agreement, despite the distortions that the heavy investment in arms is producing in Saudi Arabia, the horrific human rights record of the regime there, and the basic instability of that regime. As for the argument about oil supplies, the US, Britain and France cannot – like other western countries – buy their oil on the international market, remembering that Middle Eastern countries often need to sell the oil even more urgently than we need to buy it. It is interesting that this so-called argument of economic strategy usually comes from foreign ministries rather than ministries of finance or economics.

The UK record

The recent UK record is not all bad. In July 1997 the then new British Foreign Secretary Robin Cook stated that the new Labour government would not permit the sale of arms to regimes that might use them for internal repression. It is the least he could have said after the *Arms for Iraq* scandal. The government has fulfilled an election pledge to publish annual reports on UK's strategic export controls. These have gradually improved in quality; and the third one, issued in July 2000, has been described by Saferworld as 'the most transparent report published by any European country and one which offers a potential template for best practice through the EU.' But even this latest report is criticised for failure to provide information on ultimate end users, the absence of summary information on licences refused and lack of detailed information on actual deliveries, as distinct from licences.

The Blair government inherited various international obligations such as membership of the Australia Group of 30 countries aiming to discourage the proliferation of chemical and biological weapons. An international convention was reached in December 1997 banning the production and transfer of anti-personnel mines. This came too early to be attributed to the Labour government elected in the same year. But the new government indeed took a lead in pressing for a European Union Code of Conduct on Arms Exports which was agreed in June 1998. The Chancellor of the Exchequer, Gordon Brown, began the millennium by adding 22 new poor countries over and above the previous 41 covered by the ban on export credits 'for unproductive expenditure'.

Indonesia, however, remains off the banned list. And because the Chancellor's action was in the context of debt relief for poor countries, it did not affect Saudi Arabia, which has accounted for about one third of British arms sales. It is thus fair to say that there is still a long way to go. Amnesty International's view has been that the Department of Trade and Industry 'is not meeting its responsibility to promote trade in a manner which is not harmful to human rights.' It was also worried that this same department is responsible both for the licensing of arms sales and for their promotion. A joint report of four House of Commons committees reiterated that a serious error of judgement was made in late 1998 and early 1999 in granting several open export licences for military equipment to the government of Zimbabwe, despite that government's heavy involvement in the fighting in the Congo and its domestic infringements of human rights. The same report urged considering a stricter interpretation of the arms embargo on China and also raised issues about licences for arms to other countries.

At the height of the East Timor crisis in early 1999 there appeared a telling *Times* cartoon. On one side of the cartoon a buoyant Tony Blair was shown exclaiming: 'We need a hawk' – meaning a more determined military effort to put pressure on the government of Indonesia. On the other side he was shown piloting one of the Hawk aircraft that the UK had been delivering to Indonesia for many years for the use of the country's former military dictator, General Suharto.

Export Promotion

A popular view is that some arms sales may be undesirable, but that they help promote jobs, growth and employment. Therefore a balance has to be drawn between these two considerations – a compromise always appeals to the so-called practical man. We will thus never really stop dubious arms sales until the myth of the export drive is nailed once and for all. The root of the matter is the belief throughout the political and business establishment that exports are worthwhile for their own sake, irrespective of the terms on which they are sold and how much they have to be subsidised. It is for this reason that prime ministers, whether Thatcher, Major or Blair, time and again come down against the Treasury in favour of controversial arms deals or dubious overseas capital projects. These attitudes are a hangover from the siege economy days of Stafford Cripps (Labour Chancellor in the late 1940s) and have no place in a global market economy.

The balance of payments preoccupation goes back many centuries. Mercantilist writers in the 16th, 17th and 18th century, campaigned for a favourable balance of trade and for an inflow of gold and silver. These writers were refuted as conclusively as anything can be in political economy by 18th century members of the Scottish Enlightenment such as David Hume and Adam Smith. During the subsequent period of rapid world economic growth towards the end of the 19th century huge current account surpluses and deficits built up, far greater than any of the imbalances which commentators have bemoaned in recent decades. The origin of both the export drive and the reinvention of so-called balance of payments problem was in the immediate post-war years when sterling was on a fixed exchange rate and was also inconvertible. The financial policy regime was then one of suppressed inflation, which tended to spill over into the balance of payments, and which was held down by a mixture of controls and exchange rate overvaluation. It was, moreover, a world with strict controls over capital flows. These controls could not be severe enough to protect determined speculators from launching an attack on a suspect currency, but they were enough of a deterrent to the regular flows of capital across borders which normally finance imbalances on current account. The post-World War Two generation of political and economic leaders was brought up on slogans and posters such as 'export or die', the 'dollar drive' and even on one occasion 'exporting is fun'. By contrast we are now back in a world of relatively free capital flows. There are bound to be large imbalances between countries with high savings ratios and relatively few investment outlets and other countries, such as the United States, which have had low savings but many investment opportunities. Moreover we now have floating exchange rates.

Advanced industrial countries with floating exchange rates need never have balance of payments problems. They may suffer from unwelcome downward pressure on their exchange rate due to financial market's distrust of their policies or of fears about domestic inflation. If so, such fears should be tackled directly. In today's circumstances export drives really amount to the diversion of public resources towards special interest groups under the guise of patriotic slogans. The basic political and business fallacy is not to realise that exports, like investment, are a cost and not a benefit. If we could finance the imports that British citizens want to buy without any exports – say by interest-free loans from overseas on indefinite repayment terms – we would be better off.

Of course this would require a period of adjustment. But such adjustments are necessary after any kind of economic or industrial change. In the world as it is, exports are a waste of resources and serve no purpose if they are not paid for, or are paid for very late and on a heavily subsidised credit basis and with a strong political risk factor.

The jobs argument

The most popular argument for subsidising exports is the effect on jobs. We should be on our guard when politicians defend dubious policies by declaring 'jobs are at stake'. This is so whether it is an 'Old Labour' supporter wanting to protect manufacturing, a Tory spokesman talking about the employment provided by hunting, or a business lobbyist pushing for arms sales to dubious regimes. The argument that jobs derived from exporting weapons cannot be replaced is akin to the argument for keeping open uneconomic coalmines for the sake of employment. Yet it is often just those people who lecture us on the need for workers to change jobs, and who say that full employment cannot the same employment, who are most keen to promote the sale of arms.

Such arguments are based on the myth that there is a lump of labour that is engaged in making specific products. Then, it is supposed, if orders or output are lost in one area they cannot be regained anywhere else. But people change jobs constantly. Well over three million people leave the unemployment register each year even in recession periods, over half of them for new jobs or training. Indeed, it is almost certainly easier for arms workers, many of whom have a wide range of valued skills, to find new jobs than it was for miners, whose training was more specific There are those who ask, 'Where will the new jobs come from to replace those lost in exporting weapons?' The onus is on them to explain how it is that other jobs, on a much greater scale, arose to take the place of handloom weavers or the drivers of horse-drawn carts – or for that matter the owners of pack-asses replaced by wheeled traffic at the dawn of history. The multiplication of population and the multiple rise of productivity in the last two centuries, so far from these having caused mass unemployment, have been accompanied by a multiple increase in the number of jobs. One of the key ideas of economics is that of the circular flow of income. The point is that there is a continuing flow between purchasers who desire to buy products, the incomes received from supplying their needs, and still further purchases. The idea is so basic that economists regard it as too obvious to mention and take it for granted rather than discuss it explicitly. The smoothness of this flow can be helped by sensible policies, such as efforts by the Bank of England Monetary Policy Committee to maintain an adequate, but not excessive, flow of total spending, and by sensible exchange rate policies. The interested citizen needs to know mainly that there is or can be such a circular flow, and that there therefore need be no fear of one country being undercut in everything by another.

Terms of trade

A slightly more respectable argument is that relating to the terms of trade. A royal visit or a small amount of official publicity, or arm-twisting by the Foreign Office, might enable a company to sell more overseas at a given price or to sell a given amount of goods at a higher price. This enables the home country to exchange exports for imports on slightly more profitable terms. The argument has very little application in a highly competitive world where a country of the size of Britain has little monopoly power. If e-commerce means anything at all this should vanish completely as buyers are able to find the most competitive offer unaided by royal visits.

A further argument relates to small exporters, who might not have the resources to engage in the required market research and export promotion. But surely this kind of thing is the job of market research and advertising agencies, chambers of commerce and industry associations. If it does not pay them to engage in such promotion, it is because government support agencies are providing these services on a free or subsidised basis.

Spillover benefits

The last resort of any sector or industry whose subsidies are challenged is to say that it brings spillover benefits to the rest of the economy. Concorde was virtually launched on such arguments.

Weapons producers argue that the government should continue to support exports because the proceeds contribute to the overhead costs of firms supplying the British military. These considerations cut both ways. The drive for arms sales itself distorts the design and production plans of British manufacturers and, in the view of some defence economists, offsets the savings in overheads. In any case, only some arms exports would be affected by a ban in the spirit of our supposedly ethical foreign policy. The posited economies of scale could readily be achieved by greater specialisation among Nato counties – a process inhibited by the desire of so many governments to protect domestic firms.

The NERA report

A report on export credit by the National Economic Research Associates (NERA). There has been some misguided celebration of the fact that NERA did not recommend that ECGD should be privatised. But the more important question is whether the provision of insurance cover should be subsidised. Until 1991, the Department showed heavy cash flow losses. It was then instructed to break even in cash flow terms in line with Berne procedures. But the ECGD is still, not required to show the positive return of 6% in real terms normally required on public sector investment projects. NERA could not find any justification for the subsidy – a most important finding which the vested interests involved have contrived to bury.

NERA's first preference is for an internationally negotiated phasing out. We must also face the question of whether there is a case for the UK moving further ahead on its own. But much more important than any of these details is the fact that reports such as NERA's are based on a mutually convenient misunderstanding. Economic research organisations, trying to unearth a case for intervention and subsidy, tend to focus on lapses from perfection inherent in almost all markets: matters such as informational barriers facing potential new exporters, and which governments might be able to help overcome by activities such as trade fairs or start-up credits. NERA indeed found such imperfections.

Politicians and opinion leaders take such reports, however, as confirmation that, without export promotion, the balance of payments would go haywire, the country become bankrupt and thousands of jobs would be lost. They conveniently overlook the fact that these bankruptcy and job fears are dismissed in polite terms as fallacies not worth serious consideration. NERA for instance remarked that the last thing the overheated British economy needed was extra demand for labour. Even in the year 2001 when there was a risk of recession, selective aid to a few heavy goods or arms manufacturers would have been an extremely inefficient way of stimulating demand.

SMALL ARMS TRADE

In the age of nuclear and other weapons of mass destruction, the vast majority of all warfare continues to be conducted using conventional weapons: machine rifles, grenades, landmines, explosives, and light rockets. These small arms, and the ability to obtain them, are the operational means of warfare. The much-touted efficiency of "high-tech" warfare based on computer-guided rockets and remote-controlled war machinery has been generally successful only as bombardment in advance of ground-based attack which ultimately depends on soldiers wielding hand-held weapons. Thus, even when blessed with unlimited war capability and unlimited weaponry options, militaries such as those of the United States and Russia depend on small arms to subdue populations and control territory. So do guerilla revolutionaries and those defending themselves against their own violently abusive governments. This essay will consider the issue of the global trade in small arms, examining its scope, its global economic underpinnings, its relationships to the economies of conflict-plagued countries, its particular connections to the current war in Sudan, and finally possible initiatives for reform of the global small arms trade.

The Scope of the Problem

As recently as World War II, the ability to prosecute war depended on developing the industrial capacity to produce these "small arms." During the Cold War, the United States and the Soviet Union provided conventional weapons for their respective client states fighting "proxy" wars. The high-geared military-industrial economies of the two leviathans have stimulated France, China, Germany, the UK, Italy, Ukraine, and Israel to compete in the lucrative worldwide business of weapons export. In 2002 these nine weapons-selling countries exported $14.8 billion in conventional weapons to the rest of the world. Forty percent of this staggering volume of weapons flows from Russia; 27% is shipped from the USA. The USA, UK, and France earned more in small arms sales to developing countries in 1998-2001 than they gave in aid.

The gigantism of this industry renders it a force in national economic policies. It is in the national interest of these nations, to some degree, to promote violent conflict and war around the world. As is apparent in the case of Sudan, the economic leverage of the weapons industry, including the small arms industry, may determine whether major first-world nations support or impede peace processes in war-torn countries. This positive self-interest that weapons-supplying first-world nations have in the negative interest — the active destruction and resulting impoverishment — of third-world nations is a very dark side of the economic colonialism that typifies neo-liberal economic globalization.

Classic game-theory analyses of arms race determinants assume arms development and production to come at the expense of a nation's economic well-being. While that may actually be true in terms of benefit to an entire nation's economy, it is *always* true that war yields positive economic benefit to national military industries, and that military industries hold disproportionate power over their governments' decision-making processes. In result, the world is flooded with weapons, and the potential to pursue violence is immediately and endlessly available to all. As Mary Kaldor notes, "violence is increasingly privatized both as a result of growing organized crime and the emergence of paramilitary groups." There are reported to be more than 639 million small arms in the world today; in the case of South Asia, 80% are in civilian (non-governmental) hands.

The availability of small arms is further assured through the worldwide financial deregulation that is a cornerstone of neo-liberal economic globalization. The deregulation of financial transactions has effectively rendered the financing of war exempt from national or international governance. Arms merchants and, significantly, diaspora supporters of civil conflicts are easily able to move funds instantly and covertly behind the screens of small states specializing in such banking services, thanks to the blessings of deregulated economic globalization. Weapons procurers are similarly enabled to operate with impunity, even when supplying arms illegally to the perpetrators of humanitarian crimes and genocides. Even when legal "controls" are in effect, sales and movement of small weapons to parties in conflict can proceed unabated. The illegal arms trade is estimated at more than (perhaps much more than) $1 billion per year. Conflict entrepreneurs – weapons manufacturers, gun-runners, merchant middle-men, and the weapons users themselves, profit both from the supply of weapons and from their use in protracted conflict.

During the Cold War massive supplies of conventional and more sophisticated weapons systems were pumped into client states by the Cold War powers, providing vast stores of machinery for ensuing post-Cold War wars. Weapons fed into the Afghanistan and Cambodian conflicts have been the foundation of supply for current South Asian violence. Massive supplies of weapons supplied to the Congo and Angola wars provided the stockpile for succeeding West African wars. The killing lives of such weapons may last many years. During the Cold War, the Coordinating Committee for Multilateral Export Controls (CoCom) operated as the Western self-regulation of which weapons and technologies were to be restricted. By 1989, however, the appeal of economic gains effectively overwhelmed security concerns. CoCom was disbanded in 1994, and first-world weapons producers have since fed arms to parties in conflict with unrestricted, free-market eagerness.

SMALL ARMS PROLIFERATION: THE ARMS CONTROL CHALLENGE

Over the course of the past decade small arms have become the primary choice of weapons for political and criminal groups in fueling armed conflicts, wars, massacres, ethnic cleansing and human rights violations. That, in no small measure is due to the fact that small arms are too readily available and too inexpensive, while at the same time requiring only minimal training, logistics and support to maintain and operate. 300 manufacturers in 74 countries produce small arms, of which well over 500,000,000 are believed to be in circulation, inside or outside of state regulatory controls.

Between 1985 and 1995, there has been a twenty-five per cent increase in the number of producers. Moreover, low-end sell-offs or give-aways of "surplus" small arms increase supply as well. As a result, there is an overabundance of inexpensive small arms glutting the world market.Yet, to date the international trade in small arms remains largely unregulated.

Principal sources of small arms include: small arms acquired for legal purposes and misused (e.g. human rights violations and external aggression), small arms acquired for legal purposes and sold/stolen; small arms for crime and unintentional injuries (gray market), and illegally manufactured or trafficked small arms (black market).

Whatever the perspective, i.e. peace-building versus crime prevention or arms control, draining these supply sources is imperative. Measures must be devised to limit the access to small arms (licensing, storage, embargoes), to reduce the supply of small arms (control of manufacture, identification, tracing etc.) and to reduce the demand for small arms (amnesties, buy-backs). The weapons of violence must be brought back into the control of the state, with the state itself being made accountable for its deeds. This essentially means empowering the state at one level, and using all tools available to induce more responsible behaviour on its part, at another. The two approaches must be mutually compatible.

The permanent members of the UN Security Council alone are responsible for 85% of the global arms trade. 40% of the worldwide flow of small arms is attributed to illicit trafficking and the majority of illicit weapons are proven to originate in the licit trade. Getting these governments to tighten national controls and to accept strengthened international standards for legal arms transfers should lend itself to reducing supply, significantly. Small arms transfer policies should be designed to support transfers that do not destabilize or threaten regional peace and security. With production monitored and limited and exports restricted and tighter controlled a reduced supply should restrict access and decrease overall circulation.

Given that small arms are produced, acquired and exported for legitimate purposes it is not, as opposed to the global campaign to ban landmines, appropriate to seek a ban. Rather, EPG's overall objective is to assist in efforts to curtail the supply of illicit small arms.

Such an objective will require a constructive parallelism among a range of politically and legally binding instruments, involving operative and normative measures which pertain both to the licit as well as the illicit trade, and which address both conflict prevention and conflict resolution. As one building block toward this overall objective, the group's goal is to promote a cooperative regulatory approach built around a small arms control regime (SACR), broad in scope and global in reach and to consist of, on the preventive side, (1) a Small Arms Register, (2) strengthened national export controls, and (3) an international code of conduct. On the reduction side, to consist of weapons collection programs as integral to peace agreements and post-conflict demobilization and reconstruction programs as well as to conflict prevention strategies.

Universal, comprehensive and non-discriminatory SACR would integrate current efforts based on a variety of approaches: crime prevention, arms control, firearms regulation, human rights, development, gun safety etc. It should, therefore, not be viewed as detracting from or interfering with ongoing, local, national or regional efforts. Rather, SACR can be said to provide a set of common standards around which these efforts can be harnessed.

Cooperative arms regulation and disarmament must address security and developmental concerns as functional corollaries and must be integrated into national programs as well as into international cooperation efforts. While the task is a daunting one, many international development agencies have already taken steps to incorporate security sector reform and other conflict prevention strategies into their assistance programs. Integral to cooperative disarmament, preventive measures must pursue two objectives: first, to limit and control availability and access to small arms (supply side) and secondly, to reduce the demand for such weapons (demand side). On the supply side such an approach necessitates measures aimed at effectively regulating legal transfers between states based on a principle of responsible restraint, controlling the availability, use and storage of small arms within states, preventing and combating illicit transfers, collecting and removing surplus arms from both civil society and regions of conflict, increasing transparency and accountability, support for research and information sharing.

Correspondingly, on the demand side, the international community must commit to helping reverse cultures of violence through support for the reform of the security sector (both police and military) in affected states as fundamental to good governance, through the promotion of norms of civilian non-possession and of government restraint, by enhancing demobilization and reintegration programs for ex-combatants, by halting the abhorrent use of child fighters and by effectively combating the culture of impunity that fuels the illicit arms trade.

Also, reduction measures must be devised to secure, destroy or otherwise responsibly dispose of small arms that are already in circulation, inside or outside of legal possession. The international donor community should establish collection and buy-back programs as well as other mechanisms to identify and promote best practices and to ensure adequate financial support. This is of particular importance with respect to "surplus" military weapons during a peace process.

Integral to peace accords, combatants must be demobilized, disarmed and weapons surrendered safely destroyed. There are important lessons to be learned from small arms collection and destruction (Mozambique, Mali, Liberia) reintegration of ex-combatants into productive civilian life (Cambodia, Philippines), post-conflict reconstruction (Cambodia, Bougainville) and the reform of police, judicial and penal systems (Cambodia, Papua

New Guinea). Law enforcement efforts in States where the illicit use of small arms is particularly severe should be supported as well.

The international donor community should cooperate with affected states in the establishment of incentive-based weapons collection programs as well as other mechanisms to identify and promote best practices and to ensure adequate financial support. The UN can develop centres for excellence pertaining to certain aspects of the problem area, such as arms collection programs, security sector reform and security arrangements for post-conflict development. Technical and financial resources are needed and the UN can play a role in mobilizing these resources.

4

Economics of the Global Arms Trade

Every sensible market economist should accept that a market must operate within a framework of law and moral convention.Investment Bankers are not permitted to finance firms that sell poison and there are strong constraints on the emission of lead into rivers or on pollutants into the chain of foodstuffs.My contention is that exports of arms to dubious regimes should come within the sphere of what is out of bounds – and more decisively so than at present.

Would we have to pay a heavy economic price for such restraint? There is indeed sometimes a conflict between national self-interest and ethical actions, just as there can be a conflict between personal self-interest and moral behaviour. But in both cases this is often exaggerated. In the national case it is exaggerated by an inflated view of the role of arms and export promotion in the British economy.

The promotion and *de facto* subsidisation of arms sales is – like most other industrial subsidies – wealth destroying; there would be very little, if any, sacrifice involved in doing away with the whole effort. Behind the arms promotion lobby is the primitive belief that if one source of overseas sales dries up, the workers and other resources involved would waste away. This is rubbish in view of the millions of people who change jobs every year. If other countries want to compete with us in foolish subsidies, let them.

The ethical case

It might be best to examine the ethical case before the economic arguments. It is not my intention to argue against all arms sales. It would be absurd for each member of an alliance to try to make a full range of weapons, simply out of *amour propre,* when specialisation would pay far better. In 1998-99 the Ministry of Defence spent 13% of its equipment budget on 64 co-operative equipment programmes involving 19 partner nations. The most important of these, by far, were France, Germany, the USA, Italy and the Netherlands.

Subsidised credit for exports of arms or major capital goods have far worse effects than just the economic ones. Western nations are undoubtedly rich enough to waste some resources. As Adam Smith said: 'There is an awful lot of ruin in a nation.'

The worst effects are political and moral. They are both illustrated by the instance of the Pergau Dam in Malaysia in the mid 1990s when the Conservative government overturned a publicly minuted reservation by the Permanent Secretary of the Department of Overseas Development and insisted on supporting credits for this dam.

One of the unstated arguments for going ahead was that this would act as a sweetener to persuade the Malaysian government to buy other goods, including arms, from Britain. On the other hand arms sales are justified because they are supposed to persuade governments that buy them to use British equipment in their capital projects. Thus one bad consequence is called in aid to support another; and Third World despots are encouraged to devote still more resources to military spending on prestige projects of dubious value.

More recently, the Labour Prime Minister was said to have overruled the Foreign Secretary when he authorised a statement by Stephen Byers on 21 December 1999 that he was 'minded', subject to certain conditions, to grant export credit for the Ilisu dam project in Turkey, which will flood several valleys with sites of unique cultural and religious value to the Kurds. You can imagine what this will do to promote ethnic harmony inside Turkey. In the spring of 2001 we were still waiting for a decision.

We cannot leave out of account the enormous part that bribery plays in this trade. A forthcoming study by Joe Roeber concludes that: 'Because of the structure, complexity and capacity of the market, and above all, because of the secrecy that surrounds every aspect of its activities, the international arms trade is the most corrupt of all legal trades.' He finally asks: 'Can we justify bribing people to buy arms they may not need with money their taxpayers cannot afford, simply to inflate the number of jobs in a declining industry?'

All these follies are supported by the myth that exports are valuable for their own sake, however small the return the British nation gets from them. Business lobbyists are able to persuade a succession of prime ministers, ranging from ultra-dry Conservatives to New Labour that, if the government does not support them, their overseas rivals will win the contracts instead.

Orders of magnitude

The official estimate for British arms sales is that they amounted in 1999 to about £4bn or appreciably less 0.5% of GDP. A great part consisted of aircraft and aerospace parts. A good academic estimate of the direct cost of government support is about £400m per annum. This does not cover the arms promotion aspects of many royal, political and military visits and activities, which are ostensibly for other purposes. Indirect support for what is known as the Defence Industrial Base is a good deal larger. The number of workers employed is put at 90,000 or just over 0.33% of UK employment. There are two practical inhibitions that limit official export promotion. The first and obvious one is the Exchequer cost. Secondly there is the fear that official promotional activities will be self-defeating, and still more expensive, if all governments follow them in a competitive race. Accordingly, international organisations such as the European Union, the World Trade Organisation, the OECD and the Berne Credit Union have set rules to limit – but not stop – government support.

Unfortunately these agreements do not prevent the never-ending procession of royalty, ministers and ambassadors who promote arms sales abroad, to say nothing of the military and trade attachés. Then there is the Defence Export Services

Organisation, which provides marketing and military assistance. Above all, arms sales are often backed by the Export Credits Guarantee Department (ECGD), which provides 'insurance and finance packages for exporters of capital goods and services and political risk insurance' – in other words, taxpayer support for sales that would not pass muster on purely commercial terms. While public enterprises are set a target real rate of return of six per cent, the ECGD has to do no more than break even on average. The ECGD covers medium to long-term capital goods exports from three years up to 16 years duration. In a typical year it underwrites about £7bn of cover. The business is concentrated almost entirely on civil engineering projects and military and civil aerospace. The largest recipient is China. The military share of ECGD business has averaged over 25% in the most recent five years.

The much-maligned Treasury tends to fight many ECGD deals, but is often defeated. Huw Evans, a former Treasury deputy secretary, has said that the ECGD is too vulnerable to intensive lobbying of ministers by large corporations and that it should become an independent agency. As Andrew Tyrie MP, a former adviser to Conservative chancellors has written, 'It is illogical to indulge in a competition to give away our own exports through an auction of subsidies.'

THE GLOBAL SMALL ARMS CAMPAIGN

The humanitarian, political-economic and security dimensions of excessive and destabilizing accumulations of small arms confront civil and political society with the need for immediate action. With political awareness aroused by the human toll of illicit small arms in Africa, Asia, Europe and the Western Hemisphere, denoting the issue's global dimension, the UN is embarking on the important task to convene, by 2001, an international conference on the illicit trade in small arms in all its aspects.

A nascent global campaign is to be commended for successfully pushing small arms onto the agenda of multilateral arms control. Unlike the international campaign to ban landmines, however, the emerging "movement" is lacking in focus and direction. A plethora of initiatives notwithstanding, concerns persist that economic and political interests of the few may hinder tangible humanitarian results for the many.

The potential for diversion is immense as even basic agreement on how to define the issue remains wanting. Is it, for example, an arms control, disarmament or crime prevention issue; is one to address oneself on the supply or the demand side, the precipitating versus root causes of small arms violence? Too overwhelming, then, the dualism which connects illicit arms to the licit trade, where a majority of them originate, too daunting the interaction between the licit and illicit trade, too challenging the interconnectedness between the root and precipitating causes of civil conflict and small arms violence.

Small arms violence poses as much an arms control challenge as a humanitarian challenge. It can also be said, since a majority of weapons producers are located in the developed world and a majority of weapons recipients in the developing world, the small arms issue is, at its core, a North-South issue. In the North, the global campaign on small arms must be put in the framework of development, demilitarization and peace building. In the South, such a campaign must be put in the context of a broader justice-oriented community and human rights.

Reducing the number of small arms requires a multisectoral and comprehensive approach, encompassing a whole range of measures, both operative and normative, which must be dealt with both within the context of conflict prevention and conflict resolution. Small arms action must address both security, humanitarian and developmental concerns.

Economic development is dependent on a secure and stable political environment. Some refer to this as the "Security First" approach. But the opposite is also true: without economic development, many of the root causes of grievance cannot be properly addressed and there will be no political stability. A more appropriate-nonetheless more daunting-approach instead of "Security First" is "a proportional and integrated approach to security and development." In areas of conflict, both security and development aspects must be integrated into national programs as well as into international cooperation efforts. Whereas, however, taking a narrow approach "Security First" advances security at the expense of development, the proportional-integrated approach takes too broad a venue with respect both, to the supply of and demand for small arms, existent and future stockpiles and inherent linkages between security and development. It would appear that it strives to achieve too much in too short a period of time.

Recognizing security and development as corollaries in reducing supply the EPG compromise cooperative regulatory approach advances a constructive parallelism between both input functions without establishing ipso facto linkages which, from a bargaining point of view, should lend itself to tangible results within a reasonable time frame. The compromise approach built around a universal, comprehensive and non-discriminatory Small Arms Control Regime which centres on transparency and accountability should not be seen as an alternative, but as a minimalist position concomitant to the integrated-proportional approach.

An independent international commission the Eminent Persons Group strives to make a specific contribution to the emerging global small arms effort. While fully acknowledging the need for a broad approach, EPG pursues a cooperative regulatory approach to the international trade in small arms. As a sub-campaign and integral to the larger small arms campaign being led by the International Action Network on Small Arms (IANSA), EPG undertakes to confront the supply side of the illicit trade by making cross-border arms sales subject to arms control, export and transparency regimes.

Moreover, governments will be encouraged to limit the number of small arms approved for export, to combat illicit transfers of weapons and to assist in extracting surplus weapons which are circulating the global market. In this complex situation, a sincere abhorrence of covert wars and civilian destruction would prove conducive to putting in place the norms that would regulate state behaviour.

The attainment of the goal requires an integrated proportional approach between governments and civil society to advance elements of a realistic plan of action for the 2001 UN conference on small arms trafficking in all its aspects. Within the preparatory process for the conference, this approach consists of two tracks: first, the involvement of EPG on the inter-governmental level and secondly, the participation of EPG within the NGO community. For the two levels of action, the governmental and non-governmental, are co-dependent and mutually enhancing in building momentum for regulatory controls and micro-disarmament.

EPG's ability to remain highly visible at both, the non-governmental and inter-governmental levels of small arms action, defines the Commission's juxtaposition within the global small arms effort. The Commission's uniqueness lies in the special blending of incumbent and former officials at the highest levels of government from around the world. Members of the Commission represent both, weapons-exporting and weapons-importing countries.

This active involvement of decision-makers in the early stages of and throughout the preparatory process is essential to political advances towards curtailing small arms proliferation. It is the high caliber of members of the commission, which provides for the level of credibility and political prestige to assure serious deliberations.

With respect to the governmental level, EPG is in exploratory talks with UN member States, within the Group of Interested States (GIS), to provide for a consultative framework, affiliated with but independent of the eminent persons group. GIS is comprised of foreign ministers of those UN member States which are taking the lead on the small arms issue and which find themselves in conceptual agreement on the cooperative regulatory approach inherent in SACR.

Without prejudice to national bargaining positions, GIS facilitates consultations on a multilateral approach to small arms proliferation both, throughout the preparatory process and at the conference itself. With respect to the non-governmental level EPG is actively cooperating with and working through IANSA. At the same time, as part of its commitment to help raise the profile of small arms proliferation globally, EPG is pursuing a vigorous public diplomacy schedule.

In close consultation with UN member States, the UN Secretariat and other NGOs the group will, within the preparatory committee, advance elements of an action agenda aimed at curtailing illicit small arms by confronting the illicit trade. To be successful such an action agenda must centre on increased transparency and raised common standards and provide concrete and practical measures on the global and regional level. The group will submit to the UN conference a report on the scope and magnitude of the illicit arms trade, ways to curb it and the United Nations role in collecting and disseminating information in this area, prevention and enforcement.

ECONOMICS OF MILITARY INDUSTRIES

The creation of indigenous defense industries in developing countries is motivated by a variety of strategic, political, and economic factors. Since arms are not regarded as a purely commercial good, their production in developing countries is not governed solely by the economics of comparative advantage. A strategic motivation behind the creation of a military industry is to reduce the dependence on unreliable, or potentially unreliable, sources of arms. South Africa, for example, initiated an intense effort to build its military industry in the late 1960s and early 1970s in anticipation of an arms embargo. Brazil, from the late 1960s, pursued a political strategy of building up its defense industry not only as part of its ambitions to be a regional power and a symbol of national pride, but also in response to a US arms embargo. Yet, once political conditions change, nations reassess the benefit of defense industries to national strategic goals.

Proponents of a Domestic Defense Industry

Proponents of a domestic defense industry argue that industrial development, job creation, and export opportunities provide marginal benefits in excess of marginal costs. Ideally, the defense industry would promote the development of human capital and prevent the emigration of skilled labour. The creation of a military industry would also promote the development of a civilian industry by providing backward linkages into the economy for support industries and forward linkages by feeding into downstream industries. Offset deals, co-production and license agreements with foreign producers would promote technology transfer from more technologically advanced nations. Ideally, the country would improve its balance of payments by import substitution industrialization, substituting the imports of arms for those locally produced, and by exporting to foreign markets, thus saving foreign currency.

However, there are many hidden costs in defense production. Developing countries rely on importing raw material, parts, and technology for the industry. These imports drain the foreign exchange reserves that the defense industry generates. Arms exports and industries are often subsidized by governments. The subsidies conceal the true cost of the transactions. In general, defense industries are less productive than civilian industries and the cost of maintaining advanced technology could be prohibitive. In addition, the industries demand for highly skilled labour could deprive civilian industries of resources needed to develop.

Ladder of Production

Krause (1992) enumerates a process, an eleven step "ladder of production," by which a developing country would progress from an arms importer to a fully independent arms producer. Krause explains such models as being descriptive of the evolution, rather than the linear progression, of the defense production process. Brauer (2002) points out that some countries may chose to enter into the defense production industry at entry points beyond stage one. In addition, some countries may chose to focus on different entry points for different arms. He distinguishes between complete weapons systems production and weapons modules development. Although the US, and to a lesser extent, countries such as France, the UK, and Russia are technological

innovators in defense production, Krause (1992) argues that most arms production efforts seem to end between stage eight and nine with progress beyond limited R&D being rare. While the ladder of production is descriptive of the evolution of the defense production process, it does not capture the time progression of the development of indigenous arms industries. The time progression of the eleven steps of the ladder of production as a function of the time required to attain each level. The process is non-linear with increasing opportunity cost for a country to reach the higher stages. The production process through the first five steps can skip levels or enter at any level. However, it would be difficult for a country to ascend to higher stages by skipping lower stages. Comparative advantage would suggest that countries should produce at a level with the ratio of their marginal cost to marginal benefit equal to that of other arms producers.

Industrial Compensation Practice

Offsets, an industrial compensation practice imposed by the buyer country as a condition of purchase on the seller company, have become a popular method for stimulating domestic economic activity. While civil offset programs are not permissible for developed countries under Article XXIII of the Government Procurement Act of the World Trade Organization, offsets from defense procurement are an option available to all countries.

The offsets can be directly linked to defense contracts such as technology transfer, co-production, or local assembly related directly to the equipment purchased or they can be indirectly sourced where civilian, military goods, or services are unrelated to the defense equipment purchased. Although, the costs and benefits of offsets are debatable, no compelling evidence points to the positive impact of offsets on a domestic economy. This pattern is consistent across countries as varied as Brazil, India, and Saudi Arabia where offsets were used to stimulate a variety of economic and industrial policy initiatives.

South Africa presents a good example of progress in indigenous defense production. Batchelor and Willett (1998) divide South Africa's defense production into three distinct time periods in which civilian manufacturing employment growth exceeded that of the defense industry and where military expenditures grew faster than total government expenditure.

During the first period, 1961-68, South Africa shifted away from a heavy reliance on complete weapons systems imports to stage five of the production ladder, final weapons systems assembly and local component production. By the end of the second period, 1968-77, South Africa reached stage seven, limited R&D improvements to local license-produced arms, and was close to stage eight, limited independent production of less sophisticated weapons and limited production of more advanced weapons, in certain sections, such as ammunitions and small arms.

In the last period, 1977-89, the defense industry reached stage nine, independent R&D and production of less sophisticated weapons. The ammunitions and small arms sector were at stage ten, independent R&D and production of advanced arms with foreign components, Military aircraft, missiles, and naval vessels production were at much lower stages of the ladder.

Civilian Industry

Defense production is less efficient than civilian industry as its primary aim is raising weapons systems performance by technological improvements, rather than cost reduction through a streamlined production process. In addition, investment in defense production and poor choices of military technology led to underinvestment in civilian industries for the same countries.

The evidence in support of the economic gains from establishing military industries is quite mixed for developing countries. Devarajan, Swaroop, and Zou (1996) test whether the share allocated to various components of government expenditures is associated with higher growth. They find that defense expenditures appear to have a negative influence on economic growth whereas consumption oriented public expenditures appear to positively influence economic growth. Dunne (1996) substantiates their findings and affirms that reallocations from defense spending to other forms of government spending have been shown to increase employment in developing countries.

Analyse the Economic Significance

Batchelor and Willett (1998) analyse the economic significance of South Africa's defense industry and conclude that despite increasing numbers of highly skilled workers employed in the industry, it absorbed scarce labour resources making them unavailable to the civilian industry. Brazil's economic gains from its weapons industry are mixed Although, in absolute numbers, about 200,000 jobs were created at the height of the industry's success, a trivial amount for a country of Brazil's size. They also point out that domestic defense production remained a net user of foreign exchange with no positive impact on the country's technological performance. Foreign exchange earnings are questionable when balanced against the cost of acquiring technology and components. The resulting development and success of the Brazilian civilian aircraft industry came at a great cost and may have been achieved by direct government support rather than indirect military production promotion. In Brazil, however, the skill and technology levels of military and civilian industries are more compatible than in other countries and these industries have managed to support each other.

KADDB

In the early 1990s, Jordan's military industry expertise lay with the Royal Maintenance Corps (RMC), which was charged with maintenance, overhaul, and limited upgrades of equipment. The largest facility was the King Hussein Main Workshops (KHMW) in Zarqa. The RMC rebuilt armoured vehicles, performed some redesign on the British built Alvis Scorpion tracked reconnaissance vehicle and undertook the modernization of armoured fighting vehicles and armoured personnel carriers. The RMC outfitted some Scorpions with TOW anti-tank missiles, and others with a mortar carrier. This work was part of a plan to create an indigenous military industrial capability known as the Jordan National Industry.

In August of 1999, the Jordanians established KADDB as an independent government entity within the Jordan Armed Forces (JAF) with a Board of Directors reporting to the Private Office of the King of Jordan through the Chairman of the Joint Chiefs of Staff. KADDB's operations are funded from the defense budget and earned income. KADDB mission is to supply the JAF with a range of scientific and technical services in engineering and applied research including policy and technical advice and support, operational assessments and studies, formulation of user requirement statements, concept definition, project support, equipment trials and evaluation, and general support. In addition, KADDB is to provide training for Jordanian engineers in research, design, and development to facilitate further employment opportunities.

KADDB operates with two strategic business groups. The Engineering Group is responsible for the design, development, prototyping, evaluation, and industrialization of equipment primarily for the Jordanian armed and civil defense forces and secondarily for markets in the Middle East and North Africa. KADDB's Commercial Operations Group has two departments, Marketing and Business Development. The commercial group is responsible for the marketing of KADDB projects, technologies, and services. KADDB had expected to generate, within five years of its conception in 1999, a revenue stream enabling a self sufficient Bureau to operate without government subsidies.

KADDB's strategic direction, from its inception to 2005, was to focus on wheeled and tracked armoured fighting vehicles (AFV) design, development, integration, prototyping, testing, and evaluation to be achieved through joint venture operations. KADDB medium term plans are to expand land system capabilities to include communication systems, battlefield management systems, and air defense systems. KADDB is to develop the capability to upgrade aircraft and integrate aircraft systems. An overview of KADDB products. The companies KADDB formed, the strategic partners involved, and the employment generated.

KADDB does not have access to offset agreements to help develop its capability since Jordan currently does not have offset agreements with any of its suppliers and, quite probably, does not have the purchasing power to be able to aggressively pursue offsets. However, since the benefits of offsets, both those that are direct and indirect, are questionable, it may be in Jordan's best interest to refrain from pursuing this option; this is especially true because arms purchasers may actually pay a higher price when seeking offsets. The US has increased its military aid to Jordan since the mid 1990s, helping maintain Jordan's level of military expenditures.

Jordan currently has one of the highest military expenditures to GDP ratios for its income class. The Jordanian Armed Forces currently rely on the United States Foreign Military Financing (FMF) for a substantial percentage of their military expenditures. The Annual US military assistance to Jordan. The US level of aid has fluctuated widely over the past 10 years in response to political conditions and available aid funding. Jordan can not access FMF for domestic acquisition, and as such, KADDB does not have the flexibility to use these funds to help develop Jordan's indigenous defense industry. However, because of the fungibility of these funds, Jordan is able to maintain the same level of military expenditures with less domestic funds and at the same time support its defense industry.

KADDB and QIZ

KADDB and the QIZ are the two major economic efforts undertaken by the Jordanian government to stimulate the domestic economy. Although, the QIZ program was established three years before KADDB, comparing their performance to this point would be beneficial. In absolute numbers, even after accounting for expatriate employment, the QIZs have created more employment opportunities for Jordanians than KADDB. Most of the QIZ created jobs, however, require minimal technical skills. Data available from the Ministry of Industry and Trade for 2002 provide a rough classification of jobs available in 31 QIZs. While it is difficult to determine the level of skills required using the job description provided, by the process of eliminating obviously low skilled positions, it is estimated that, at a maximum 6% of domestic jobs generated by QIZs, about 1200, require some technical expertise. Although, the available information for the jobs KADDB created is not complete, it would not exceed 1250 positions and presumably a high percentage of them require some technical skills and a fair percentage would require some form of higher education.

The level of technology used in the QIZs does not extend beyond garment assembly (sewing, ironing and washing). As such, the technology transfer from the QIZs into Jordan is minimal. Applying Krause's production ladder, the QIZs probably operate at an equivalent of level one with the ability to perform simple maintenance work. KADDB, using Krause's "ladder of production" has reached level five by having attained the capability of performing final assembly of less sophisticated weapons with some local component production and to a small extent may have reached level six of co-production or complete licensed production of less sophisticated weapons. KADDB has started operating at level seven of limited R&D improvements to local license produced arms for some systems. KADDB is clearly transferring more technology into Jordan than the QIZs. Comparing the technology transferred by KADDB and the civilian sector into the country, it appears to be at about the same level for equipment manufacturing and assembly. However, the IT transfer into the country appears to be higher than that available in the civilian sector.

Little evidence exists to confirm the QIZ or the KADDB success in creating strong backward and forward linkages into the economy because of Jordan's narrow industrial base. QIZs essentially transform imported raw material into a finished product. Little of what goes into creating a final product originates domestically and the value added comes from the transformation (i.e. fabric into clothing). The number of subcontractor companies created in the QIZ zones to support QIZ activites. All these companies are connected in some way to the garment industry. There is no employment or sales data available for these companies. As it takes very little capital investment to establish a garment facility, these industries are easy to relocate to other countries. The concern is that the QIZs located in Jordan could migrate to Turkey, Morocco, or Egypt, nations with a larger domestic industrial base, when these nations conclude similar arrangements with the US. KADDB seems to make a policy of partnering with a domestic civilian entity for its projects. As such, these civilian entities may be able to transfer their knowledge and experience into the civilian economy. What is not clear at this time is the extent of these industries reliance on defense work and whether they have been able to branch out into the non-defense sector.

QIZ generated exports increased from $2.44 million in 1999 to $919.94 million in 2004. These constituted 23% of all exports from Jordan in 2004. All QIZ exports are directed to the US and it is highly unlikely that Jordan exports to the US would have increased at this rate without the QIZ arrangements. What is not clear at this time is Jordan's success at cultivating the EU and regional markets for QIZ type products. At this point, it is impossible to gauge KADDB's success in exporting since KADDB does not disclose its sales figures. However, KADDB reports some success exporting to Algeria, Iraq, Libya, Saudi Arabia, Sudan, Yemen, and UAE. KADDB also reports sales to the JAF. Again, sales figures were not made available.

Neither the QIZs nor KADDB have been successful in attracting regional capital. The QIZ companies have generated about $182 million in Foreign Direct Investment (FDI). Approximately 88% of the capital is classified as non-Arab and 5.7% as Jordanian with the balance of 6.3% being regional capital. None of the KADDB joint venture companies list a regional partner and KADDB does not report figures regarding the amount of FDI resulting from non-regional partners.

DEFENCE INDUSTRY AND THE ECONOMIC CHARACTER

The transformation of China's defence establishment into a system capable of independently sustaining modern armed forces was one of the major goals of the military modernization program. In the late 1970s and 1980s, defence spending remained relatively constant despite the shift in resources in favour of overall economic development. Reforms focused on reorganizing the defence research-and-development and industrial base, more closely integrating civilian and military science and industry, and selectively utilizing foreign technology. China sold arms for hard currency to provide additional funds for defence industries. The PLA continued to play its role in economic development by participating in selective construction projects, providing dual-use training, and producing most of its food needs.

Military Expenditures

In the 1980s Chinese statistics indicated that defence spending represented a decreasing percentage of government expenditures, falling from 16 percent in 1980 to 8.3 percent of the state budget in 1987. However, United States Department of Defence studies suggested that the published budget figures understated defence spending by about one-half. With the growth of the Chinese economy under the modernization program, defence spending also represented a smaller percentage of the gross domestic product (GDP) than previously. United States Central Intelligence Agency analysts estimated that defence expenditures in 1978 absorbed 8 to 10 percent of GDP; in 1986 United States Department of Defence analysts estimated that China's military expenses fell within the range of 6 to 8 percent of GDP. Comparison of indices of defence procurement spending and industrial production from 1971 to 1983 revealed that the former increased by 15 percent, whereas the latter rose by 170 percent. These studies indicated that Chinese leaders have indeed subordinated military modernization to economic development. United States Department of Defence officials in 1986 estimated Chinese defence spending by resources and force categories for the 1967 to 1983 period. Roughly 50 percent of defence expenditures were for weapons, equipment, and new facilities; 35 percent for operating costs; and 15 percent for research, development, and testing and evaluation.

By service, these costs broke down to 25 percent for the ground forces; 15 percent for the Navy; 15 percent for strategic air defenses; 5 percent for ballistic missile forces; 5 percent for tactical air forces; and about 35 percent for command, logistics, personnel, intelligence, medical care, administration, research, development, testing and evaluation, and other support. Beginning in the late 1970s, China devoted more resources to its Strategic Missile Force, indicating an effort to increase its strategic security while modernizing the economy, and to national command and support activities, reflecting an emphasis on modernization of the defence structure.

MILITARY R&D AND NDSTIC

The National Defence Science, Technology, and Industry Commission was the coordinating body for military research and development and industrial production. The NDSTIC reported to the party Central Military Commission's National Defence Industries Committee and the State Council's Leading Group for Science and Technology. The NDSTIC supervised weapons research and development, coordinated military production of defence industries, and controlled funding for weapons procurement. The establishment of the NDSTIC was a reform measure designed to break down the barriers between civilian and military research and development and industry. Military science and industry previously had been secretive, segregated, and privileged sectors, having material, financial, and personnel resources superior to those available to the civilian sector. The creation of the NDSTIC was one measure by which Chinese leaders hoped to facilitate the transfer of technology between the military and civilian sectors. The NDSTIC, in particular through its trading arm, China Xinshidai Corporation, coordinated procurement of foreign technology for military purposes.

Defence Industry

Beginning in 1978, Chinese leaders set out to transform the defence industries, which had a huge excess capacity and were criticized for having a "golden rice bowl" (rich but always begging for more). To utilize this excess capacity better and to break down the barriers between military and civilian industry, the machine-building ministries were reorganized, and civilians were appointed to manage them.

The civilianized, renamed ministries and their responsibilities consisted of the Ministry of Nuclear Industry—nuclear weapons; Ministry of Aeronautics—aircraft; Ministry of Electronics Industry—electronics; Ministry of Ordnance Industry— munitions and armaments; Ministry of Astronautics—ballistic missiles and space systems; and China State Shipbuilding Corporation—naval construction.

In 1986 the Ministry of Machine Building, which produced civilian heavy machinery and industrial equipment, and the Ministry of Ordnance Industry were consolidated into the new State Machine-Building Industry Commission as a way to strengthen the unified management of the national machine-building and weapons enterprises.

In 1987 little information was available about this new commission or its relationship to the NDSTIC or to the State Economic Commission, whose Defence Bureau coordinated the civilian production of the defence industry. Further changes in defence industry structure occurred in 1986 and 1987, when inland defence enterprises were either relocated closer to transportation links or cities, closed down, or transferred to local civilian control and production.

Weapons Production

In 1987 China adopted a new contractual system for weapons research, development, and production. It was not clear from available information how this contract system would affect the role of the NDSTIC as the coordinating body for defence science and industry. Previously, the NDSTIC controlled procurement funding, reviewed proposals for weapons requirements funneled through the General Staff Department's Equipment Subdepartment, and coordinated with defence industries to produce the needed equipment. Under the new system, the state divided defence research and development funds into three categories: military equipment research, basic and applied sciences research, and unidentified technological services. The first type of appropriation went to military arms and services, which signed contracts with research institutes or enterprises to develop and manufacture the required weapons.

The contract system involved the PLA, which had been removed to a large extent from such activities, in the development and manufacture of the weapons it would use. The second category of funds was devoted to basic research and applied science to help modernize the defence industry. The third category went to technological services necessary for research programs. This reform was another measure designed to integrate military and civilian industry by placing the military production of defence industries within the framework of the planned-commodity economy. The new system further sought to provide the military with better equipment at a minimum cost, to force the defence industry to upgrade weapons designs and improve production, to improve the management of weapons research and development through state application of economic levers, to promote cooperation between research institutes and factories, and to increase the decision-making powers of the enterprises.

Procurement of weapons and equipment represented 45 percent of the defence budget during the 1967 to 1983 period. This figure included 25 percent for aircraft, 15 percent for ground forces weapons, and about 10 percent each for naval and missile systems. China's military-industrial complex, the third largest in the world, produced a wide variety of weapons, including light arms and ammunition, armor, artillery, combat aircraft, fast-attack craft, frigates, destroyers, conventional and nuclear submarines, electronic equipment, tactical missiles, and ballistic missiles.

With the notable exception of China's indigenously produced nuclear submarines, nuclear missiles, and satellites, most Chinese weaponry was based on Soviet designs of the 1950s and 1960s. Much of this equipment was obsolete or obsolescent, and beginning in the late 1970s China made great efforts to upgrade the equipment by changing indigenous design or by incorporating Western technology. The greatest weaknesses were in conventional arms, precision-guided munitions, electronic warfare, and command, control, communications, and intelligence. China attempted to address these weaknesses by focusing military research on electronics—essential to progress in the previously mentioned areas—and by selectively importing key systems or technologies.

INDIAN DEFENCE MANUFACTURE

A nation's military strength is determined by its economic might. Industry provides the military with the wherewithal to fight the nation's wars. Since independence the policy relating to Strategic Defence Production has been evolving. For too long, India depended on foreign industries for its military hardware. The desire to achieve self-reliance has always been there. Constraints of technology and resources prevented the process from fructifying to the extent desired. The first phase, was characterized by the State led industrialization. Since the era of liberalization, which began in 1991, the role of private sector and also that of competition, both domestic and international is playing a much greater role in the national economy. Naturally, this also meant changes in policy for Defence production.

Production of defence equipment has been under the purview of Government right from its inception. The Industrial Policy of the country had kept defence production in the public sector since First Industrial Policy outlined in the Industry Policy Resolution of 1948. The Industries (Development & Regulation) Act, 1951 gave statutory base to the Industrial Policy. Under this policy, the Defence Industry, which required heavy investments, strong R&D backing and on which there could be total reliance because of its criticality, remained under Government Control at all times. The control over defence industry was exercised under the Industries (Development & Regulation) Act, 1951, which made licensing compulsory. As a consequence of the then industrial policy, a large infrastructure for Defence production consisting of 39 Ordnance Factories, 8 Defence PSUs and 50 Research & Development laboratories was created in the country.

However, contrary to the common perception, the Private Sector has been playing significant role in the Defence industry sector as sub contractors and ancillary industry. The private sector mainly has been involved in supply of raw materials, semi-finished products, parts and components to Defence PSUs and Ordnance Factories to a great extent and also to Base Workshops of Army and Base Repair Depots of Air Force and the Dockyards of the Navy. Defence PSUs and Ordnance Factories are outsourcing their requirements from private sector (mainly SMEs) in the range of 20-25%. Out of this outsourcing, about 25% requirement is met through small-scale sector.

Several hi-tech equipments have also been successfully produced by the private sector. In the quest for self-reliance in the crucial sector of defence, the Government has been continuing its efforts to indigenize defence equipment wherever technologically feasible and economically viable. It has been a part of indigenization efforts to locate and develop broad-based indigenous supply source – both in the public sector and in the civil trade for many complicated and intricate equipments. The economic liberalization in 1991 resulted in the high degree of deregulation and allowed the private industry to progress more rapidly. With the initial difficulties encountered by the Indian Industry today one has witnessed positive impact of this liberalization. There has been tremendous growth in the private sector and today many Indian companies are global players.

After considering the capital intensive nature of defence industry sector as also the need to infuse foreign technology and additional capital including FDI, Govt. decided in May, 2001 to open Defence industry for private sector participation up to 100% with FDI permissible up to 26% - both subject to licensing. Now with this policy change all defence related items have been removed from Reserved Category and transferred to the licensed category, as a result of which private sector can manufacture all types of defence equipment after getting a licence. Consequent to the Government's announcement about the policy change, Department of Industrial Policy & Promotion (DIPP) in consultation with Ministry of Defence, issued detailed guidelines regarding the modalities for consideration of applications for grant of Industrial Licence.

After the announcement of policy changes, there has been a paradigm shift in the role of private sector in the field of indigenisation, i.e., from the role of supplier of raw materials, components, sub-systems, they have now become partners in the manufacture of complete advanced equipment/system. The basic objective of allowing private sector participation is to harness available expertise in the private sector towards the total defence efforts and search for self-reliance. In-built advantages of the private sector are its reservoir of management, scientific and technological skills coupled with its ability to raise resources. The involvement of private sector with its world-class expertise and high technology would not only augment India's indigenous defence production capability but also lead to creation of employment and infrastructure in the country, giving a strong impetus to the economy. It must be acknowledged that the policy change of May 2001 for allowing private industry to produce any defence item under licence was a logical outcome of liberalization initiated in India in 1991. The private sector industry in India is now just beginning to become significant partner in production and development of Defence items.

After opening up of defence production for the private sector, the industry has shown keen interest in this field. Many large industries have shown definite inclination to invest both in R&D and infrastructure to develop capabilities in defence production to assume the role of system integrators.

5

The International Arms Trade: Difficult to Define, Measure, and Control

The international arms trade apparently has weathered the financial crisis quite well. Available data indicate that the impact to date on the volume of orders and deliveries has been limited.

As has been shown in the past, financial resources—from domestic budgets or foreign military assistance—are not the only factor that influences arms acquisitions. Perceived internal or external threats to national security, the need to replace or upgrade military inventories, demonstrations of international status, development of domestic arms industries via licensed production and offsets, the desire to strengthen ties with suppliers, and the influence of the military play important roles in the arms acquisition process. Before permitting exports of arms and military equipment, suppliers will assess the potential economic gains and the potential impact of the transfer on their strategic interests and foreign policy. Will the transfer harm or help friendly states or the supplier's international commitments, reputation, or standing?

For several reasons, there is no straightforward answer to the question, "How big is the international arms trade?" First, there is no globally agreed definition of "arms." States and international organizations that seek to measure or control the arms trade use lists of items that vary in their complexity and coverage, most notably with regard to their inclusion of "dual-use goods," items with both military and civilian applications. Second, there is no common agreement on what types of activities constitute the arms trade. Examples of areas where differences exist include arms leased to other states; gifts and donations; the transfer of technology to produce arms and military equipment; and upgrades, parts, and services related to the transfer of arms and military equipment. Third, the lack of openness and transparency by many arms suppliers and recipients regarding the value and volume of their arms exports and imports makes it difficult to collect accurate data. As a result, a variety of different definitions of the international arms trade and estimates of its scale exists. This has implications for efforts to establish controls on arms transfers via a future international arms trade treaty (ATT). This article will outline some of the challenges in defining, measuring, and controlling the international arms trade.

Definitions and Estimates

The national lists of arms and military equipment to be subject to export controls (control lists) maintained by most states and all major arms exporters provide a useful starting point for defining "arms" and the international arms trade. The Munitions List and Lists of Dual-Use Goods and Technologies of the Wassenaar Arrangement on Export Controls for Conventional Arms and Dual-Use Goods and Technologies provide the basis for the control lists of the 40 states that are members of the group. The Munitions List covers a wide range of arms and military equipment, from small arms to ships, as well as ammunition, information and communication technologies, training equipment, and equipment for producing arms. Several significant arms-exporting nonmembers, including China, have fully or partially aligned their national control lists with the Munitions List. As a result, all of the top 10 arms suppliers during 2005-2009 have control lists derived from the Wassenaar Arrangement.

National control lists serve as the basis for national reports on arms exports. As of January 2010, 32 states had published at least one national report on arms exports since 1990, and a further nine states provided information on the value of their export licenses and exports to the 2009 European Union (EU) Annual Report on

Arms Exports. These reports vary in detail but, at a minimum, tend to provide data on the financial value of arms export licenses or arms exports. Several major exporters (e.g., Russia) do not produce such reports, but do release official data on the financial value of their arms exports. Using national reports and official statements, the Stockholm International Peace Research Institute (SIPRI) has attempted to provide estimates of the financial value of the international arms trade.

The now-defunct U.S. Arms Control and Disarmament Agency (ACDA) created the following comprehensive definition of the arms trade, which has been widely used by researchers: weapons of war, parts thereof, ammunition, support equipment, and other commodities designed for military use.... Dual-use equipment...when its primary mission is identified as military. The building of defence production facilities and licensing fees paid as royalties for the production of military equipment.... Military services such as training, supply operations, equipment repair, technical assistance and construction are included where data are available.

A similar definition of the arms trade is used to compile the U.S. Congressional Research Service's (CRS) annual report, "Conventional Arms Transfers to Developing Nations." In spite of the name, the report contains estimates for the value of the global arms trade, not just trade with developing countries. The CRS estimated the financial value of deliveries of arms to be $34.5 billion for 2007. Despite using a narrower definition of arms transfers than the CRS, SIPRI's accounting of official financial data contained in national reports and official statements for 2007 generated a figure of $51.1 billion for arms exports, representing 0.3 percent of world trade. This figure is likely to be lower than the true figure because a number of significant exporters, including China, do not release data on the financial value of their arms exports. The difference between the SIPRI and CRS estimates is a further demonstration of the difficulty of estimating the financial value of the international arms trade.

The SIPRI arms transfers database provides information on international arms transfers from 1950 to the most recent calendar year. Its coverage is narrower than that of the ACDA, CRS, and national control lists; for example, it does not include transfers of most small arms and light weapons (SALW). However, it provides information on the number of units transferred and employs a unique pricing system to measure the volume of arms transfers. The SIPRI trend indicator value allows researchers to track developments in transfers to and from different suppliers, recipients, and regions. SIPRI data form the basis for the discussion below.

Arms Trade Trends

The volume of international arms transfers in the post-World War II period peaked in 1982. Following the end of the Cold War, there was a steady decline in global arms transfers. They reached their lowest point in 2002, when transfers amounted to only 38 percent of their Cold War high. This decline has reversed, and the volume of international transfers of major conventional weapons during 2005-2009 was 22 percent higher than during 2000-2004.

One of the most marked aspects of the international arms trade has been its dominance by five suppliers. During 1980-1984, when global arms transfers were at the highest level, the Soviet Union (37 percent), the United States (29 percent), France (8 percent), the United Kingdom (5 percent), and the Federal Republic of Germany (5 percent) accounted for 84 percent of all exports. The five largest suppliers of major conventional weapons during 2005-2009 were the United States (30 percent), Russia (23 percent), Germany (11 percent), France (8 percent), and the United Kingdom (4 percent), collectively accounting for 76 percent of exports.

The governments of these major suppliers are actively engaged in assisting the export efforts of their domestic arms industries in the competitive international arms market. Some governments also provide military equipment to allies at beneficial rates as a key plank of their foreign and defence policies, something that often has clear benefits for commercial arms manufacturers based in these states.

Since 2001, the United States has increased foreign military aid for allies in regions of tension or conflict. President Barack Obama has maintained the Bush administration's pledge to increase foreign military financing aid for Israel, which is set to reach $3 billion in 2012. Egypt and the members of the Gulf Cooperation Council have been the recipients of increased assistance as well.

Russia has announced its willingness to develop and produce arms jointly with other countries to help strengthen ties, accept payments through barter, participate in joint economic projects, and offer credit and exchanges of debt for arms. In 2009, Russia extended a $2 billion line of credit to Venezuela for arms purchases. In addition, it agreed to cancel Vietnam's debt to Russia and help modernize its shipbuilding industry in exchange for Vietnam's commitment to purchase 20 Su-30MK combat aircraft and six Type-636 Kilo-class submarines and further expand the involvement of Russian companies in the exploration and extraction of Vietnamese oil.

In 2007 the French government simplified and modernized France's arms export licensing system and began taking a more active role in promoting exports abroad. It has demonstrated a willingness to engage in far-reaching technology transfer agreements in order to win contracts. In September 2009 French President Nicolas Sarkozy visited Brazil to conclude an almost $10 billion deal to supply four conventionally powered submarines and technology to assist in the development of Brazil's first nuclear-powered submarine.

Attempts by countries beyond the traditional major producers to develop their own arms industries and increase their share of global arms exports have typically had limited success, largely because of high technological barriers or an inadequate civilian industrial base. Yet, many countries still seek to increase their levels of autonomous capability in arms production, with some developing state-of-the-art products for particular niche items. For example, Israel is widely recognized as a leading producer and supplier of unmanned aerial vehicles (UAVs), supplying systems and licenses for production for more than 100 UAVs to 18 states, including all of the top five suppliers, during 2005-2009.

In addition, licensed production agreements have led to an increase in the number of states that are capable of manufacturing less-advanced weapons systems, particularly small arms and light weapons. Although licensed production agreements often include controls on who can receive the weapons produced, this is not always the case, or the agreements are not enforced. Soviet Avtomat Kalashnikov (AK) and German Heckler and Koch G3 assault rifles serve as classic examples of cases in which licensed production has led to exports being made without the express permission of those issuing the original license. Russia perceives the production of Kalashnikov rifles in a number of former Warsaw Pact countries to be unlicensed and illegal, claiming that arrangements concluded during the Soviet era have expired. The decision to give designs and information on product technology to Warsaw Pact states and clients during the Soviet era therefore remains a source of concern. Nonetheless, Russia continues to issue licensed production agreements for Kalashnikov rifles, revealing recently that 10 states had applied to build factories. The possibility remains that today's license holders could produce or export Kalashnikovs without the express permission of Russia in the future.

In contrast to the largest suppliers, the largest recipients of major conventional weapons have varied considerably over the years. During 1980-1984, the five largest recipients of military equipment—Iraq (7 percent), India (6 percent), Libya (5 percent), Syria (5 percent), and Egypt (4 percent)—accounted for 27 percent of total imports. The five largest recipients of major conventional weapons during 2005-2009 were China (9 percent), India (7 percent), South Korea (6 percent), the United Arab Emirates (6 percent), and Greece (4 percent), accounting for 32 percent of total imports. After the end of the Cold War, China imported a large volume of aircraft, ships, submarines, air defence systems, and missiles from Russia, but Chinese arms imports from Russia have declined dramatically in recent years. One explanation for this drop is that China appears to have overcome many of the problems that have dogged its arms industry and is now able to manufacture advanced weapons systems domestically. There are persistent allegations that many of China's "indigenous" weapons systems are actually copies of other countries' designs. It continues to rely on imports of components and subsystems for a number of its weapons systems, but is regarded as an example of a country in which arrangements for licensed production and technology transfers as part of arms import deals have helped with the development of an indigenous arms industry. India has sought to develop its own arms industry and decrease its reliance on arms imports but with limited success to date. It is expected to replace China as the largest arms importer in the coming years.

Recent acquisitions by states in Latin America, the Middle East, North Africa, and Southeast Asia indicate the possible emergence of reactive arms acquisition patterns that could develop into regional arms races. The volume of deliveries to Southeast Asia nearly doubled during 2005-2009 compared to 2000-2004. Deliveries were 722 percent higher to Malaysia, 146 percent higher to Singapore, and 84 percent higher to Indonesia. In 2009, Malaysia received six Su-30MKM combat aircraft with advanced missiles from Russia, two Scorpène submarines from France and Spain, two MEKO-100 frigates from Germany, and 21 PT-91 tanks from Poland. Singapore received eight F-15E combat aircraft with advanced air-to-air and air-to-ground missiles from the United States, two La Fayette frigates from France, and 40 Leopard-2A4 tanks from Germany.

There is limited empirical evidence to suggest a direct causal link between an increase in the volume of arms imported and the outbreak of conflict or an increase in the intensity of conflict. It has been suggested, however, that states that acquire significant quantities of military equipment may be more prone to use armed force to resolve disputes. For example, the recent conflicts in Sri Lanka and Georgia, both of which are relatively minor arms importers, were preceded by significant increases in transfers. In both cases, governments sought to restore what they perceived to be their state's territorial integrity against forces that were seeking independence and had established high levels of autonomy to some degree within clearly defined regions.

As the graph on this page demonstrates, the volume of Georgian imports of major conventional weapons in the years preceding the August 2008 conflict in South Ossetia increased significantly, with the largest volume of arms imports for Georgia, excluding acquisitions by forces in Abkhazia and South Ossetia, taking place in 2007. Significant increases in arms imports and military spending were perceived by some as indicating that the Georgian government was preparing to use force to restore Georgia's territorial integrity.

TRADE CONTROL EFFORTS

At present, UN Security Council arms embargoes are the only global, legally binding prohibitions on arms transfers. Since 1990, the United Nations has imposed 28 arms embargoes against targets in 17 countries and one nonstate entity (Osama bin Laden and al Qaeda). The most recent new arms embargo was introduced against Eritrea on December 23, 2009. Recent UN arms embargo resolutions recognize that nonstate actors play an important role in the contemporary arms trade and in the facilitation of arms transfers to "undesirable" end-users. States retain primary responsibility for enforcing arms embargoes and controlling the activities of arms brokers and dealers operating from their national territory or registered with their national authorities.

Sanctions committees and panels of experts charged with monitoring arms embargoes have documented the role different states have played in violating arms embargoes, such as in the case of Eritrea's involvement in transfers to Somalia. Also, states have been accused of giving shelter to individuals and entities accused of violating embargoes and of failing to investigate alleged violations but in such instances have not been sanctioned themselves. Stronger transfer control policies and increased political will are of central importance for preventing violations of UN arms embargoes.

States have long been reluctant to give up any element of national control in the field of arms transfer controls. Yet, the Iraqi invasion of Kuwait in 1990 and the scandals involving Western states and companies in the arming of Iraq prompted the development of the guidelines for conventional arms transfers, under which the permanent members of the UN Security Council agreed to exercise restraint in exports of conventional arms transfers. Suppliers were required to ensure that exports met only the "legitimate self-defence" needs of the recipient and did not contribute to conflict or regional instability or introduce "destabilizing military capabilities in a region." There is no international agreement on what constitutes legitimate self-defence or "destabilizing military capabilities."

Efforts to improve controls on international arms transfers have primarily been driven and directed by suppliers in North America and Europe. Motivations have included protecting national industries by preventing the spread of technologies and limiting potential adversaries' access to key technologies. The prevention of conflict and human rights abuses also has long been at the heart of efforts to control the arms trade. States, export control regimes such as the Wassenaar Arrangement, and regional organizations (e.g., the Economic Community of West African States, the EU, the Organization for Security and Cooperation in Europe, and the Organization of American States) have developed various sets of best-practice guidelines and model legislation to help ensure that arms exports do not provoke or exacerbate conflict and are not used to commit violations of human rights and humanitarian law. In addition, efforts have been undertaken to prevent the diversion of arms to terrorists, criminals, and armed groups.

Experience with existing regional mechanisms and export control regimes demonstrates some of the problems that an ATT is likely to face when it comes to ensuring harmonized interpretations of the criteria it puts in place. Despite developing agreed export criteria and mechanisms of consultation and information exchange, members of the Wassenaar Arrangement have demonstrated contrasting attitudes toward exports of arms and military equipment to a range of destinations.

Although the EU and the United States have arms embargoes against Iran, Myanmar (Burma), Sudan, and Zimbabwe, Russia continues to supply weapons systems to these states. Meanwhile, Russia has repeatedly called for restraint on arms transfers to Georgia, but Wassenaar Arrangement members the Czech Republic, Turkey, and Ukraine have continued to supply arms to Georgia. It appears that bilateral pressure on nonmembers Bosnia and Herzegovina, Israel, and Serbia led to some deals to Georgia being canceled.

Even within the EU, where states have agreed that their export license decision-making should be guided by eight criteria relating to issues such as conflict prevention, human rights, and economic development, there appear to have been differences of opinion among members regarding exports to Georgia. EU member states reported issuing licenses worth more than $180 million between 2004 and 2007 for exports of arms and military equipment to Georgia and making exports worth almost $96 million during that period. Also during this period, EU member states denied 41 export licenses for arms and military equipment for Georgia because of concerns about the potential impact of the transfer on the possibility of conflict within Georgia. In several cases, EU member states denied an export license for the export of a particular type of military equipment that other EU member states had exported.

Researchers have found evidence of a correlation between the introduction of the politically binding EU Code of Conduct on Arms Exports in 1998 and a decline in arms exports from EU member states to countries in conflict or considered violators of international human rights and humanitarian law, but differences in decision-making on "responsible" recipients continue within the EU. In this regard, the impact of the EU arms exports code and the legally binding Council Common Position 2008/944/CFSP, defining common rules governing the control of exports of military technology and equipment, which replaced the EU arms exports code, continues to illustrate the challenges of reaching agreement on how to interpret and implement a set of agreed common standards among (supposedly) like-minded states. Disagreements in the Wassenaar Arrangement show the difficulties in achieving similar objectives when the group is composed of states that hold very different opinions on what constitutes a responsible end-user.

INTERNATIONAL TRANSFERS OF SMALL ARMS AND LIGHT WEAPONS

Since the mid-1990s global attention has become increasingly focused on transfers of SALW, which have come to be regarded as the type of conventional weapon that can cause the most instability in a country or region. Governmental transparency in international transfers of SALW continues to lag behind transparency levels for other types of conventional weapon transfers, although advances have been made in recent years. For example, in December 2003 the UN General Assembly invited member states to provide information on SALW transfers to the UN Register of Conventional Arms (UNROCA), which had previously covered only major conventional weapons, and in 2006 states were invited to do so using a standardized reporting form.

As of 31 December 2008, 56 states had submitted data to UNROCA on their SALW transfers on at least one occasion since 2003. The major suppliers and recipients according to UNROCA data. However, the information submitted to UNROCA covers only a fraction of international transfers of SALW because many significant exporters (e.g. China, Russia and the USA) have not submitted data. In addition, since a high proportion of European states have submitted SALW data to the UNROCA, they are over-represented among exporters.

The only other regularly updated source of information on the global trade in SALW is the customs data that states submit to the UN Commodity Trade Statistics Database (Comtrade). The Norwegian Initiative on Small Arms Transfers (NISAT) collects and collates customs data from Comtrade and compiles an annual register of international SALW transfers.

However, this source is also far from complete. For example, many countries omit data related to arms exports in their reports to Comtrade or omit information about the destination of arms exports.

RECENT TRENDS IN WORLD MILITARY EXPENDITURE

There is no necessary, direct relationship between global military spending and the volume or value of the global arms trade. Movements in one do not necessarily correlate to movements in the other. For example, the majority of most states' military budget is spent on personnel costs, rather than equipment acquisitions. Among member states of the North Atlantic Treaty

Organization (NATO), the median share of military spending allocated to equipment purchases was 17.6 per cent in 2008. Also, many of the world's biggest spenders, including Russia and the USA, acquire the majority of their equipment domestically, and so increases in their procurement costs will not lead to a rise in international arms transfers. In addition, many states, particularly in the developing world, often exclude money spent on arms acquisitions from published military budgets. Such purchases may be funded through non-military budget lines or simply may not accounted for in the budget. Finally, many states receive considerable amounts of military equipment in the form of military aid, which would not necessarily be reflected in the recipient states' military budget.

Nonetheless, a general increase in military expenditure in a particular region or worldwide is likely to be a strong indication that arms procurement expenditure has also increased, whether on-or off-budget. In addition, many states, particularly in the developing world, rely on arms imports, rather than domestic production, as their main source of military procurement, and increases in their military spending may well translate into increases in the global arms transfers. While patterns over previous time periods vary, since 2001 there have been consistent year-on-year increases in the SIPRI data on both international arms transfers and global military expenditure.

Over the first decade following the end of the cold war (1989–98), world military spending fell in real terms by more than one-third. Many states downsized or restructured their armed forces while making deep cuts in procurement. The deepest cuts took place in Russia and the other former members of the Warsaw Treaty Organization; there were smaller reductions in Africa, the Americas and Western Europe. However, military spending continued to rise in Asia (by 27 per cent) and the Middle East (by 17 per cent). Since 1998 the downward trend in military spending has reversed. Global military spending increased by 45 per cent in real terms over the 10-year period 1998–2007, reaching $1339 billion in 2007. This corresponded to 2.5 per cent of world gross domestic product (GDP) or $202 for each person in the world. The increase in spending has accelerated since 2001, with an annual average increase of 5.3 per cent, compared with 2.2 per cent during the period 1998–2001.

The factors driving increases in military spending since 2001 constitute a mixture of foreign policy objectives, real or perceived threats, armed conflict and policies to contribute to international peacekeeping operations. However, the primary driver of the high rate of growth has been the USA, which accounted for 63 per cent of the post-2001 increase in global spending and 45 per cent of total global military spending in 2007. While much of this increase is attributable to spending on military operations in Afghanistan and Iraq, the core military budget has also risen significantly. Many other states have also increased their military spending since 2001. Around two-thirds of countries that make data available increased their military spending annually between 2001 and 2006. Of the 121 countries for which such data was available, 88 had higher military spending in real terms in 2007 compared to 2001. The following regional trends can also be observed.

In Eastern Europe military expenditure rose by 162 per cent over the period 1998–2007, the highest increase in any subregion. It was also the region with the highest increase in 2007, at 15 per cent. Russia, with a 13 per cent increase in 2007, accounted for 86 per cent of this regional increase. In North America military expenditure rose by 59 per cent over the period 1998–2007. This rise was driven almost exclusively by the recent increases in US military spending. By 2007, US spending was higher than at any time since World War II.

In the Middle East military expenditure rose by 62 per cent over the period 1998–2007. There have been strong increases in all Gulf Cooperation Council member states apart from the UAE. There have also been significant increases in military spending in Iran, Jordan and Lebanon.

In South Asia military expenditure rose by 57 per cent over the period 1998–2007. The upward trend was largely due to a real-terms increase of 64 per cent in Indian military spending. In Africa military expenditure rose by 51 per cent over the period 1998–2007. This increase was largely driven by a 97 per cent increase in Algeria's military spending. While military budgets in much of

Africa remain low by global standards, the economic burden that they represent can be considerable. For example, in 2005 military spending in Angola and Burundi represented 5.7 and 6.2 per cent of GDP, respectively, among the highest proportions in the world. Angola and Burundi also have some of the lowest human development indices.

In East Asia military expenditure rose by 51 per cent over the period 1998–2007. Three countries increased their military spending by more than 50 per cent during this period: China, by 202 per cent, Indonesia, by 100 per cent, and Malaysia, by 153 per cent. While China increased its military spending threefold over the decade, its rapid economic growth, means that the economic burden of military spending is still moderate, at 2.1 per cent of GDP in 2006. The subregions with the lowest growth in military spending over the period 1998–2007 were Western Europe (6 per cent) and Central America (14 per cent).

RECENT TRENDS IN WORLD ARMS PRODUCTION

The global arms industry, especially the production of modern major weapon systems and technologies, is dominated by North America and Western Europe, although significant capabilities also exist in Australia, China, Israel, Japan, South Korea and Russia. There are no available reliable estimates for the overall size of the global arms industry. However, SIPRI produces an annual list of the top 100 arms-producing companies (the SIPRI Top 100), which captures the majority of the financial value of the global arms industry. The total value of arms sales (military-specific goods and services) by the Top 100 companies was $315 billion in 2006, a 60 per cent increase on the 2002 value. This rapid rise is mostly linked to increases in US military expenditure. US-owned companies accounted for 63.5 per cent of the 2006 total and West European-owned companies accounted for 29.2 per cent. These shares have not changed greatly over the past few years. 19 Following the end of the cold war the global arms industry contracted significantly due to the substantial decreases in military expenditure by both NATO members and former members of the Warsaw Treaty Organization.

In the USA and Western Europe, while this decline led to substantial job losses, it took place at a fairly managed pace and was accompanied by largescale consolidation of the industry. In the USA a few giant companies were formed through mergers such as those of Northrop and Grumman in 1994 and of Boeing and McDonnell-Douglas in 1997. In Europe consolidation led to the creation or rapid growth of BAE Systems in the UK, Thales in France, Finmeccanica in Italy, and the trans-European company EADS.

These four companies are the only non-US companies among the world's 10 largest arms producers. In some countries, particularly the UK and the USA, the reductions in spending on military equipment were to some extent mitigated by the growth of outsourcing of services formerly performed by the military. The period of post-cold war consolidation in the Western arms industry had largely ended by the early 2000s, which was also when US military expenditure began to increase significantly, especially following the terrorist attacks on the USA of 11 September 2001.

The rapid growth of US military expenditure has led to increasing efforts by overseas companies to access the US markets through acquisitions of US companies. British companies, due to the UK's close political relationship with the USA, have been most successful in acquiring US companies. Led by BAE Systems, which is now one of the top 10 sup pliers to the US Department of Defence, many British companies now carry out as much or more of their operations in the USA as in the UK.

Continental European companies have been far less able to make acquisitions in the USA, but in 2008 an Italian company broke this pattern with the acquisition for $5.2 billion of DRS Technologies, a US military electronics company. In Russia, the former Soviet arms industry virtually collapsed as Russian military spending fell to just 6 per cent of the former Soviet level. While in recent years the Russian industry has revived somewhat, helped by strong export performance, and is beginning to receive new injections of state capital and domestic orders, it still suffers from severe problems of aged equipment and obsolescent technologies. The Russian arms industry is currently undergoing a major reorganization, with the creation of a few large stateowned holding companies to consolidate different sectors of the arms industry. These include the United Aircraft Corporation, the United Shipbuilding Corporation and Rostekhnologii.

Attempts by countries outside the traditional major producers to develop their own modern arms industries have typically had limited success. This is in large part due to the high technological barriers to producing modern major weapons systems and, in many cases, an inadequate civilian industrial base. However, many countries are continuing efforts to increase their levels of autonomous capability in arms production, sometimes with increasing success.

China is increasingly able to produce a wide range of modern weapon systems, including fourth generation-plus combat aircraft, although in most areas it is still one to two generations behind the most advanced technology. Israel has for some time now maintained an advanced arms industry. In some areas, such as unmanned aerial vehicles (UAVs), it technology is among the best in the world and is sold to major Western powers. South Korea has had considerable success in a number of areas in recent years. In 2007 Turkey signed a $459 million deal to buy 40 KT-1 Woong-Bee trainer aircraft from South Korea, reflecting the country's emergence as a significant arms exporter. India is pursuing a strategy of off sets to obtain technology transfers when importing arms, as a way of developing its indigenous capabilities. It is too early to judge how successful this strategy will be. Brazil had the most successful arms industry in Latin America during the 1980s and was the 11th biggest supplier in the world for the period 1984–88. Its industry contracted rapidly in the early 1990s, but the Brazilian Government is placing a strong emphasis on revitalizing the sector. South Africa developed a significant military industry during the apartheid era and has sought to keep the sector going in the years since. As of 2008, Denel Group, South Africa's largest arms-producing company, had about 7300 employees.

While countries in other parts of the world may lack modern defence industries, they can still act as sources of surplus or second-hand equipment or of newly produced but less technologically advanced weapon systems, such as SALW and their ammunition. According to one estimate, at least 1249 companies in more than 90 countries are involved in some aspect of SALW production. The means of producing weapons and military systems, particularly SALW, has spread through the licensed and unlicensed transfer of production facilities around the world. The level of technological know-how attained by the host country through licensed production is highly variable. In some cases the host country is responsible for no more than the final assembly of components made by the licensing country, while in other cases it may be used as a step towards mastering the full production process. According to one estimate, 60–80 per cent of all military rifles, assault rifles and carbines are manufactured by producers that acquired the necessary technology from elsewhere. Examples of countries that lack a significant defence industry, but which nonetheless maintain some level of SALW production capacity, include Colombia, Indonesia, Jordan, Nigeria and Sudan.

RECENT TRENDS IN EXPORT CONTROL MECHANISMS

Arms export policies are policies that govern 'The dispatch of conventional weapons, weapon platforms and related equipment (that would normally be found on a military list of controlled goods) from one country to another'. 32 Along with other defence- and security-related issues, the development and implementation of such policies is almost universally considered to be the exclusive prerogative of states. States have traditionally pursued widely divergent arms export policies and, with the exception of multilateral arms embargoes, have been reluctant to give up any element of national control in this area.

Nonetheless, numerous states have also sought to increase the level of coordination and harmonization in this area—as a means of both increasing international standards and off setting the commercial costs of maintaining a more restrictive system than other states. Such efforts have intensified in recent years. While they have largely focused on regional organizations such as the

Organization for Security and Co-operation in Europe (OSCE) and the EU, the UN has also made extensive and long-standing efforts. Numerous UN Security Council and General Assembly resolutions have reiterated the importance of states maintaining functioning controls on the export of military goods. For example, under the 2001 Programme of Action to Prevent, Combat and Eradicate the Illicit Trade in Small Arms and Light Weapons in All Its Aspects (POA), states have agreed to ensure that they have adequate laws, regulations and administrative procedures to control transfers of SALW.

Transfer prohibitions and guidelines

At present, arms embargoes imposed by the UN Security Council are the only global, legally binding prohibitions on arms transfers. UN arms embargoes are imposed by resolutions adopted under the authority of Chapter VII, Article 41, of the UN Charter. Like all Security Council resolutions, embargoes require the affirmative votes of at least nine of the 15 members of the Security Council, and each of the five permanent members (China, France, Russia, the UK and the USA; the P5) has a veto. As of 1 January 2009 there were 11 mandatory UN arms embargoes in force. However, according to the sanctions committees and panels of experts monitoring these embargoes, many UN arms embargoes have been repeatedly violated, by both states and private individuals.

The development of regional and global guidelines for conventional arms transfers has been on the international agenda since the 1920s. In 1925 the League of Nations produced a draft convention on the arms trade, but it was never adopted. While global conventions govern the transfer of nuclear, biological and chemical weapons, there is currently no equivalent, global mechanism covering the transfer of conventional weapons. During the cold war the two competing blocs and individual countries used conventional weapon transfers in order to establish or maintain spheres of influence. At the regional level, the coordination of export control policies was mainly focused on preventing transfers to members of the opposing bloc. For example, in 1949 the Western bloc formed the Coordinating Committee for

Multilateral Export Controls (COCOM) to manage an embargo on transfers of arms and related technologies to the Eastern bloc. COCOM was disbanded in 1994.

In the early 1990s states concluded that the accumulation of major conventional weapons in Iraq in the period preceding the 1990 invasion of Kuwait had contributed to Iraq's decision to invade. Partly as a result, during the early and mid-1990s different state groupings developed several sets of guidelines or principles on arms transfers. Rather than targeting specific groups of states, they sought to lay down rules that would apply to all conventional arms transfers, regardless of their destination.

In October 1991 the P5 adopted a set of guidelines for conventional arms transfers which called on the P5 and other arms exporters to export conventional arms only in line with the legitimate self-defence needs of recipients and appropriate and proportionate responses to security threats. It was also agreed that transfers that were likely to prolong existing conflicts and tensions, introduce 'destabilizing accumulations' or contravene international commitments, such as arms embargoes, would be avoided. In November 1993 the OSCE reaffirmed its commitment to a similar set of principles governing conventional arms transfers.

Other principles emphasized in these guidelines include the need to prevent transfers that might contribute to destabilizing military build-ups, prolong or aggravate an armed conflict, or fall into the hands of terrorists. However, the guidelines lack enforcement mechanisms, and their interpretation has been left entirely at the discretion of individual states. Concerns such as these have played a significant role in the recent push for the development of an international arms trade treaty. A 2006 draft UN General Assembly resolution states that the 'absence of common international standards on the import, export and transfer of conventional arms is a contributory factor to conflict, the displacement of people, crime and terrorism'.

Export control regimes and other regional mechanisms

The post cold-war period has also seen the development of more formal mechanisms aimed at coordinating the policies of supplier and recipient states. These mechanisms involve the application of guidelines and principles, but they also include some level of coordination between the states involved to try to ensure some level of harmonization in how they are implemented. Other mechanisms cover exports of missiles (e.g. the Missile Technology Control Regime), nuclear technologies (e.g. the Nuclear Suppliers Group) and chemical and biological agents (e.g. the Australia Group). The Wassenaar Arrangement on Export Controls for Conventional Arms and Dual-Use Goods and Technologies was established in 1996 in an attempt to replicate some of the benefits of COCOM but on a broader and non-adversarial basis. It currently has 40 participating states, including Russia, the USA, most members of NATO and most former members of the Warsaw Treaty Organization. The Wassenaar Arrangement was designed to promote transparency and responsibility in transfers of arms and dual-use items in order to prevent 'destabilizing accumulations'. Participating states exchange information on their exports and discuss policies on particular regions or destinations.

The EU's Common Rules Governing Control of Exports of Military Technology and Equipment (known as the Code of Conduct on Arms Exports until 2008) was first formally adopted in June 1998.41 It consists of eight criteria on which EU member states should base their export licensing decisions, relating to issues such as conflict prevention, human rights and economic development. Under the EU Common Rules, governments agree to exchange, in confidence, information on any application for an export licence that is denied, including the reasons for the refusal. If a member state is considering granting an export licence for a transaction that it believes might be 'essentially identical' to one that has previously been denied, then it is obliged to consult the state that previously issued the denial in order to clarify the situation. In 1998 members of the Economic Community of West African States (ECOWAS) adopted a moratorium on the manufacture, importation and exportation of SALW. A 2002 evaluation report highlighted a number of weaknesses in the moratorium and cases where certain states had failed to uphold its principles. In response, the ECOWAS Convention on Small Arms and Light Weapons, Their Ammunition and Other Related

Materials was adopted in June 2006. The convention retains the moratorium's prohibition on SALW imports, but states can apply to the ECOWAS Commission for exemptions 'in order to meet legitimate national defence and security needs, or to participate in peace support or other operations'. The convention also requires that participating states provide detailed information to the ECOWAS Commission on any SALW import.

ARMS PRODUCTION, EXPORTS AND CONTROL IN THE ASEM PROCESS

Arms production and arms trade should be addressed within the political and security pillar of the ASEM process. Three of the EU ASEM countries are among the most prominent arms exporters - France, the UK and Germany. Of the top importers three countries are from East Asia: China, South Korea and Taiwan. Only China is itself a significant arms exporter. However, the flow of arms trade is like a river going one direction - towards Asia. Despite the fact that some recipient states embarked long ago on the creation of a domestic defence industry, they are still dependent on importing supplies.

There is an Asian as well as a European side to arms exports and production of the countries participating in the ASEM process, but this only tells a partial story. Significant differences exist both within and between regions. Europe is home to three of the ten biggest arms manufacturers worldwide. The Japanese Mitsubishi Heavy Industries with a military turnover of US$ 3.6 billion lies just behind the military industries from the US, the UK and France/ Germany, making it by far the biggest arms manufacturer of Asia.

Arms production within both Europe and Asia is too diverse to be analysed as one single region. For instance, weapons production in South Korea cannot be compared with Cambodia and Greece (a top ten arms importer) and Germany are playing a very different role in the arms market. Furthermore, the provision in the Japanese constitution against arms trade is not matched in any of the EU countries. These differences indicate the need for further research in establishing the significance of the arms trade and arms production in the ASEM process and for identifying the arms trade connections between the European Union and Asia ASEM countries.

Enhanced Partnerships

In the European Commission Framework document for 'Enhanced Partnerships between Asia and Europe' the latest outline of Europe's Asia policy is given. One of the few remarks on arms trade in the document identifies arms trafficking as a common concern on the level of Ministries of Justice and Home Affairs. Arms traffickers are working across boundaries and co-operation in this field is essential to tackle the illegal flow of arms. One example from 1999 illustrates how an Israeli businessman transported 40 armoured personnel carriers from Germany to Iran. The arms followed a route through the Netherlands, Britain and Singapore before reaching Iran. The Israeli businessman was in close contact with a South Korean arms dealer known to sell arms to Iran. To tackle this kind of flows concerted action between law enforcement bodies of all involved countries is essential.

The Framework document also states that co-operation should exist "for the early and comprehensive ratification of major international Instruments such as the Comprehensive Test Ban Treaty or the Conventions on small arms and anti-personnel mines." Regional and global security is certainly helped by an orchestrated implementation of those conventions. Landmines are a hidden killer and the removal of those weapons from the stocks of armies is essential for the security of those wanting to use the land for productive purposes such as agriculture, leisure and transport. Illegal small arms are causing death and destruction in all parts of the world and their wide distribution leads to killings by criminals, gangs and paramilitaries. The small arms convention is also addressing those used by resistance groups.

The killings by armies, democratically controlled or not, are outside this Convention and so its implementation is limited to law enforcement and control by the government. The scope of arms control is too limited when it stops at the level of law enforcement and nuclear testing. Such an approach uses a narrow concept of security - that is military security. Arms trade is a way of beefing-up allies, with consequences for regional balances of power and relations between nations and as such part of the conservative security debate. Moreover, major arms deals involving hundreds of millions or even billions of dollars of government expenditure cannot be left out of a genuine people's oriented security debate. Arms trade and acquisitions are part of such a security debate and for this reason should be part of the Framework document.

Finance Packages and Debt

When the EU adopted a strategy on Asia in 1994, it clearly identified the increase in the ambitious armament programmes in the Asian region as one of the factors "which could disrupt world equilibrium and thereby impinging on Europe's Common Foreign and Security Policy objectives." In the 2001 update of the Asia Strategy however, there is less attention to the security dimension of the relationship, with the exception of the issue of small arms trade and nuclear testing.

There can hardly be any justification for this omission. Although the impression exists that arms trade to the ASEM countries declined due to the economic crisis of 1997, this is not yet reflected in the figures given by SIPRI for 1999. Because the negotiations for arms deliveries in general take a long time it is possible that there will be a significant decrease visible in the near future. Another reason the economic crisis is not yet reflected in the figures, is that Arms companies made financial arrangements with governments and banks, such as low interest loans and favourable re-payment schedules to back up ongoing arms deals and negotiations. 'Buy now, Pay later' became the modus operandi of both arms exporters and importers. An official of the British Ministry of Defence explained it in this way: "In the United Kingdom, we view innovative financing packages as a key factor in any likely success". The Defence business was not willing to let existing deals collapse and used financial flexibility to secure additional new deals. Sales did not stop and some were merely postponed. This of course has led to further public debt. Conveniently, the international attention on the burden of debt on state budgets was put aside in order to continue arms trade.

Growing Demand

Besides, the long term effects of the crisis will be downplayed by new developments. Analysts see a growing demand for arms in South East Asia. The Malaysian Defence Minister Najib Razak told the well attended Defence Services Asia (DSA) arms fair: "With the economy of most of these countries back on track there will be a projected increase in the defence expenditure to procure platforms, weapon systems and solutions to meet national requirements." Defence companies likewise felt rewarded for participating in the DSA 2002. Malaysia alone ordered weapons valued US$ 958 million in April 2002. According to an Australian analyst, the process will go more rapidly in Southeast Asia than in the nineties: "Those that haven't started to move with new fighters, new surface combatants, new subs, are very quickly going to."

Issues raised in the nineties are very much back in the debates on arms trade in Asia. Is an arms race ongoing or not?. Do the acquisitions find their logic in modernisation, overhaul or refurbishment? Is it old shopping lists which now materialise? All these questions which had been set aside for five years are once again on the agenda.

However, there are also new issues with the turmoil in Indonesia being an important new factor. What is not yet very much back in the discussion is the ASEAN Regional Forum (ARF) or any other initiative on genuine regional security co-operation. Military exercises with the US and Australia are the most developed forms of regional military co-operation at present. The absence of a multilateral framework for regional security co-operation seriously hampers confidence among the countries in the region and arms acquisitions of one country are followed by similar acquisitions by neighbouring countries.

9/11 Becomes a New Sales Pitch

According to Malaysia's Defense Minister Razak when he defended the Malaysian arms acquisitions during the DSA arms fair "The 9/11 attack drastically changed the outlook toward national security". By invoking the 9/11 terrorist attacks, he was joining those government leaders who have used the 9/11 events to popularize a new sales pitch for arms acquisitions.

The strike on the World Trade Center and Pentagon is a weak rationale for placing submarines and fighter aircraft on the shopping list of many East and Southeast Asian countries. These are not the best weapons in the fight against terrorism.

The current weapons acquisitions are high-tech buys demonstrated during the Second Gulf War on Iraq (1990-91). Furthermore, the latest orders and wish lists follow the images of US technology shown on the Afghan battlefield: the integration of remote operation, new observation techniques, state of the art Information Technology, improved precision guided munitions, and lasers. According to an Australian expert, "we will see increasing sophistication, not only of the platforms, the ships, tanks and aircraft, but of the weapon systems that go with them."

The 9/11 attacks and the creation of US led coalition against terrorism provided the rationale for lifting arms embargoes and relaxing arms export policies on more advanced weapon systems as a reward to countries for their participation.

This applied to the Middle East, South Asia, and also in Southeast Asia e.g. Indonesia. The restrictions on military co-operation between Jakarta and Washington (developed between 1994 and 2000) have been under pressure ever since. Likewise the Philippines has received 100 million US$ in military assistance, and has allowed the intervention of US Special Forces in Mindanao.

An additional factor for further militarisation in the region is Missile proliferation and the re-emergence of the US Star Wars programme - pushing military budgets ever higher.

According to John Chipman, Director of the International Institute for Strategic Studies in London, " The nature of missile proliferation in the region holds in prospect the kind of arms race that was not seen in the first half of the 1990s"

Defence Industry in East and Southeast Asia

The economic crisis of 1997 did change the picture of the defence industry in Asia. Domestic defence industries in Southeast Asia are opening their firms to foreign investment to build equity and market links with Western nations for capital, technology and markets. Malaysia recently indicated that it wants to become a regional hub to help international defence firms to penetrate Asian markets and most of the ASEAN defence industries are eager to find a foreign partner to attract market access as well as capital. This path is also followed by South Korea. The French Thales company has a joint venture with Samsung. Taiwan wants to build the submarines offered by the US in 2001 at the China Shipbuilding Corp. as well as import the technology from abroad. All this is underlining dependence on Western funds and weapon technology, developed with large sums on Research & Development programmes (R&D) -estimated at US$ 39.3 billion in the US and at US$ 9.1 billion in Europe annually.

Singapore Technologies follows another route similar to what Western firms do - buying what it needs mainly in the US. This excludes the real state-of-the-art technology because this is prevented from foreign participation even by key allies. Of the six ASEAN countries which are producing small arms at home, only Singapore Technologies has a sound economic policy and export record. It exported ordnance, machine guns and assault rifles to a wide range of regions of tension. Other countries produce arms against higher market prices - which has more to do with national pride than with sound economics and the rule of the market.

The Chinese defence industry still produces obsolete weapon systems. It is not yet able to start the reorganisation process demanded to generate the capacity needed for the technological advanced weapon systems which the Chinese military want to possess. There has been little change in the Japanese weapons industry. However, as a result of the economic recession the Japanese car industry was opened up to foreign investment. Renault took this opportunity and its investment in Nissan resulted in the sale of the military division of Nissan Motor Corp. to Ishikawajima-Harima Heavy Industries. This reflects the imperative to keep arms production in Japanese hands.

6

Economic Globalisation of Small Arms in South Asia

SMALL ARMS IN SOUTH ASIA

The proliferation and illicit use of small arms in South Asia can never be understood in isolation. This is as much a theoretical position, as it is a practical one. In view of recent developments at the local and global levels, particularly with the arrival and reproduction of globalisation, small arms had a qualitative transformation with respect to its proliferation and use. Never did the world see such an easy availability and at the same time grandeur yet demonic use of weapons that have been conventionally categorised as 'small.' It seems that the humane call of Bhupen Hazarika that 'We are in the same boat, brother!' has come to haunt us-from Chicago to Chittagong, from Jaffna to Johannesburg, from Bosnia to Baghdad-indeed, more dramatically yet more painfully. But lest we make a mistake in understanding the dynamics informing, influencing and reproducing the proliferation and illicit use of small arms, it is important that we take a critical account of the meaning of globalisation and its practical implications locally, nationally, regionally, and of course, internationally.

Globalisation, mainly because of its birth from a complex combination of multiple interactions, has given rise to a multiversity or multiple universes of knowledge and practices. Three precise modes could easily be identified. First is economic globalisation, second is reverse globalisation, and the third is subaltern globalisation. In each of these modes small arms play a precise and distinctive role. A closer exposition will make this clear.

ECONOMIC GLOBALISATION

The Globalisation meaning has been best captured by an OECD publication which, while crediting the term to Theodore Levitt who first used it in 1985 in his book, The Globalisation of Markets, sees globalisation as 'a seamless or borderless, global economy.' More concretely, it is informed by precise sets of economic activities with precise characteristics on a world scale. There exists a subtle difference between the 'internationalisation of economy' and 'globalisation' according to this perspective. While the former primarily refers to the internationalisation of trade and later on, the internationalisation of finance and investment, each coming in the wake of precise historical moments of capitalism, globalisation refers to the complex combination of all these but more importantly one that is inclusive of a thoroughly transformed production structure. The latter can be best described as the organisation and development of a denationalised form of production.

That is, multi-national or rather transnational companies now collect resources in several countries, process them in another several countries and finally, export the finished products to the rest of the world. A fully finished product, therefore, no longer has one single birthmark; it has multiple birthmarks since several countries have gone to produce it. A Compaq computer, in that sense, is no longer entirely American, or a Toyota car fully Japanese. The final product of both these items will have components made in several countries of the world. Put differently, unlike the previous internationalisation of things, in the globalisation phase of capitalism the thing itself is the product of the international or global market.

In this newer configuration, the non-state enterprises are often more critical than the state-oriented or state enterprises in the reproduction of capitalism. The need for safeguarding the non-state enterprises, therefore, is as vital as protecting the state enterprises. The outcome has been greater policing and diffusion of licit weapons, which often for reasons of pilferage and structural leakage end up in the market as illicit commodities.

Reverse Globalisation

The second meaning of globalisation is very much intrinsic to the developing country's craze for modernity, principally the organisation of the (post-colonial) nation state in the image of the modern 'Western' state. In some respect this has been well described by Nirad C. Chaudhuri as early as 1926 when Chaudhuri, while referring to 'a clash of civilisation' between the East and West, sarcastically noted that 'the real cultural role of the (colonised Indians) is to assimilate the ways of Europe' (1996:1,5). Put differently, if OECD's definition could be referred to as economic globalisation, the modernist aspirations of the developing or less developed countries could be referred to as reverse globalisation.

The global reach of Bollywood (India's film industry) and Indian restaurants are good examples of reverse globalisation, where the non-state forces of the East or that of the South are no less critical in channelising the development of the (culturally and intellectually colonised) less developed or developing countries. One critical outcome of reverse globalisation has been to develop militarily in the image of the modern West, bringing with it not only the military hardware, including small arms, developed in the West but also the impetus to produce such weapons at home. Often this has taken the form of joint collaboration between developed and developing countries with many of the small arms like AK-47, M16, G3, and even grenades produced and marketed as globalised items. Again, for reasons of pilferage and structural leakage many of these weapons end up in the market as illicit commodities.

Subaltern Globalisation

There is yet another type of interaction informing and reproducing globalisation. This is a complex mode and therefore requires greater care in its exposition. Critics have already referred to the mushrooming of global networks resisting economic globalisation as 'globalisation from below'. The latter includes a diverse group of people environmentalists, NGOs, religious groups, small farmers, labour unions (incidentally of both the developed and developing countries), women's movement, consumerists, African debt relief campaigners, anti-sweatshop activists, and the like, all one way or another either critical of or directly suffering from and struggling against the impact of economic globalisation. Here the forces of the seemingly disempowered non-state have creatively joined hands to overcome the exploitation of the empowered non-state, i.e. the forces of economic globalisation. The subaltern nature of the resistance movements, particularly the networking, can hardly be minimised.

But then, there is a further subaltern variant to the whole notion of globalisation from below. This refers to the deepening of relationship between and amongst the 'dubious groups' and 'shadowy activities' ranging from smuggling of goods and people, illicit production and trading of small arms, money laundering, narco-production and trading, terrorism, and the like, and that again, across and beyond national, ethnic, racial, and even religious affiliations. The subalterns, particularly the poverty-ridden and marginalised population, become easy target of such groups and activities, but more importantly the state of being itself becomes a factor for certain groups of (relatively well off) people to rally support and even clandestinely work for their cause.

A protracted nature of poverty and marginality and a lack of substantive global concern also push them to seek informal or even criminal means to reproduce their lives or redress the situation. The complex networking at this level and in combination with the resistance movements against economic globalisation could be best referred to as subaltern globalisation. Here the subalterns, including their ardent supporters and sympathisers, are no less creative and empowered when it comes to organising and reproducing their activities at the global level, and that too often by challenging the overly empowered forces of economic globalisation.

Two things are worth pointing out here. First is the subtle connivance of the state machineries with the dubious forces in reproducing subaltern globalisation. In fact, the state machineries go on to empower the subaltern networks almost to their own peril, which brings us to the second point. Indeed, if economic globalisation is in the business of weakening the power of the state, the practices of subaltern globalisation are no less menacing and destructive to the state. According to Mittelman (2000: 214): '(Criminal) groups are alternative social organisations that, in some respects, challenge the power and authority of the state to impose its standards, codified as law. These groups constitute an alternative system by offering commerce and banking in black and gray markets that operate outside the regulatory framework of the state; buying, selling, and distributing controlled or prohibited commodities, such as narcotics; providing swift and usually discreet dispute resolution and debt collection without resorting to the courts; creating and maintaining cartels when state laws proscribe them; and arranging security for the so-called protection of businesses, as well as sheltering them from competitors, the state and rival criminals. There is no reason to doubt the destructive potential of subaltern globalisation. Even those resisting economic globalisation and joining ranks with the subalterns may find themselves at risk if and when the destructive potential of subaltern globalisation is played out with full ferocity and demonic intent. The use of small arms can hardly be underestimated here. A quick look at some of the practices of subaltern globalisation would provide credence to our contention.

SUBALTERN GLOBALISATION AND THE ARMING OF THE NON-STATE

The element of subalternity in the resistance movements against economic globalisation (and the case could also be stretched to reverse globalisation) cannot be denied. The anti-globalisation protests in Seattle, Rome, Prague or Washington all tend to indicate that the subalterns or marginalised forces have been put into a dire situation because of economic globalisation. The protests are otherwise meant to highlight the grievances of the subalterns worldwide.

The resistance movements however in and by themselves do not reproduce the life and living of the subalterns. Mittelman has already indicated that 'where poverty is severe, criminal gangs flourish' (2000: 209). The link between poverty and criminality is less linear than what is seemingly suggested here. A state of subalternity in fact creates conditions that make people disinterested in the business of reproducing the power of the state. Mis-governance otherwise becomes the (dis)order of the day. People, particularly the subalterns, increasingly start depending on informal, often criminal, means for reproducing their livelihood. Even when requiring business or personal security they fall back on the power of the 'godfathers,' hired goons, mastans, and the like, than on the otherwise inept, often corrupt, governmental machineries.

A shadowy network of things and transactions gets reproduced and in the process destabilises not only the power of the state but also the power of the subalterns, indeed, making them more vulnerable and disempowered. This further creates grounds for fresh recruits and creative but demonic ventures for organising and reproducing subaltern globalisation.

Narco-terrorism

Narco-production and trading is a lucrative business in this region. In 2001 Myanmar surpassed Afghanistan as the largest producer of illicit opium and heroin in the world. To provide some knowledge of the amount, 865 metric tons of opium was produced in Myanmar in 2001, almost all of which were processed into heroin and sold to the illicit market both within and outside the region (BCB, 2002:1). This is more than double the amount of illicit opium that is available in other heroin-producing countries, such as India, Columbia, Mexico, or Laos (ICB, 2002:2). It may be mentioned that there exists a vibrant but complex relationship between opium growers and heroin producers, drug dealers and consumers, security and custom officials, high-risk investors and money launderers, and that again, not only nationally but also regionally and globally. As the following U.S. Drug Enforcement Agency report suggests (BCB, 2002:1):

'Opium poppy cultivation and heroin refining take place in remote, mountainous border regions. Armed ethnic groups such as, the United Wa State Army, the Kokang Chinese, and the

Myanmar National Democratic Alliance Army control the cultivation areas, refine opium into heroin, and also produce methamphetamine. Associates of these organisations from other Asian nations have shipped tons of heroin from Burma to the United States within the past decade. The largest single heroin seizure in the United States consisted of 486 kilograms of Burma-produced heroin that the US Customs Service discovered in a containerised shipment of plastic bags from Southeast Asia, via Taiwan, en route to a warehouse in Hayward, California, in May 1991'.

But Myanmar, apart from being a member of the infamous 'Golden Triangle', is also close to yet another major narco-producing region, the 'Golden Crescent.' In smuggling heroin from Myanmar beyond the region and the continent both India and Bangladesh are used as transit points (BCB, 2002:4). This further exacerbates problems related to narco-terrorism in the region. In fact, one critical problem arising out of the confluence of two major narco-producing and trading regions is the cementing of a diabolic relationship between insurgent groups, arms dealers and narco-terrorism. Such a relationship is quite common in and around Thai-Myanmar, Indo-Myanmar and Bangladesh-Myanmar borders. Not that all the insurgent groups engage in narco-production or narco-trafficking but it has been found that almost all of them have regularly taxed and exhorted money from the traffickers while providing protection to the latter for conducting trafficking in drugs. There are several critical implications of this.

Firstly, the transnational narco-networks, now backed by armed insurgents, make anti-narco-production or anti-narco-trafficking drive immensely difficult. And given the terrain (both physical and topographical) in which the insurgents and the traffickers operate there is now all the more reason to believe that the nationally-organised military or coercive solutions may not be the correct way of overcoming the menace of narco-terrorism.

Secondly, weapons, particularly small arms, in the hands of both the insurgents and traffickers become more rampant, indeed, to the point of threatening the law and order situation in the vicinity. A large portion of the money received from taxing and extorting the narco-traffickers goes on to purchase small, at times sophisticated, arms for the insurgents.

Finally, subaltern aspirations get entwined between insurgency and narco-terrorism, almost to the point of blurring the distinction between the two. While this becomes handy for the state machineries in the strategy of depicting the insurgents as narco-traders and winning back the support of the members of the dissenting communities, it often leads them to quick-fix remedies with little or no results. As the World Bank-sponsored study on Indo-Bangladesh border smuggling once pointed out that 'Ordinary men, women and even children participate in smuggling as couriers, porters and rickshaw pullers' (Nandy, 1995), which only indicates that the subalternity of smuggling or even narco-terrorism is far more complex than what is readily understood. There is therefore no guarantee that the narco-menace would discourage the subalterns from joining the trade.

Money Laundering

Narco-terrorism would not make much headway without the practice of money laundering. It is the latter that provides the required funds for the production and later on, shipments of the narcotics across regions and continents. The weakness and corruption prevalent in the banking system of the region remain easily susceptible to money laundering. Often drug traffickers invest their drug profits in the country's infrastructure and legitimate businesses (BCB, 2002:11). The drug trafficker cum money launderer otherwise with the connivance of the bank and the state end up running legal businesses! When such a structure comes into being it becomes impossible to eradicate narco-trafficking and all the corroborating agencies, including money laundering and terrorism, unless and until the state itself goes through a sustained period of reforms and restructuring.

At times certain other structural factors are also responsible in reproducing money laundering, as is the case with the stateless but relatively well off Rohingyas living abroad. As stateless and few licit areas to invest, these Rohingyas have no option but to launder money to various Rohingya nationalist or insurgent groups, mainly to fulfil their subaltern aspirations in the northern Arakan region of Myanmar. That a part of this money would be used in purchasing arms and later on in insurgent or terrorist activities can never be ruled out.

Let me at this stage clarify one point. Once a subaltern struggle takes a military or violent turn, it cannot escape from being linked to the various networks of subaltern globalisation. This is because in order to sustain the subaltern movement through military means there is a dire need for both cash and arms, indeed, over and above the committed recruits of fighters. Often the funds as well as the arms come via the network of dubious groups and shadowy activities.

In recent times, more so in the post-cold war era, this has been the case practically with all the militant groups, including those directly involved in subaltern movements. Tamil Tigers is a good instance, which despite having being funded by the Tamil diaspora, did not hesitate to enter into the business of selling heroin and hashish for financing arms purchases (Shah, 1998:515). Again, take the case of Kachin Independence Organisation, a militant group fighting for the interests of the Kachin people within Myanmar, which with five thousand regular 'armed' soldiers remains 'heavily involved in the heroin trade' (FAS, 2003). This is not something unexpected in view of the protracted nature of these movements and the cost that is involved in sustaining them. Even a modest costing will show that the need for cash is quite substantial. For instance, if we take that a militant group is made up of 3000 fighters or terrorists and that each is paid a monthly allowance of Rs. 5000, the need for cash just for paying the terrorists every month comes to Rs. 15,000,000 (or USD 319,148 at the current exchange rate), which is quite substantial in local standards (Swami, 2003:7). Often the militant groups for the sake of maintaining their freedom and this is more so in the aftermath of the cold war shy away from a particular source of funding. Instead, they now prefer diversifying fund-raising, which at times includes money from taxing the narco-traders or even joining in the business of selling drugs and arms. The following report is a good indicator of the militant groups' involvement in arms trafficking and making money from it (TDS, 2002:12):

Around 100 AK-47 rifles reached different gangs of criminals in the port city (of Chittagong) and its surrounding areas from the insurgents of Arakan state of Myanmar staying in deep forests across the Bangladesh border.... Arakan insurgents sold the rifles and some other sophisticated weapons to these gangs through a clandestine channel of local kingpins of arms dealers and smugglers on various occasions in the past few years. This brings us to the third and final area, the issue of illicit small arms.

A GLOBAL DIFFUSION OF SMALL ARMS

For many years, the global trade in major conventional weapons has been well documented. By comparison, the global trade in small arms and light weapons has proved much more difficult to track. Few national governments publish statistics on the sale or transfer of light weapons or release information about the sales activities of private companies. Moreover, much of the trade—perhaps 25 percent—is carried on through illicit and black-market channels of one sort or another.< 4 >

In the absence of uniform statistics on the trade in light weapons, researchers must rely on anecdotal information and what little fragmentary data is available from government and trade sources. Fairly reliable estimates of the global trade in such weapons range from $5 billion to $7 billion a year, with some estimates running as high as $10 billion a year.< 5 > And while official statistics indicate that the trade in major weapons systems has fallen sharply with the end of the Cold War, many analysts believe that global transfers of light weapons have increased during this period.

The global spread of small arms and light weapons has been facilitated by the emergence in many states, including a dozen or more developing countries, of a domestic capacity for the manufacture of such weapons. Whereas the fabrication of major weapons systems is highly concentrated, with only a dozen or so states capable of producing modern tanks, planes and warships, some 50 nations now manufacture light weapons and/or ammunition of various types. The production of modern assault rifles, for example, occurs in many of the industrialized nations as well as in Argentina, Brazil, Chile, Egypt, India, Indonesia, Iran, Iraq, Israel, Mexico, North Korea, Pakistan, Saudi Arabia, Singapore, South Africa, South Korea, Taiwan and Turkey. Many of these countries produce arms for export as well as domestic use, greatly adding to the number of sources from which a potential belligerent can obtain weapons of war.

The large number of production sites contributes not only to the expansion of national arsenals, but to the spread of arms within societies via theft, bribery and corruption. The multiplicity of trade channels leads to the diffusion of light weapons within societies—extending not only to governments and state-owned entities but also to private armies and militias, insurgent groups, criminal organizations and other non-state actors.

Accordingly, any analysis of the trade in light weapons must take into account both the sharp increase in the number of producers and suppliers and how their weapons are being transferred to an ever-expanding array of states and non-state actors in every region of the world.

The following list of legal, illegal and covert methods by which small arms and light weapons are sold, transferred and exchanged underscores the complexity of the problem:

- Grants or gifts by governments to allied governments abroad;
- Sales by governments to client governments abroad;
- Commercial sales by private firms to governments and private dealers in other countries;
- Technology transfers associated with domestic arms production in the developing nations;
- Covert transfers by governments to friendly insurgent and separatist groups in other countries;
- Gifts by governments to armed militias and paramilitary organizations linked to the ruling party or the dominant ethnic group;
- Black-market sales to the governments of "pariah" countries and to insurgent and separatist forces;
- Theft of government and privately owned arms by insurgent, criminal and separatist forces; and

- Exchanges between insurgent and criminal organizations, whether for profit or in pursuit of common political objectives.

Legal Channels. Currently, there are over 300 manufacturers of light weapons and related equipment in 50 countries around the world, a 25 percent increase in the last decade alone.< 6 > Until the end of World War II, the major producers of these weapons were the industrialized nations. In recent decades, however, these established producers have been joined by China, Israel, South Africa and many developing countries. Estimates of some common models produced by these countries in the past few decades show the enormity of the problem: 5 million to 7 million Belgian FAL assault rifles produced in 15 countries; 35 million to 50 million Soviet/Russian AK assault rifles manufactured by Soviet/Russian factories and licensees; 7 million German Heckler & Koch G3 assault rifles made in 18 countries; 8 million U.S. M-16 rifles produced in seven countries; and 6 million Chinese-made AK-type assault rifles.

These numbers, as alarming as they are, do not include the millions of surplus arms that have been sold or given away as the world's major military powers have reduced their forces and/or found themselves with excess production capacity following the end of the Cold War. Because small arms and light weapons have few moving parts and are extremely durable, even weapons that are 10-to 20-years old are often fully operational and as effective as newly produced weapons. Accordingly, countries such as the United States, Russia and Germany (especially with the dismantling of the East German army) have been able to sell or transfer millions of light weapons to their allies and clients abroad.

Covert and 'Gray-Market' Channels. In addition to legal sales and military assistance programs, small arms and light weapons are disseminated through covert and "gray-market" channels (that is, channels that operate with government support even though in violation of official government policy), most often by government intelligence agencies or private companies linked to such agencies. During the Soviet occupation of Afghanistan, the CIA helped to supply some 3 million AK-47 assault rifles (mainly

Chinese and Egyptian models) to rebel *mujahideen;* thousands of these weapons have since turned up in fighting in Kashmir and elsewhere in South Asia, and as far away as Southeast Asia and the Middle East. In addition, the United States and the Soviet Union supplied arms to rebel groups in Central America and sent massive amounts of weapons to various factions in Angola and Mozambique.

Since the end of the Cold War, Washington and Moscow have discontinued many of these activities. But it is widely believed that military commanders and managers of military factories in Russia and some of the other newly independent states of the former Soviet Union have engaged in large-scale covert sales of weapons to clients in neighboring states and beyond. Government officials in other states have also been accused of smuggling arms to allied groups in other countries, whether for profit or to advance particular political or religious objectives. Officials in Zaire, for instance, reportedly bought large quantities of weapons on the international market and sold them to UNITA forces in Angola for profits running into the hundreds of millions of dollars—most of which is believed to have wound up in the overseas bank accounts of former President Mobutu Seso Seko and his associates.

Another form of gray-market transfers entails the delivery of weapons from government stockpiles to political entities and ethnic militias associated with the ruling clan or party. Prior to the 1994 genocide in Rwanda, for example, the Hutu-dominated government distributed small arms and machetes to government-linked militias. Once the killing began, the Rwandan military sought to crush any organized Tutsi resistance while the militias slaughtered unarmed Tutsis and moderate Hutus. A similar pattern was evident in Haiti in the early 1990s, when the ruling military junta organized and armed the Front for the Advancement and Progress of Haiti (FRAPH) to suppress popular support for ousted President Jean-Bertrand Aristide.

Illicit and Black-Market Channels. The third major category of light weapons transfers includes illegal sales through black-market channels, the supply of arms in defiance of international embargoes and other legal sanctions, and the theft of arms from government stocks or private citizens. In recent years, there has been a striking growth in the operations of black-market dealers to satisfy the needs of non-state actors in ethnic and internal conflicts.

Because such actors are normally barred from purchases on the legal munitions market, they must acquire their weaponry from illicit sources. The growing number of UN arms embargoes has also produced an increased demand for black-market arms. Although it is impossible to estimate the value or scale of all such transactions, some estimates place 1993 black market sales to the belligerents in Bosnia alone at $2 billion or more.< 8 >

The black-market trade has been facilitated by the existence of vast stockpiles of surplus arms in the states of the former Soviet bloc—arms which in many cases are guarded by near-destitute soldiers and officers who are all too eager to conspire in their theft by black-market dealers or to enter the illicit trade themselves. Moreover, there are strong linkages between the illegal narcotics trade and black-market arms trafficking. These underground networks have developed sophisticated methods for the procurement, transportation and sale of small arms and light weapons, at times with the connivance of governments or corrupt public officials. Finally, theft of weapons from military and police warehouses is a major problem in countries afflicted by civil war or insurgent violence. As civil strife spread across Albania in the spring of 1997, thousands of weapons were looted from military depots by insurgents, criminals and civilians. These weapons not only increased the levels of armed violence in Albania, but reportedly were also being smuggled across the border into the Serbian province of Kosovo, where 2 million ethnic Albanians pose an irredentist challenge to Serbian authority. In South Africa and Colombia, stolen weapons contribute to a culture of violence and criminality that undermines the stability of the state and the cohesion of society.

SMALL ARMS PROLIFERATION

The proliferation of small arms is a complex and increasingly international issue. There are important linkages between the nonproliferation, arms control and disarmament dimensions of small arms problems, on the one hand, and firearms regulation (i.e., gun control and criminality) dimensions, on the other. The problems caused by small arms are primarily regional, sub-regional and internal (i.e., within states) in nature.

As a result, while useful things may be done on a global level, a primary focus for practical solutions would appear to be in regional, sub-regional and internal action. It is important, therefore, to develop a body of relevant case studies of the impact of small arms proliferation in particular regions as a basis for policy action. This project will examine the extent of small arms trade and proliferation in two geographical areas of East Asia — Southeast Asia and the Russian Far East. These two areas have significant possibility of experiencing small arms proliferation problems because of ethnic, cultural and political diversity, decades of post-colonial violence, and inadequate policing in both regions, and the emergence of major organized crime in the latter. The general problem of sub-state weaponry is not unique to the two regions, of course, but it is a particular aggravation to government and social order there. From Canada's perspective the problem may become larger as arms sales directly affect maritime trade and state stability in the regions, enter or pass through our territory, or involve criminal organizations within Canada.

The topic of our research is illicit trafficking of small arms and light weapons, as defined by the UN General Assembly. However in some cases it is hard to draw a distinct line between illicit and "legal" arms proliferation, in cases when high-rank state structures are involved in the above activity. The latter cases are also included into the scope of this research.

The Case of Southeast Asia

Southeast Asia saw a perverse "peace dividend" of small arms proliferation as early as 1975, with the end of the Vietnam War. An unknown quantity of weapons flowed out of Indo-China at that time into surrounding states, to guerrilla groups and pirates who plied the waters of Southeast Asia. The uneven development between major cities in the region and the more traditional rural regions, combined with the relatively weak presence of state police and military power in rural areas, and the mobility of watercraft, provided opportunities for arms traders to carry on their commerce undisturbed. Reports of rogue Chinese military trading in small arms must also be examined. Fallout from the recent "financial meltdown" in the region may also exacerbate crime growth in the near future.

The Case of the Russian Far East

The end of the Cold War has had a direct effect on the phenomenon of small arms proliferation in Asia and elsewhere. The arms buildup in the Soviet Union was both in nuclear and conventional weapons, and with the end of Communism, the rationale for the heavy armaments declined precipitously.

Moreover, the demoralization and impoverishment of Russian society and the Red Army has weakened government control over weaponry, which has become a commodity of trade in many cases. The socalled Russian Mafia, which had existed throughout the Soviet period, was lured by the illicit arms trade to facilitate the export of weapons.

Implications

The widespread demand for small weapons has been exacerbated by breakdown of local security and easy access. Relatively simple technology also means that manufacture and assembly does not require advanced industrial techniques.

The model of the drug trade may be applicable, and indeed, one of the findings of the research is the linkage of the drug and small arms trade through the same trafficking routes and criminal organizations (not unlike the Latin American experience).

Drugs and arms share some of the following characteristics in the two regions under study:

1. Widespread demand for the product;
2. Relatively high value per unit;
3. Relative ease of transportation;
4. Relative difficulty of detection;
5. High profit margin;
6. Corrosive effects on law enforcement within states;

7. Manufacture, shipment, and distribution requires illicit networks, which further undermine law and order; and
8. Long-range harm to society in the diversion of scarce resources to non-productive ventures.

Arms and drugs both have legitimate roles in society, when controlled and used for positive ends – police and defence in the former, and medical purposes in the latter (opiates are used for painkilling and sleep inducement). To the extent that the drug trade model is applicable to small arms proliferation, the above eight characteristics can provide entry points for reducing small arms flows, as follows:

1. Reduce supply and demand for the product;
2. Interdict transportation;
3. Improve detection capability and technology;
4. Clean up police and government corruption; and,
5. Improve enforcement capabilities, including international cooperation.

The Japanese have been successful in practically eliminating small weapons from society, and some lessons for Asia can be learned there. Unless the problem of small arms proliferation is brought under control, civil disorder and violence may become more widespread in the East Asian region. Drugs and small weapons are criminalized because they encourage and facilitate further crimes. Drugs create a dependency which can drive persons to engage in robbery and prostitution to acquire illegal substances, moving out of productive and responsible habits necessary to sustain social integrity. Guns decrease the vulnerability of criminals who undertake greater risks and anti-social actions, knowing that their weapons escalate the cost of challenging their actions.

But drugs also have major differences with small arms. Some trade in the latter is legitimate, as long as there is government sanction, while the illicit drug trade is practically proscribed universally.

Also, illicit drugs have accelerated the spread of diseases such as hepatitis and HIV, affecting individuals far beyond users. The indirect effect of small weapons is much more limited. Finally, the end users of weapons are usually men, and these tend to have profiles of greater criminality and aggressiveness than the average population, while drug users tend to be more passive and of both sexes. Most importantly, the trade in small weapons is an area which lends itself best to detection and reduction in the experience of arms control and verification. The legitimate production, distribution, and deployment of large and small weapons has been the jurisdiction and central interest of the arms control community. Accounting for disposition of large as well as light weapons, for example, has been one of the activities of the Neutral Nations Supervisory Commission (NNSC) under the 1953 Military Armistice Agreement in Korea. Other arms control agreements in other areas of the world have also included small weapons in their provisions.

SOUTHEAST ASIA

Scope of Research

The illicit movement of small arms and light weapons into, within and out of Southeast Asia, predominantly through illegal channels and the black market, is a dangerous phenomenon. Borrowing the definition used by the United Nations, illicit trafficking is the movement of weapons that is "contrary to the laws of States and/or international law." This phenomenon is of growing concern because it has the potential to undercut government efforts at establishing stability and order. Also, its potential disruption towards legitimate commercial activities can cause serious harm to economic and social development within the region. The illicit movement of small arms is a human security concern since it has the potential to fuel increased numbers and levels of violent crimes. This perception mainly arises from the fear that there would be a surge in criminal activities resulting from increased economic hardship, which is induced presently by the region's financial turmoil. Violent crimes, in turn, could present a destabilizing force undermining state sovereignty. Governments in Southeast Asia (and the rest of Asia, in general) are worried about the growing illicit trade in small arms because a number of factors have allowed it to flourish steadily:

- inadequate controls against illicit weapons production, exports and imports at the national level due to poorly trained and/or corrupt officials;
- financial and technological difficulties in implementing effective controls;
- lack of coordination and cooperation among regional states in monitoring the circulation and supply of weapons from within and outside of the region; and,
- non-existence of international or regional agreements on controlling the small arms trade (licit and illicit).

The security impact of illicit small arms movement is not confined to the region. Regional ports are becoming popular sites for transshipping weapons around the world, including destinations in the Middle East and possibly North America. Taking this argument into consideration, the small arms proliferation in Southeast Asia could have significant implications for Canada.

China

The People's Republic of China (PRC) may be one of the major sources of small arms proliferation in Southeast Asia. According to media reports, Chinese arms manufacturers are known to be involved in illegal production. The central government determines levels of production for each manufacturer, but many of the factories have produced quantities beyond these levels. Surplus arms are sold through illicit channels for the sake of profits. Officials in Beijing blame this condition on the lack of centralized regulations. However, regulations alone will not solve the problem. Although China recently adopted strong laws against the illicit possession, production and transfer of small arms, such laws may only limit the growth of "cottage" production (which has been growing rapidly). The laws' ability to make an impact against the wellconnected, larger state manufacturers remains doubtful. For example, two firms, Poly Technologies and China Northern Industries (Norinco), are connected to central government officials. The former is a defence conglomerate controlled by the General Staff of the People's Liberation Army (PLA) while the latter reports to the State Council under the Prime Minister. Having entered an era of capitalism, small arms production in China is also increasingly governed by the market — the demand for such weapons within China and in neighbouring states have grown as well as the profits to be had. Current conditions in the arms manufacturing industry contribute to this trend:

- factory managers resort to illicit sales to make up for capital shortages resulting from a decline in "legal" demand for small arms;
- the lack of competitiveness, which result from outdated technology, leads to dumping of weapons; and
- corruption among officials and lack of supervision of surplus weapons result in increased thefts. Beijing attempts to manage the problem through identifying and halting proliferation at its sources, increasing border and port controls as well as launching a campaign to seize banned weapons. Nevertheless, the obstacles are daunting.

North Korea

Weapons from North Korea have also circulated throughout the region and beyond. Some have been confiscated in Hong Kong and most of these were believed to be destined for the Middle East. North Korean weapons range from small arms (machine guns, rifles and grenade launchers) to high tech missile components. Specific information about arms production in the DPRK is scarce, and efforts to assess small arms transfers from North Korea are difficult. North Korea has the additional incentive of needing weapons sales to earn hard currency to buy food to alleviate the ongoing famine as well as other goods.

Russia

Many of the small arms that have been intercepted and confiscated point to Russia as another major source of supply. Some of these weapons were left over from past conflicts in Indochina (Cambodia and Vietnam), but there are signs that new Russian small arms are also in circulation. Cambodia and Vietnam import Russian weapons for defence purposes, but there is a possibility that theft and corruption among military officials have allowed weapons to fall into non-military hands. Such conditions may be more prevalent in Cambodia, where stability has been uncertain since last year's coup.

Vietnam and Cambodia

Vietnam is another source of small arms in the region. Seizure of weapons from Vietnamese trawlers (some of the Vietnamese "fishermen" appear to be former military personnel) in the South China Sea raises the possibility that Vietnamese military stores are being looted by soldiers and that weapons leftover from past conflicts are making their way into neighbouring states. There is demand for small arms in Vietnam, but the country is increasingly becoming a transshipment area for weapons originating from China and Russia. The weapons enter Vietnam through its porous northern borders and move to its ports before they are loaded onto cargo ships. Russian weapons are also arriving directly at Vietnamese ports where they are further dispersed throughout the region and possibly beyond. Cambodian weapons originate from left over caches of the war against Vietnam as well as continued Khmer Rouge insurgency which had made the country a "killing field" from the mid 1970s until early 1990s. Last year's coup, the ensuing violence and the breakdown of the UN peace-building mission may not have changed these conditions. The demand for small arms has probably risen as the sense of national security diminishes and Cambodians seek personal security through the possession of firearms.

Establishing Patterns of Proliferation

Patterns of proliferation described in this chapter should not be assessed as hard data, and are based on analysis of media reports of intercepted small arms movement throughout the region. According to one source, in general the proliferation of small arms is "not random but highly patterned" and it can be controlled effectively through identifying likely channels of supply. Another characteristic of weapons movement through a particular channel is that such a movement often goes in both directions. For example, when illicit Chinese-made machine guns are confiscated in Vietnam, it is apparent that Vietnamese weapons could enter China through the same channel of supply. By keeping these factors in mind, our understanding of the small arms proliferation in the region would be more comprehensive. Small arms proliferation in Southeast Asia is often linked to the drug trade. It is believed that drug cartels in Myanmar are receiving small arms from Chinese sources. This claim may be valid considering that the southwestern corner of China is known as the "Dark Channels" of illicit activities.

It is possible that Chinese weapons are traded for drugs; although information on this remains sketchy. Burmese drug lords have also been receiving small arms from Cambodia. These weapons are usually transported overland through Thailand. The Thai government has attempted to step up controls but high levels of corruption among customs and security officials has undermined such efforts. Chinese weapons are also making their way into Vietnam. However, it is unclear whether the weapons are intended for Vietnamese markets, or if Vietnam is only used as a transshipping site. This is important considering that Vietnam is already saturated with small arms left over from past conflicts as well as those which recently occurred in neighbouring Cambodia. Furthermore, Chinese sources claim that the Vietnamese are smuggling weapons into China, reinforcing the "dual-direction" argument of small arms smuggling.

Small arms from Vietnam have been found on fishing trawlers off the coast of Malaysia on the South China Sea. Malaysian officials argue that these cases do not represent a serious threat because the coastal guards have only confiscated fourteen small weapons from 1990 to 1994. Malaysian optimism is countered by the fact that such confiscations occurred on several occasions, indicating a patterned movement. Actual interception may indicate only the tip of the iceberg. Vietnamese small arms have also been reported circulating in the Philippines, with weapons making their way through methods similar to those in the Malaysian case above. In most cases, illicit weapons were found after the Vietnamese trawlers had been detained for illegal entry. Manila points to rebels in the southern island of Mindanao as the most likely recipients of these weapons. One of the rebel factions, the Moro National Liberation Front (MNLF), admits to obtaining small arms from abroad but has not identified a country source. These patterns of small arms proliferation do not exhaust those in the region, but do indicate some of the better-known channels of supply.

East Asian Ports

The region's ports play a major role in facilitating proliferation. The lack of controls on the movement of goods often allows the ports to be used as sites for transshipping small arms. Arms dealers see these ports as effective channels for dispersing their merchandise throughout the region and beyond. Hong Kong, Taiwan and many of the ports in ASEAN countries share this problem because of the following characteristics:

- the large volume of goods passing through the ports daily;
- frequent corruption and lack of professionalism among customs and security (the military, police, coast guard) officials;
- states' reluctance to impose harsh controls for fear of losing competitiveness;
- financial and technological deficiencies which prevent the development of effective control measures; and
- lack of coordination and cooperation among the region's customs and security officials.

In the case of Hong Kong, former British security officials have noted the problem. Although the demand for small arms in Hong Kong is not high, the territory is a magnet to weapons because its docks are used for licit and illicit transshipment. Hong Kong is strategically located at the crossroads of Northeast and Southeast Asia as well as being the region's gateway to Europe, North America and the Middle East. Although officials claim that Hong Kong's shipping controls are very effective, the port's high volume of traffic is enough reason for arms dealers to take the risk. A tight security net around Hong Kong is neither viable nor seen as desirable because it would severely restrict legitimate trade. The weapons that are transshipped here not only originate from mainland China but also from neighbouring countries such as North Korea. In 1995, a third of the Chinese weapons confiscated originated from PLA sources and have ranged from small arms to high-tech missile components. The situation is worsening because China's harsh internal crackdown on illicit small arms trade has resulted in a surge of weapons movement from the rest of the country to the southern provinces and into Hong Kong. In Guangdong and other areas around Hong Kong violent criminal activities have been on the rise in the last two years.

In addition to Hong Kong, small arms are making their way to Taiwan. Suspected weapons carrying ships from mainland China have been reported unloading cargoes at several ports on the island. It is still not clear whether Taiwan is the final destination of these weapons or if it simply serves as a transshipping site or both. There have been examples of Taiwan serving as a transit point: the 2,000 AK-47 machine guns that were confiscated in San Francisco about two years ago had been transported by Chinese and Taiwanese citizens. The demand for small arms in Taiwan is high among criminal elements and a report in 1996 also suspects that the Chinese government may be supplying prointegration groups on the island. In addition to the discovery of Chinese weapons, the Taiwanese security apparatus has also found caches of small arms that originate from Sabah, Malaysia. The existence of weapons supplier other than just the Chinese supports the view that Taiwan is a possible hub in a network of illicit small arms trade in the region. Ports in Southeast Asian countries have been identified as having some of the least effective antismuggling controls in the world (especially against drugs and small arms). The United States has pressured members of the Association of Southeast Asian Nations (ASEAN) to increase control mechanisms at their ports. However, the ASEAN countries have not been responsive. As in the situation in Hong Kong and Taiwan, the lack of effective anti-smuggling controls is a result of the factors. Most of the ASEAN states, especially Singapore, argue that increased controls would seriously hamper legitimate trade and make their ports unattractive to shipping companies.

SUGGESTIONS FOR NAC AND CBMS IN SOUTH ASIA

The current state of nuclear affairs in South Asia leaves much to be desired. In fact, the challenges enumerated on earlier can only be surmounted if the relevant participants share an equal sense of the dangers presented by nuclear weapons and urgency of lengthening the fuse of any crisis. It is with the hope that such a day will dawn, sooner rather than later, that some suggestions are offered below. These range from reciprocal measures aimed at enhancing confidence by facilitating conceptual clarity, to more specific suggestions on weapon systems. Each recommendation would be useful for addressing either first strike instability, arms race instability, or both.

Clarity on Nuclear Doctrines and Force Structures

While India formulated a written nuclear doctrine and put it in the public domain in 1999, Pakistan never reciprocated. Greater transparency in nuclear doctrines and force structures can be useful for achieving arms race stability. Confidence in understanding the nature and direction of the other side's forces provides a certain amount of transparency and predictability. Thus, it alleviates concerns of arms racing. For instance, the character of India's nuclear forces, per its doctrine, is "effective, enduring, diverse, flexible, and responsive." Such a clear statement provides notice on the capabilities and aims to remove ambiguity. It announces that India focuses on operationalizing its delivery capabilities via mobile long range missiles, including SLBMs, and the establishment of a robust command and control system. As countries improve their space surveillance technology, a certain transparency of the force structure is inevitable. But a negotiated approach is useful to understand the future trajectories of development plans so that both sides need not hedge against presumed adversary capabilities.

Transparency in Survivability Measures

A secure second-strike capability forms the bedrock of stable deterrence. Hence, development of, and transparency regarding, survivable capabilities, can alleviate pressures for preemption. This improves crisis stability by credibly promising assured retaliation. The construction of missile silos, operationalization of sea based deterrence, and increased C2 robustness for also do so. Countries moving in the direction of these developments and maintaining a certain transparency about them foster strategic stability and lower the chances of deterrence breakdown.

Formalizing Low-Alert Statuses

Washington and Moscow's NAC agenda includes measures that lower the alert levels of their nuclear arsenals. Since both countries maintain a significant part of their force on hair-trigger alert, de- alerting and de-mating warheads increases crisis stability. Fortunately, China, India, and Pakistan's arsenals are already in such a state.

However, an agreement that formalizes the low-alert status of each country's arsenal could be a further step towards stability. If verification could be part of the agreement, it would also be a huge confidence booster. Yet, the political and logistical feasibility of such an agreement poses significant hurdles.

Exchange of Information on Nuclear Safety and Security

Given that the threat of nuclear terrorism looms large over the region, South Asia's nuclear states have an opportunity to enhance confidence by exchanging information on their practices and procedures for maintaining nuclear safety and security. Adherence to the many international conventions in these areas as well as a joint regional center focused on the threat is a possibility worth exploring. This center could distribute region wide information on safety and security best practices.

Joint Study on Effects of Nuclear Explosions

No significant attention has been paid to the likely effects of a nuclear weapons exchange in any of the three countries identified above. Given the regions' high population density and the fact that modern mega cities use material that could maximize the thermal and blast effects of a nuclear explosion, it may be useful to conduct a joint study to assess the damage that nuclear arsenals would inflict on population centers. Such a study could be an effective method of calculating the cost- benefit aspects of nuclear war. This would enhance deterrence by making China, India, and Pakistan understand and appreciate the likely extent of damage if nuclear weapons were used.

Limits on BMD

Defense and deterrence have long been thought mutually exclusive. The ability to defend against another's nuclear strike is believed to lessen its sense of vulnerability, tempt it toward nuclear pre-emption, and thereby degrade the other's deterrence. Consequently, during the Cold War years, the United States and Soviet Union agreed to keep each other mutually vulnerable by severely restricting their deployment of anti-ballistic missile (ABM). For instance, the ABM treaty of 1972 mandated that both sides defend no more than one site each with no more than 100 interceptors.

Turning to South Asia, one sees that BMD is beginning to make its presence felt. Given Pakistani doctrine and the danger of inadvertent use, India perceives BMD as an insurance measure to reduce damage should the worst happen. At the same time, China's ABM capability is deployed with America's nuclear arsenal in mind. This development obviously casts a shadow over Indian doctrine and makes Indian BMD a sort of necessary evil. In Islamabad, however, the Indian step has been perceived as destabilizing: it degrades Pakistan's nuclear deterrence posture and fears arise that BMD enables India to engage in limited nuclear war. Pakistan's obvious response has been to increase the number and sophistication of its missiles so as to saturate Indian BMD. In turn, Pakistan's actions raise Indian threat perceptions, especially given the reality of the Sino-Pak strategic nexus. This three way nuclear relationship and the induction of BMD complicates the situation.

Despite BMDs complicating effects, NAC can still be attempted. At one level with China, an ABM treaty that allows BMD over a fixed number of mutually agreed upon sites should be explored. Given that both countries have similar nuclear doctrines premised on no-first use and deterrence by punishment, BMD should logically be used for retaliatory capabilities—including command and control structures. Such an agreement would not only stabilize deterrence but also help alleviate arms race instability. If BMD can be mutually deployed to improve the survivability of retaliatory assets and nuclear command authorities, an agreement could increase deterrence stability by ruling out the possibility of a disarming first strike. At the same time, all sides would evade the defense-offense spiral. With Pakistan, NAC in an environment where BMD exists could occur through the fostering of better understanding and clarity on nuclear doctrine. For instance, it is important for India to explain that an NFU doctrine with BMD in no way increases the chance of pre-emption. Also, an India-China agreement on the subject could go a fair distance in psychologically alleviating Pakistani concerns on the matter.

Controls on MIRVed Missiles

China is believed to have MIRV technology but it is unclear whether Beijing has deployed it. Meanwhile, India is certainly moving toward MIRVs and it is only a matter of time until Pakistan also develops or acquires MIRV missiles. Once China, India, and Pakistan deploy MIRVs, strategic stability will suffer because this capability produces a temptation for pre-emption. With their greater accuracy, multiple warheads become essentially first strike weapons. For the attacking state, a MIRV provides the promise of being able to carry out a disarming counter-force strike. Meanwhile, missiles with many warheads also become attractive targets for the adversary too, creating an urge to strike MIRV missiles before they are launched. Therefore, the use or lose dilemma is heightened. Moreover, in a crisis, the states with MIRV technology might be tempted to strike first in hopes of gaining a war-winning advantage.

An agreement whereby all sides agree not to develop MIRV missiles would contribute to fostering crisis stability. Single warhead missiles present much less tempting targets: a pre-emption strategy would require more warheads be expended than could be destroyed. It would be far more worthwhile for India, China, and Pakistan to arrive at a mutual understanding on this technology rather than follow the dangerous path taken by Washington and Moscow. The three South Asian powers would only arrive at the realization that the United States echoed in its latest Nuclear Posture Review, which mandates the de-MIRVing of its missiles as a step towards strategic stability.

The case for mutual agreement on MIRV missiles may appear unfeasible because countries with 'minimum deterrence' doctrines might find it more useful to have smaller numbers of MIRV missiles. But some strategic stability must be established. In this case, it may be worthwhile to link MIRV capabilities with NFU. Doing so will rule out pre-emption since it reduces risks generated by the existence of MIRV arsenals and functions as effective NAC.

SOUTH ASIA AND THE MIDDLE EAST: PROLIFERATION LINKS

While an analysis of proliferation in the Middle East is outside the scope of this study, it is necessary to highlight existing and potential links between the Middle East and South Asia, apart from the A.Q. Khan network mentioned above. Khan's network provided significant know-how to Iran in the late eighties and early nineties (including centrifuge technology), though the full extent of these transfers has still not been confirmed. While nuclear links between Iran and Pakistan have ended for now, Islamabad's nuclear connection to the Middle East remains, such as through possible collaboration with Saudi Arabia.

From the South Asian proliferation perspective, the close ties between Saudi Arabia and the development of Pakistan's nuclear program is a crucial development. News reports as well as official U.S. government analyses have claimed that Riyadh provided considerable financing for Pakistan's nuclear and missile program in the past, but some reports now suggest a more proactive role by Saudi Arabia-in terms of nuclear energy development itself. This is in line with the announcement in November 2006 by six Arab states-Saudi Arabia, Morocco, Egypt, Algeria, Tunisia, and the United Arab Emirates-that they would develop civilian nuclear programs. Earlier, in 2005, Saudi Arabia applied for and was granted exemption from nuclear inspections through the IAEA's 'small quantities protocol.' Before that, a widely quoted 2003 report in The Guardian stated that Riyadh was considering three nuclear options: (a) building a nuclear deterrent, (b) allying with a nuclear power, or (c) working toward a nuclear weapon free zone in the Middle East. Recent developments suggest that a combination of the first two options might be adopted given that it is highly unlikely that Iran and Israel relinquish their nuclear programs in the near future. This is where Pakistan's role could be significant. German news reports stated in early 2006 that Pakistani scientists assisted Saudi efforts to develop a nuclear program and that this was done under the guise of pilgrimages to Saudi Arabia between 2003 and 2005. Several high-ranking Saudi royals as well as government officials are among the few non-Pakistanis who have toured Islamabad's nuclear facilities.

These include defence minister Prince Sultan (now also crown prince) who visited the Kahuta uranium enrichment facility in 1999, and a son of the current Saudi ruler, King Abdullah, who attended a test of the nuclear-capable 950-mile range Ghauri missile in 1999. These developments suggest that if Riyadh decides to acquire nuclear weapons, the spotlight could be on Pakistan as one of the sources. A factor that could prompt Saudi Arabia to pursue nuclear weapons would be if Tehran unambiguously builds it own nuclear weapon, prompting Israel to shed the opacity over its arsenal.

While disincentives for Pakistan to go along this route are considerable (most notably, U.S. opposition), there are also incentives for Islamabad to aid the Saudis in their quest-cheap oil from Saudi Arabia, and a favorable endorsement for the Musharraf regime (or a successor regime) from powerful conservative Sunni religious and political groups within Pakistan. A 2003 news report quoted an anonymous Pakistani official who claimed that Riyadh and Islamabad had concluded a secret agreement under which Pakistan would receive subsidized oil in exchange for transferring nuclear technology. In 2004, Iranian government sources also claimed that they had information that confirmed this agreement, but there was no further corroboration of this from other sources. Therefore, even if there is no immediate possibility of such a transfer, Saudi Arabia could pursue this with Pakistan in the future to hedge against nuclear developments in the Middle East.

A key incentive for Pakistan could also be to use Saudi Arabia for strategic depth purposes. Islamabad's traditional geographic buffer against Indian military campaigns was Afghanistan, but that was lost after the fall of the Taliban in 2001. Ostensibly, Pakistan requires strategic depth to protect its forces (conventional and nuclear) from an armored offensive by the Indian military, which could cut off the country similar to the 1971 war. Saudi Arabia could provide a base for stationing Pakistani nuclear devices that would be safe from the reach of Indian missiles and give Islamabad a semblance of second-strike capability. This idea of looking towards the Middle East for strategic depth is not new. In the 1990s, former Prime Minister Benazir Bhutto, skeptical of the reliance on Afghanistan, recommended Iran as a more useful ally for purposes of strategic depth.

Apart from the Pakistan-Saudi Arabia link, concerns have also been expressed (especially in the U.S. Congress) over India's ties to Iran, at a time when the IAEA and western powers led by the United States are working toward controlling Tehran's uranium enrichment program. These concerns have arisen during the broader debate in Washington on the nuclear agreement with India. In particular, attention has focused on India's long-standing political and diplomatic relationship with Iran as well as the imposition of sanctions on two private Indian companies suspected of transferring chemicals meant for rocket fuel as well as chemical weapons. The Indian government claimed that both companies (Balaji Amines Ltd. & Prachi Poly Products) were doing legitimate business with Iranian firms. Balaji Amines insisted that they had been supplying products used for manufacturing life-saving drugs such as ampicillin and other antibiotics, but nevertheless, New Delhi ordered the company to stop all trade with Iran.

Both India and Pakistan have attempted to ensure that they are in compliance with the latest international regulations against Tehran's nuclear program. In February 2007, Pakistan froze assets of several individuals and other entities connected to Tehran's nuclear and missile projects in accordance with UN Security Council resolution 1737. In the same month, New Delhi banned exports of equipment and technologies to Iran that could be used in nuclear and missile development projects.

The Iran nuclear issue has been an important point of discussion in context of the Indo-U.S. nuclear agreement. The Hyde Act, passed by the U.S. Congress in December 2006, endorses nuclear cooperation between India and the United States, but it also states that New Delhi should assist the international community in clamping down on Iran's nuclear program. Furthermore, in May 2007, a group of U.S. senators sent a joint letter to Indian Prime Minister Manmohan Singh articulating their dissatisfaction over India's military ties with Iran, especially a 'joint defence working group' between the two countries. Nuclear ties between India and the United States are not limited to nuclear trade between the two, but also extends to discussions over restricting proliferation elsewhere.

Prime Minister Manmohan Singh has stated in the past that New Delhi does not favour another nuclear power in the neighbourhood, and India voted against Iran at the IAEA in September 2005 and February 2006. However, two factors have restrained the Indian government from opposing Iran's nuclear weapons program more forcefully. First, the scramble for energy resources has made the Iran-Pakistan-India (IPI) natural gas pipeline a crucial economic issue for India. Stern Indian opposition to Iran's nuclear program would jeopardize the proposed IPI pipeline from Iran to India. The pipeline is considered to be of crucial importance to India in order to sustain high economic growth rates in the coming years. Thus, economic imperatives, specifically the need for energy sources, are an important factor in nonproliferation positions of countries such as India and China. In this context, New Delhi has reiterated that the construction of the pipeline will proceed in spite of pressures from Washington to cancel the project.

Second, for New Delhi, another variable is satisfying domestic political constituencies that are skeptical of the nuclear overtures from Washington that come at the cost of long-standing ties with Tehran. Since the Congress Party-led coalition government depends on parliamentary support from Communist parties, the government is obliged to periodically hold positions on contentious issues such as the Iranian nuclear program.

The Manmohan Singh government has stated that it would be guided by India's national interest on the Iran nuclear issue, but this does not clarify to what extent India would be willing to go along with the United States on this issue. Some recent reports have also stated that New Delhi could play a more formal role in mediating the growing tensions over Iran's nuclear program in conjunction with the UN Security Council. However, it is unclear what form this would take.

In sum, nuclear issues in South Asia cannot be examined in isolation from developments elsewhere. Historically close political ties have existed between the South Asian subcontinent and the Middle East, and therefore, regional rivalries and bilateral relations play an important role in shaping decisions that impact broader nuclear issues, including horizontal proliferation.

Indo-U.S. Nuclear Cooperation

Since July 2005, when the U.S. and Indian governments unveiled their nuclear cooperation agreement, a debate has risen over its impact on the global nonproliferation regime. This agreement will allow India to acquire nuclear technology and materials from the United States and other suppliers. In return, New Delhi will designate which of its nuclear facilities are for civilian use and which are for military use. The former list would be opened up for international inspections. Prior to implementation, New Delhi will have to conclude a safeguards agreement with the IAEA, while the Nuclear Suppliers Group (NSG) will have to effect changes in its rules to enable nuclear cooperation between its member states and India.

The Hyde Act passed by the U.S. Congress in December 2006, authorized the Bush administration to bring into place a nuclear cooperation mechanism with India, after concluding a bilateral agreement under Section 123 of the U.S. Atomic Energy Act. Negotiations on the '123' agreement began in early 2007, but as of early June, talks were stalled on a few contentious issues. The disagreement is over five main items; (i) the right to reprocess spent fuel, (ii) the conversion of a voluntary moratorium on nuclear testing into a legal commitment by India, (iii) the assured supply of fuel by the United States, (iv) the return of all equipment to the United States if India conducts a nuclear test, and (v) the level of inspections of Indian facilities.

The nuclear deal reflects an influential view in India that the nonproliferation regime embodied in the NPT is defective.

According to Indian Prime Minister Manmohan Singh, the regime is ineffective and that the international community should introduce measures that restrict nuclear proliferation more effectively without suppressing peaceful uses of nuclear energy. At the same time, the contention is that India is a responsible nuclear state that has adhered to the guidelines of nonproliferation (without legally being part of the NPT regime) through strict export controls and denying nuclear assistance to other states, unlike the record of some nuclear weapon states.

A basic feature of this agreement is that by acquiring uranium from foreign sources (to free up domestic supplies) and by placing a set of nuclear facilities on the military list, India can increase its fissile material production for weaponization purposes. However, a different line of analysis examines the implications of increased uranium supplies in the context of India's fledgling nuclear submarine project. This perspective views that rather than increasing nuclear warhead production, New Delhi would use the expansion of its uranium supplies and enrichment capability to fuel its nuclear submarine project, a key element of India's desire to achieve a secure second strike capability under its credible minimum deterrence doctrine.

There are two separate lines of criticism of the deal; the first focuses on the nonproliferation objective, and the second on India's strategic needs. The first perspective is that the agreement will weaken the global nonproliferation regime by condoning India's nuclear weapons program.

The argument is that by introducing India-specific changes to global as well as domestic U.S. nonproliferation laws, it will be more difficult to prevent nuclear transfers involving other countries such as China-Pakistan and Russia-Iran.

A further objection is that even with 14 reactors under safeguards, 8 others will remain on the military list, free to manufacture plutonium for several nuclear weapons annually. Additionally, critics have stated that the agreement so far does not commit India to eschew nuclear testing formally, or to end fissile material production. The second criticism comes most notably, from members of the nuclear scientific community in India, who contend that elements of the agreement would in effect cap India's nuclear program and constrain its thorium-based three stage nuclear project.

They argue that while New Delhi has maintained a unilateral moratorium on nuclear testing, it does not want such a clause legalized in a bilateral treaty. The argument here is that India might have to reconsider its moratorium in the event that China or Pakistan conducts a nuclear test.

In addition, India's scientific community and government have insisted that it be explicitly granted the right to reprocess spent fuel for the three stage nuclear project that exploits the ample thorium reserves in the country (about 30% of the global supply). The Indian government wants to retain reprocessing rights as part of an advanced nuclear fuel cycle. This would involve recycling uranium oxide fuel while the consequent plutonium would be used with thorium in fast breeder reactors. However, some Indian scientific experts have stated that even if reprocessing rights and technology are not granted under the 123 agreement, it is likely that the initial reactors bought by New Delhi will come from Russia and France, rather than the United States. It is entirely possible that trade with these two countries, especially Russia, will involve reprocessing rights and sale of reactors and fuel. On the other hand, Indian analysts criticize the reported objective of the U.S. government of insuring that India's nuclear trade with other supplier states has equally rigorous conditions attached. Finally, Indian analysts have faulted the U.S. position of not allowing assurances of fuel supplies and of prohibiting India from stockpiling nuclear fuel.

Thus, the nuclear agreement between India and the United States has been criticized on the grounds of its potential impact on the global nonproliferation regime as well as its impact on India's strategic nuclear program.

It must also be noted that since the bilateral 123 agreement between India and the United States is still under negotiation, it is too early to assume the eventual direction of the nuclear agreement framework. Even if the two countries conclude the 123 agreement satisfactorily (for both sides), India still must obtain approval for nuclear trade from the NSG and has to negotiate a safeguards agreement with the IAEA.

The China Issue

Several rationales have been offered as justification for the nuclear agreement (such as economics, strategic alliance, and nonproliferation benefits), but perhaps the most intriguing is one has been left largely unstated by the two governments-that of balancing China.

Both India and the United States are concerned about the future direction of Chinese foreign and security policy. For the United States, aiding India through nuclear cooperation as well as a strategic partnership, Washington would be able to balance China more effectively in the region. In the process it would divert China from its main security issue-Taiwan. For India, the agreement is a significant diplomatic and strategic addition to its capabilities vis-à-vis China, with both the possible increase in fissile material production and a strengthened strategic partnership with the United States.

One argument supportive of the Indo-U.S. agreement stresses that China has built up Pakistan as a counter to India for several decades, a policy that involved transfers of nuclear and missile technology. It must also be noted that more than a year before the Indo-U.S. nuclear agreement was first announced in July 2005, there were reports in March 2004 that China was planning to provide Islamabad with a nuclear reactor.

The implication is that that the Beijing-Islamabad nuclear partnership might have continued in any case. Nevertheless, it is important to consider the current pattern of nuclear cooperation between China and Pakistan in the light of the Indo-U.S. deal. Regardless of the pros and cons of the deal, it can be used by Beijing to lay the grounds for legitimizing continued nuclear collaboration with Pakistan. A sign of this has been China's argument that any changes in the NSG rules should be criteria-based rather than country specific.

In December 2005, China began construction of the 300 MW second phase of the Chashma Nuclear Power Plant (contracted in

May 2004), subsequent to the commissioning of the first phase in September 2000. Parallel to the Indo-U.S. deal, China and Pakistan also reportedly agreed to a nuclear cooperation arrangement under which as many as six nuclear reactors of at least 600 MW capacity would be provided to Islamabad. As of now, no other details are available so it is not clear what kind of safeguards will be installed, though some sources have stated that this initiative is being opposed by the NSG.

Reports of a possible Beijing-Islamabad nuclear agreement gained ground ahead of Chinese President Hu Jintao's visit to Pakistan in November 2006. However, no such deal was announced during the visit, leading to a conclusion that Beijing is possibly waiting to see the final shape of the Indo-U.S. agreement to gauge its impact on China. However, one influential Pakistani analyst stated that the lack of a public nuclear cooperation agreement between Beijing and Islamabad does not mean that such an arrangement will not come about; China can supply Pakistan with the required nuclear technology at a more politically convenient time.

Pakistan's desire for a stronger and more public nuclear relationship with China is in part because Islamabad failed to obtain a similar arrangement with the United States. Some Pakistani commentators have in fact argued that their country needs nuclear cooperation with the United States (and other suppliers, for that matter) more than India because the gap between existing energy supplies and future energy requirements is far more serious for Pakistan that it is for India.

A senior Pakistani official connected to the nuclear program, stated in October 2006 that Washington's nuclear policy should be guided by a "criteria-based" approach rather than one geared toward a single country. However, U.S. government officials have stated that they have no intention of considering a similar agreement with Pakistan.

It is likely that this refusal has much to do with the activities of the A.Q. Khan network as well as Islamabad's reluctance to allow a full interrogation of Khan by U.S. experts that would shed light on some unanswered questions related to the network.

Islamabad has cited the fact that Washington declined to offer Pakistan a nuclear cooperation agreement as a motivation for increased self-reliance on nuclear energy, through indigenous fuel manufacturing capabilities.

In this context, government officials in Pakistan stated in April 2007 that the country would set up an installation for fuel testing for use in nuclear plants in a quest for "complete technological capability." As highlighted previously, Pakistan's overall agenda is to redress the perceived widening of the nuclear imbalance with India. Nevertheless, Pakistani experts have admitted that Islamabad's quest for increased nuclear capability is a result of the tacit rivalry between Beijing and New Delhi and the latter's desire to catch up with China. Apart from the impending nuclear technology transfers from Beijing, recent reports have also stated that the Musharraf regime has commenced construction of a 1,000 MW heavy water reactor that will potentially produce adequate plutonium for as many as 50 warheads per year. In addition, Islamabad is setting up a commercial scale nuclear reprocessing plant to allow production of weapons grade plutonium. Such activities would enable Islamabad to stockpile as much fissile material as possible before a future FMCT comes into force.

These developments suggest that Islamabad is attempting to diversify its nuclear weapons program through plutonium, as opposed to its traditional reliance on uranium as fissile material. Plutonium allows for more compact weapons and provides increased flexibility for the arsenal. For Islamabad, this is critical for developing a second strike capability against India. However, some Indian scientific experts have stated that even with the new Pakistani reactor, India will still be able to maintain an insurmountable lead in fissile material production through unsafeguarded reactors under the nuclear agreement.

Chinese support is key to Pakistan's quest for some strategic benefits vis-à-vis India, especially if the U.S.-India nuclear agreement reaches the implementation stage. In a possible attempt to reduce Chinese opposition to the nuclear deal with Washington, New Delhi has committed itself, in principle, to civilian nuclear cooperation with Beijing, a declaration announced during President

Hu's visit to New Delhi in November 2006. This could be viewed as an incentive from Beijing to dissuade India from a potential anti-China partnership with Washington. Nuclear trade between India and China is not necessarily an empty proposal; it has a precedent.

In 1995, India acquired low enriched uranium from China for the Tarapur nuclear reactors. The official Chinese position is opposition to any NSG amendments that would adversely effect the non-proliferation regime, and that they would consider viable arrangements at the NSG, and not bilaterally. Beijing's response reiterates its view that any exceptions should not be India-specific and should include other states.

Interestingly, Indian Foreign Minister Pranab Mukherjee stated in November 2006 that New Delhi does not have any problem with a similar nuclear agreement between Pakistan and China. If this attitude is indeed the Indian government's position, the implication could be that New Delhi is confident that the benefits it will accrue from the agreement with the United States far outweigh the possible increase in nuclear cooperation between China and Pakistan.

Commercial Issues

The Indo-U.S. nuclear agreement also demonstrates that changes in the nuclear supplier regimes will not be restricted only to bilateral nuclear trade between the United States and India. Nuclear energy firms from several countries other than India are already lining up to negotiate commercial nuclear deals with India. NSG member states such as Australia are considering approval of changes in the group's rules to permit nuclear cooperation with New Delhi. Even though Australia (a major uranium producer) has not yet agreed to revoke the prohibition of supply to India, Australian companies such as BHP Billiton are anticipating lucrative sales. Other important members of the NSG have also supported civilian nuclear cooperation with India, within the appropriate IAEA safeguards framework. French and Canadian companies have also contacted the Nuclear Power Corporation of India (one of the main government nuclear energy entities), in connection with the supply of light-water nuclear power related equipment. Thus, nuclear energy companies are important players in the future of this agreement as well as the broader nonproliferation regime. Firms such as General Electric and Bechtel have lobbied the Bush administration in favour of the agreement. Besides deals in the nuclear energy sector, the expectation is also that such cooperation will facilitate contracts in the conventional military sector, especially with respect to the impending deal for 126 fighter aircraft for the Indian Air Force, a deal worth about $9 billion. Aerospace giants such as Lockheed Martin and Boeing are among the contenders for the contract. Therefore, the implication is that the incentives go well beyond the nuclear energy sector.

Finally, it is instructive to consider the scenario if the nuclear agreement between India and the United States is scrapped, either because of insurmountable differences over the 123 agreement or later in the implementation stage. In India, several members of the influential atomic energy scientific community have expressed reservations over the agreement as have the communist parties and the opposition Bharatiya Janata Party (BJP). In the United States as well, there has been considerable opposition from nonproliferation experts as well as sections of the political establishment.

It is not certain if the reservations expressed by the Indian government towards certain clauses of the December 2006 Hyde Act will be rectified in New Delhi's favour in the bilateral 123 agreement, which again has to be approved by the U.S. Congress. Given these complicating factors, the implications of scrapping the agreement are immense; affecting broader bilateral ties between India and the United States, the nonproliferation regime in general, and the global nuclear energy market.

IMPACT OF GLOBALIZATION ON MILITARY EXPENDITURE AND ARMS TRANSFERS

Although the term 'globalization' did not appear until recently, the notion of globalization has existed for a long time. The concept is being used for a wide variety of phenomena and trends and the descriptions of current trends in globalization and the conclusions as regards its impact differ accordingly. There exists not one discourse of globalization but several. In a recent survey of the debate and the literature, five major discourses on globalization are identified, basically falling into the areas of economics, sociology, political science, culture and ecology. All these aspects of globalization, together with the globalization of technology, have an impact of the trends and patterns in military expenditure and arms transfers, directly or indirectly by their impact on the causes of military expenditure, arms production and arms transfers.

The process of globalization has gone through several phases during which the various aspects have assumed different importance. During the cold war period, the political aspects were predominant. The impact of this phase of globalization on trends and pattern of military expenditures and arms transfers was significant and is well documented. During the subsequent, current, phase of globalization, the politico-military dynamic of the cold war has been overtaken by a mainly financial phase. It began in the second half of the 1980s, with the enormous expansion of trading in foreign currency after the breakdown in the 1970s of the international Bretton Woods currency system, and has resulted in the abolishing of state controls of capital markets and opening up of new financial world markets, in privatizations of public enterprises and services, in a break-up of national champion monopolies, and in a general encouragement of global competition. Simultaneously with the globalization of financial and economic activities, the end of the cold war has meant a deglobalization of political action.

These factors, around the existence of which there is fairly broad consensus, have an impact on military expenditure and arms transfers in several ways, perhaps primarily through its effect on the arms industry. While the military sector has been the sector most resistant to privatization, commercialization and reduced political control, all these trends are currently affecting the production, procurement and international transfers of arms. The arms industry is increasingly being privatized and commercialized. The European arms industry is going through a process of internationalization, until now relatively limited and primarily through cross-border joint ventures, but more recently (during 1999) also through cross-border mergers of arms producing companies. European companies are also acquiring armsproducing companies in other continents, recent examples include Australia, South Africa and South Korea, while transatlantic military-industrial links are still rare in spite of the lively debate on both sides of the Atlantic about their potential.

The increasing privatization, commercialization, competition and internationalization of arms production, have resulted in an increased pressure from the arms industry to export their excess supply of weapons, and thus to increased commercialization also of the arms trade, in which marketing and generous sales terms play an increasing role. At the same time, increased internationalization means reduced possibilities for national governments to implement national arms export regulations, since companies can choose to export their products from a business unit in another country with more liberal export regulations. For this reason, national export laws are becoming increasingly irrelevant. This points to the need for common or international export rules.

However, globalization may render also international control more difficult. The globalization of technology in general, and in the context of a gradual closing of the gap between military and civil technology, will make it increasingly difficult to control the international transfer of militarily relevant technologies in the future. The challenge is to achieve international limitations in the transfer of military technology without resorting to controls which will inhibit international transfers of all types of advanced technology, that is, also civil technologies which would benefit economic growth in the recipient countries.

A relatively new development is the impact of globalization on armed conflict and the financing of these. The fragmentation and decentralization of the state has produced a new type of wars and with it increasingly financing of wars outside traditional government defence budgets. As described by Mary Kaldor, these new wars take place in the context of extreme globalization, under which territorially-based production has more or less collapsed and production continues only of a few valuable commodities (diamonds, emeralds, drugs), which provide a source of income for whoever can provide 'protection'. These wars are fought by various types of fighting units, public and private, state and non-state, including regular armed forces or remnants thereof, paramilitary groups, self-defence units, foreign mercenaries, and regular foreign troops, usually under international auspices. During these conditions governments, like privatized military groups, need alternative sources of funding for their military activities, many of which involve criminal activities. These fall into the following categories: 1) 'Asset transfer', i.e. the redistribution of existing assets to benefit the fighting units (such as loot, robbery, hostage-taking, and deriving profits from control over market prices); 2) 'war taxes' or 'protection' money from the production of primary commodities and various forms of illegal trading; and 3) external assistance, in particular for imports, such as (a) remittances from abroad to individual families, b) direct assistance from the Diaspora living abroad; (c) assistance from foreign governments; and 4) humanitarian assistance diverted by governments and warring factions for their own use. For countries involved in such new wars, data on government military expenditure are irrelevant for measuring military expenditure. What is more important is that the set of social relationships which are formed by these systems for financing wars constitute strongly resisting factors for the ending of war.

Privatization of security is an increasing trend also in countries which are not involved in regular armed conflict but where there is a demand for more security services than the government can offer. There is an emerging group of private security companies whose main task is the provision of security in many Third World countries, especially in Africa. The demand for private security services has emerged from a combination of factors, including from western governments seeking to reduce defence budgets, African governments in search of security, international mining corporations and rebel movements. They provide a variety of services, ranging from guarding installations, protecting convoys, supporting humanitarian assistance operations to performing reconnaissance and intelligence services, providing logistical and transport support, military training, strategic planning, and engaging in combat. These companies have developed to fill the need for security in the current context of conflict in Africa, in weak states with limited government legitimacy and with limited economic resources, and in which the international community is increasingly reluctant to intervene.

NUCLEAR ARMS RACE

The nuclear arms race was a competition for supremacy in nuclear warfare between the United States, the Soviet Union, and their respective allies during the Cold War. During the Cold War, in addition to the American and Soviet nuclear stockpiles, other countries also developed nuclear weapons, though none engaged in warhead production on nearly the same scale as the two superpowers.

GLOBALIZATION, DESTABILIZATION AND THE ILLICIT ARMS MARKET

The rapid globalization of international economies and the concomitant spread of neo-liberal ideologies in the 1980s and 1990s had a distinctly destabilizing effect on much of the world. Conflicts that had been held in check by superpower politics, and a clear distinction between "industrialized" and "third-world" nations, broke out around the world. Wars in the former Yugoslavia, Africa (Rwanda, Somalia, Democratic Republic of the Congo, Sierra Leone, and Liberia), Colombia, and Asia (Afghanistan, Chechnya, Myanmar, Sri Lanka, East Timor) raged in the 1990s.

Economies and political systems, which had previously been "regulated" and controlled by the United States, Europe, China and Russia, became fractured, economies became weaker, and governmental institutions eroded. "Weak" states began to proliferate, and in some cases those governments became "failed states" (where governments had virtually no control over what happened in their territory), or "captured states" (which became sanctuaries for arms trafficking, drug trafficking, money laundering, human trafficking and the panoply of organized crime activities).

Weak states became havens for organized crime activities and focal points for regional military conflicts, or "new wars" (Kaldor, 1999). The inability of these states to provide sufficient funding through taxation to support effective law enforcement or a competent military, along with the organizational weakness of the state itself, encouraged the growth of regional warlords, guerrilla armies, terrorist groups, or private armies serving corporations and large landowners. The result, as has been seen in Colombia, the Balkans, Africa and parts of Asia, has been armed conflict.

Weak states and new wars have two vital implications for organized criminality. First, they are havens for all manner of illicit activities. Drug trafficking in particular thrives in many of these areas like Myanmar (opium), Colombia (opium and cocaine), and Afghanistan (opium). Second, they are all markets for arms traffickers. In those states where drugs and armed conflict coincide, drug and arms have become "currencies" of exchange creating a new and robust international arms-for-drugs trade.

Crime Networks, Illicit Arms and the State

One of the newest and most profitable transnational criminal enterprises is arms trafficking. Organized crime has always, to a limited degree, dealt in weapons, mostly weapons for personal use or for organizational requirements. While syndicates of the past may have supplied a few "clean" handguns, today's illicit entrepreneurs provide spare parts for large weapons systems; small arms, including assault rifles, and portable antitank and antiaircraft weapons; and ammunition for both small arms and larger artillery and armor systems. In some cases transnational organized crime groups have also gained access to larger military systems, which have been placed on the black market for resale.

A basic and fundamental aspect of the arms trade is that organized crime networks are no longer serving the needs of individual patrons. Their customers, their clients, and to a large degree their sponsors are nation-states, the entities that are supposed to control organized crime. For example, in the late 20th century, millions of dollars worth of illegal weaponry was sold to clients in Afghanistan and the countries of the former Yugoslavia, including helicopters and fighter aircraft. Organized crime networks brokering arms acquired weaponry in many ways and many locations, but much of it is military equipment and "small arms" from the United States. It is clear that the crime networks those clients were serving were not participants in your local drug, gambling, and prostitution rackets. The clients were governments, or factions within those governments. It is equally clear that such large-scale arms trafficking could not occur without at least tacit approval by governments of source nations, like the United States.

The largest market for illegal contraband from the United States is the international market for firearms, munitions, and defense related technologies. Illegal trafficking in U.S. manufactured firearms creates enormous problems for other countries, and is often regarded as the most serious organized crime in many parts of the world. Firearms from U.S. gun manufacturers are used to supply narcotics traffickers, organized crime groups, insurgent and terrorists worldwide. Organized criminals operating in the arms trade, simply put, do so with explicit state sanction at both ends of the trade.

In addition, arms trafficking requires a new and different modality of supply and smuggling. There is a clear and discernible difference between smuggling a suitcase full of cocaine, and smuggling tanks, aircraft and helicopters. In order to accomplish this task, organized crime syndicates have to redefine themselves either as "employees" of legitimate corporations or as those corporations themselves. Almost all illicit arms transfers are accomplished through "gray market" transactions. The gray market in arms is dominated and controlled by large companies who provide both the cover and the means to make the transfers. Gray market arms trafficking involves the use of the legitimate export licensing process, which requires a "legitimate" arms brokering company. A transfer of arms in the gray market simply involves one of four techniques: (1) fraudulent documents, issued by the company, may be used to disguise the actual customer; (2) fraudulent documents may disguise the military nature of the goods; (3) false declarations by the company may hide the actual identity of the supplier; and, (4) the arms transfer may be disguised as "humanitarian aid.." All of these techniques require the participation of "legitimate" businesses involved in the weapons trade because they are all part of the normal exporting process. Furthermore, a legitimate company must be involved because the arms trade depends on both normal and legal modalities of payment and transportation. These multi-million dollar transactions are a normal part of international commerce.

In addition to the enormous profits involved, the arms trade is important to organized crime because it fundamentally changes the nature of organized crime. Instead of initiating criminal enterprise, organized criminals now become functionaries or "professionals" available for hire by international corporations, or are those corporations themselves. In addition, instead of being in an adversarial position with governments, organized crime is operating at the behest of those governments and frequently as temporary "employees" of those governments.

Guns for Drugs

Examples of the trade of arms for drugs are legion, but a few examples are illustrative. In Brazil, Luiz Fernando Da Costa operated a lucrative arms-for-cocaine business through the 1990s. Da Costa purchased large weapons caches in Paraguay. His syndicate traded guns to FARC rebels in Colombia in exchange for cocaine. Russian organized crime groups have also opened a lucrative trade in guns for both drugs and trafficked women in Brazil. The women are transported to Europe and Israel to work in Russian organized crime owned brothels, while the cocaine is transported for sale in Europe. The women and drugs are paid for with AK-47 and AR-15 semiautomatic rifles shipped into Brazil from Russia.

Another good example of this trade involves Albanian organized crime groups and the Kosovo Liberation Army in the Balkans. Heroin, primarily obtained from Turkish traffickers, is traded for guns and women. The arms were used to fuel the "new wars" in the Balkans, while the heroin and women were traded to organized crime groups in Western Europe. Organized crime revenues, particular heroin and human trafficking, with the tacit support of the United States and its allies in Europe funded the Kosovo Liberation Army (KLA). The multibillion-dollar narcotics trade in the Balkans played the major role in financing the war in Kosovo in the late 1990s.

In Afghanistan the war against Russia waged by the mujahedeen was in large part financed by the heroin trade with drugs moving out of Afghanistan through Pakistan, and arms moving back in through the same routes, all with the tacit approval of the CIA and the U.S. government. To a large degree the same heroin-for-arms trade helped to finance the activities of Al Qaeda and the Taliban in Afghanistan. And, of course, the notorious cocaine-for-guns operation, which funded Ronald Reagan's "secret" war against Nicaragua in the 1980s, has been the subject of numerous Congressional investigations and journalistic exposes.

The Source of Illicit Arms

In the United States, we know very little about the source of weapons trafficked in the illicit market, because we are forbidden by statute from knowing. In the United States the Tiahrt Amendment (named for Kansas Representative Todd Tiahrt) bans the public release of comprehensive information about guns traced to crime scenes contained in ATF's firearms tracing system database. The net result is that Congressman Tiahrt and his colleagues shield terrorists, warlords, organized criminals, and common murderers from exposure.

However, a review of ATF initiated federal prosecutions provides enough data to identify the most common sources of illicitly trafficked weapons emanating in the United States:

It is clear, just from this review of federal prosecutions that the majority of weapons illegally sold on the gray and black markets come from "legal" and protected U.S. arms sellers and brokers. That assertion is confirmed by joint reports from the ATF and Mexican law enforcement on weapons sold to Mexican drug cartels. In addition, the weapons of choice which are marketed reveal the military intent of their use.

7

Nuclear Arms Race and Military Development

India's defeat in war in 1962 was quickly followed by another uncomfortable military development for India, China's explosion of a nuclear device in 1964. This may have been carried out by Beijing primarily with the US and perhaps the Soviet Union in mind. However, one side effect was that India was now faced not only with a territorial foe, but also a nuclear foe, an uncomfortable power imbalance from India's point of view.

There may have been some limited moves toward reducing Sino-Indian hostilities following Rajiv Gandhi's trip to China in 1988, but relations still remained quite cool in the 1990s. Underlying perceptions of mistrust were very clear on India's side, as well as a sense of having been overtaken in the global pecking order and estimation. China was firmly in Indian sights in the late 1990s, as someone to be strategically matched, something of an ongoing quest. At the time, 1997, Mohan felt that given "the national determination in India to liberate itself from the current second class status in world affairs ... New Delhi will find it impossible to give up its search for global status similar to that of China"; in which "New Delhi is most unlikely give up its determination to acquire a functional nuclear deterrent against Beijing ... India will remain committed to building a small but functional deterrent against China." China's installation of CSS-5s medium range missiles in Tibet, with a range of about 1,333 miles, was highlighted in the Indian media during 1997 as targeting India.

Raja Mohan's 1997 predictions were quickly met, as India moved in 1998 toward transforming its implicit 1974 nuclear capability into an explicit realized capacity. The Prime Minister Atal Bihari Vajpayee was blunt concerning China factors behind the Pokhran-II tests by India:

We have an overt nuclear weapons state [China] on our borders, a state that committed armed aggression against India in 1962. Although our relations with that country have improved in the last decade or so, an atmosphere of distrust persists, mainly due to the unresolved border problem. To add to the distrust, that country has materially helped another neighbour of ours [Pakistan] to become a covert nuclear weapons state.

Vajpayee may not have intended this letter to the US president to be publicized; but the sentiments were clear enough, objectively and subjectively. Indian commentators like General Amarjit Kalkat, who had commanded the Indian peace keeping forces in Sri Lanka in 1987, were also clear at the time where the message of India's nuclear explosions was aimed. It was not a local regional demonstration against Pakistan. Instead, Kalkat argued that: What strikes me as being particularly significant is their effect on India-China relations. These will be put on an even footing ... The tests are really an attempt to correct the current military and technological imbalance vis--vis China, which is already in the threshold of being a world super power ... Countries tend to respect equals and nuclear parity does help provide the level playing field needed to build such an equalitarian relationship. China has been a nuclear power for long, but India was not till it showed its capability this week.

Similar logic was apparent with India's successful testing of an Agni-II medium range (2,500-3,000 kilometers/1,550-1,860 miles) missile in 1999. Dinkar Shukla at the Government of India's Press Information Bureau asserted that "Pokhran-II and Agni-II are a symbol of a resurgent India," in which "the Pakistani threat is only a marginal factor in New Delhi's security calculus. Agni is at the heart of deterrence in the larger context of the Sino-Indian equation." Such considerations were why Chellaney argued in 2000 that "a major motivation for India's 1998 nuclear tests was the growing military asymmetry with China." IR theory enters the picture with regard to China's differing responses in 1962 and 1998. Whereas China took military action against India in 1962, it initially responded fairly mildly to India's nuclear explosion in 1998. Lei Guang argues that different perceptions were in play.

In 1962, China could feel that its identity was at stake through India refusing to negotiate over what China considered was an unequal treaty imposed on it in earlier times of weakness. Guang argues that "given the centrality of territory to the Chinese national identity, what constituted the border between China and its neighbour was no longer simply a matter of administrative marking." Instead, there was a threefold challenge to China, to its perceived territory, sovereignty and legitimacy. Consequently, this "triple assault on China's fundamental identity as a nation-state contributed to its final decision to resort to violence in 1962." Such consideration are rightly seen by Guang as an example of IR constructivism.

Conversely, China took a more subdued and restrained approach to India's nuclear testing in 1998. Guang explains this difference by arguing that China's core identity was not particularly threatened by this event; India's nuclear explosion "did not constitute a frontal attack on the PRC's identity in 1998. On the contrary, it testified to China's nuclear power and affirmed its position as a major power in the region." This did not mean that China was not concerned about India's nuclear explosion. What it did mean was that China responded in different ways and at a different pitch than in 1962. As Guang argues, "a main thrust of the Chinese reaction to India's nuclear tests in 1998 was geopolitical in nature. Unlike in 1962, what was at stake for China in 1998 was its national security, not its fundamental identity as a modern nation-state." Its power advantages enabled a cooler calculated restraint in 1998.

Nuclear rivalry continues to affect Sino-Indian relations. A nuclear arms race, and its "nuclear security dilemma" dynamics, adds a competitive spiral element to their relationship. Even as the dust from India's Pokhran-II tests was settling, further deployment of Chinese missiles was causing alarm in India,

Chellaney pointing out in 2000 that "India's largest neighbor [China] is conducting the biggest expansion of missile capabilities anywhere in the world. The first of these new missiles, the Dongfeng (DF) 31, last tested in July 1999, can reach every corner of India but little of U.S. territory." Chellaney's own sense of the political context of China's nuclear program was stark, "India's existing modest deterrent capabilities will be gravely undermined as China builds up its nuclear and missile armories. The Sino-Indian asymmetry will increase ... India will have every incentive to acquire similar assets that play a primary role in power-projection strategies." An offensive weapons spiral was in the offing from both sides. Whilst welcoming US attempts to develop a AMD (Anti-Missile Defence) system, Chellaney acknowledged and concluded that "nevertheless, the likely response of those states whose security will be directly affected, particularly China, will significantly affect India's interests. This is what India has to worry about"; even though "in due course, the action-reaction cycle triggered by missile defenses could drive India closer to the United States." Strategic alignment between India and the US is Beijing's nightmare.

In terms of power projection, China's control of Tibet has seen its installation of various medium and intermediate range missile systems. These missile systems are irrelevant to curbing domestic discontent inside Tibet, but do literally and strategically point outside Tibet toward India, its capital Delhi and other major Indian cities. Indian analysts are acutely aware of these implications. For Mahapatra, this military buildup in Tibet is "not only aimed at overwhelming India militarily, but to enable Chinese coercive diplomacy in respect of the border dispute."

Asymmetrics is in play. Installation of intermediate and medium range ballistic missiles enables China to immediately and easily threaten India; whereas the main centers of China, Beijing, Shanghai, Guangzhou remained far away from India. Back in 1999, Kanwal was lamenting that "realistic deterrence against China can only be achieved by developing a demonstrated capability to target major Chinese cities such as Beijing and Shanghai with nuclear weapons."

However, India's successful testing of the Agni-III intermediate range ballistic missile in 2007 and 2008, with a range of 3,500 kilometers (2,170 miles), for the first time brings many of China's main cities within range of India's nuclear strike capability. The Agni-I short range ballistic missile is clearly oriented towards Pakistan, Agni-III is equally clearly oriented towards China, "China-specific" in Pandit's eyes. India's nuclear mobility is strengthened by the submarine based Sagarika ballistic missile launches carried out in 2008. India is set to test its augmented Agni-III+/IV missile system, with a range of 5,000 kilometers (3,110 miles) in early 2009, enabling India to target all of China for the first time. From China's point of view, this increases its nuclear encirclement, in part from India, in part from India in conjunction with the United States.

Of course, India's and China's modernization and expansion of their nuclear and missile capability is not necessarily just aimed at each other. India has its ongoing concerns with Pakistan, China has its own set of concerns with the United States. Nevertheless, India and China also feed off each other's nuclear programs.

The final twist in the nuclear relationship is India's drive to establish an effective anti-ballistic MDS (Missile Defence System), in part through collaboration with the United States, but in part under its own efforts. Following successful interceptor missile tests in 2006 and 2007, India claims to have developed an ABM (Anti-Ballistic Missile) capacity, with operational deployment scheduled by 2011. Classic security dilemma dynamics operate here. As admitted by Mohanty, "China would watch India's growing missile defence capability very carefully ... there is hardly any doubt that both China and Pakistan would most likely try to strengthen their missile strike capabilities to maintain the strategic deterrence." From India's point of view, China's close nuclear links with Pakistan remains a further exacerbating and exasperating factor in Sino-Indian relations, and is part of their respective encirclement and alignment scenarios to which we now turn.

WORLD WAR II

The first nuclear weapon was created by the American Manhattan Project during the Second World War and was developed to be used against the Axis powers. Scientists of the

Soviet Union, then an ally of the United States, were aware of the potential of nuclear weapons and had also been conducting research in the field.

The Soviet Union was not officially informed of the American experiments until Stalin was briefed at the Potsdam Conference on July 24, 1945. The Americans did not trust the Soviets enough to keep the information safe from German spies but also distrusted the Soviets and their intentions generally, despite their wartime military alliance. Even during the war several government and military figures in the USA saw the USSR as a potential enemy in the future.

Despite their official ignorance, the Soviets were well aware of the program due to a ring of spies operating within the American nuclear program. The atomic spies (including Klaus Fuchs and Theodore Hall) kept Stalin well informed of American progress. When U.S. President Harry S. Truman informed Stalin of the weapons, he was surprised at how calmly Stalin reacted to the news and thought that Stalin had not understood what he had been told. In fact Stalin had long been aware of the program. The program was top classified meaning even Truman did not know about it or the weapons until he became president.

In August 1945, atomic bombs were dropped on Truman's orders on designated Japanese cities. The first bomb was dropped on Hiroshima, and later another bomb was dropped on Nagasaki by the B-29 bombers *Enola Gay* and *Bock's Car* respectively.

Early Cold War

In the years immediately after the Second World War, the United States had monopoly on specific knowledge of and raw materials for nuclear weaponry. Initially, it was thought that uranium was rare in the world, but this turned out to be wrong. American leaders hoped that their exclusivity would be enough to draw concessions from the Soviet Union, this proved ineffective. Behind the scenes, the Soviet regime was working on building their own atomic weapons. During the war Soviet efforts had been limited due to a lack of uranium, but new supplies in Eastern Europe were found and provided a steady supply while the Soviets developed a domestic source. While American experts had predicted that the USSR would not have nuclear weapons until the mid-1950s, the first Soviet bomb was detonated on August 29 of 1949, shocking the entire world. The bomb, named "Joe One" by the West, was more or less a copy of the bomb the United States had dropped on Japan, "Fat Man".

Governments spent massive amounts to increase the quality and quantity of their nuclear arsenal. Both nations quickly began working on the hydrogen bombs and the United States detonated their first of these on November 1, 1952. Again, the Soviets surprised the Americans by exploding a deployable thermonuclear device next August, though it was not a real multi-stage hydrogen bomb, which followed in 1955.

The most important development in terms of delivery in the 1950s was the introduction of intercontinental ballistic missiles, ICBMs. Missiles had long been regarded the ideal platform for nuclear weapons, and were potentially a more effective delivery system than strategic bombers, which was the primary delivery method at the beginning of the Cold War. On October 4, 1957, the Soviet Union showed the world that they had missiles able to reach any part of the world when they launched the Sputnik. The United States launched their own satellite on the 31 October 1959. The Space Race showcased technology critical to the delivery of nuclear weapons, the ICBM boosters, while maintaining the appearance of being for science and exploration.

This period also saw some of the first attempts to defend against nuclear weapons. Both superpowers built large radar arrays to detect incoming bombers and missiles. Fighters to use against bombers and anti-ballistic missiles to use against ICBMs were also developed. Large underground bunkers were constructed to save the leaders, and citizens were told to build fallout shelters and taught how to react to a nuclear attack. These measurements were called civil defense.

Mutual Assured Destruction (MAD)

None of these defensive measures were secure, and in the 1950s both the United States and Soviet Union had nuclear power to obliterate the other side. Both sides developed a capability to launch a devastating attack even after sustaining a full assault from the other side (especially by means of submarines), called a second strike. This policy was part of what became known as Mutual Assured Destruction: both sides knew that any attack upon the other would be devastating to themselves, thus in theory refraining them from attacking the other.

Both Soviet and American experts hoped to use nuclear weapons for extracting concessions from the other, or from other powers such as China, but the risk connected with using these weapons was so grave that they refrained from what John Foster Dulles referred to as brinkmanship. While some, like General Douglas MacArthur, argued nuclear weapons should be used during the Korean War, both Truman and Eisenhower opposed. Both sides were unaware of the capacity of the enemy's arsenal of nuclear weapons. The Americans suffered from a lack of confidence, and in the 1950s they believed in a non-existing bomber gap. Aerial photography later revealed that the Soviets had been playing a sort of Potemkin village game with their bombers in their military parades, flying them in large circles, making it appear they had far more than they truly did. The 1960 American presidential election saw accusations of a wholly spurious missile gap between the Soviets and the Americans. On the contrary, the Soviet government exaggerated the power of Soviet weapons to the leadership and Nikita Khrushchev.

An additional controversy formed in the United States during the early 1960s concerned whether or not it was certain if their weapons would work if the need should occur. All of the individual components of nuclear missiles had been tested separately (warheads, navigation systems, rockets), but it had been infeasible to test them all combined. Critics charged that it was not really known how a warhead would react to the gravity forces and temperature differences encountered in the upper atmosphere and outer space, and Kennedy was unwilling to run a test of an ICBM with a live warhead. The closest thing to an actual test was 1962's Operation Frigate Bird, in which the submarine USS *Ethan Allen* launched a Polaris A1 missile over 1,000 miles to the nuclear test site at Christmas Island. It was challenged by, among others, Curtis LeMay, who put missile accuracy into doubt to encourage the development of new bombers. Other critics pointed out that it was a single test which could be an anomaly; that it was a lower-altitude SLBM and therefore was subject to different conditions than an ICBM; and that significant modifications had been made to its warhead before testing.

Initial nuclear proliferation

In addition to the United States and the Soviet Union, three other nations, the United Kingdom, People's Republic of China, and France also developed far smaller nuclear stockpiles. In 1952, the United Kingdom became the third nation to possess nuclear weapons when it detonated an atomic bomb in Operation Hurricane in Australia on October 3, 1952. During the Cold War, British nuclear deterrence came from submarines and nuclear-armed aircraft. The Resolution class ballistic missile submarines armed with the American-built Polaris missile provided the sea deterrent, while aircraft such as the Avro Vulcan, SEPECAT Jaguar, Panavia Tornado and several other Royal Air Force strike aircraft carrying WE.177 gravity bomb provided the air deterrent.

France became the fourth nation to possess nuclear weapons on February 13, 1960, when the atomic bomb Gerboise Bleue was detonated in Algeria, then still a French colony [Formally a part of the Metropolitan France.] During the Cold War, the French nuclear deterrent was centered around the Force de frappe, a nuclear triad consisting of Dassault Mirage IV bombers carrying such nuclear weapons as the AN-22 gravity bomb and the ASMP stand-off attack missile, Pluton and Hades ballistic missiles, and the Redoutable class submarine armed with strategic nuclear missiles.

The People's Republic of China became the fifth nuclear power on October 16, 1964, when it detonated a uranium-235 bomb in a test codenamed 596. Due to Soviet/Chinese tensions, the Chinese might have used nuclear weapons against either the United States or the Soviet Union in the event of a nuclear war between the United States and the Soviet Union. During the Cold War, the Chinese nuclear deterrent consisted of gravity bombs carried aboard H-6 bomber aircraft, missile systems such as the DF-2, DF-3, and DF-4, and in the later stages of the Cold War, the Type 092 ballistic missile submarine.

Richard Nixon's Program of Détente

Economic problems caused by the arms race in both powers, combined with China's new role and the ability to verify disarmament led to a number of arms control agreements beginning in the 1970s. This period known as détente allowed both states to reduce their spending on weapons systems. SALT I and SALT II limited the size of the states arsenals. Bans on nuclear testing, anti-ballistic missile systems, and weapons in space all attempted to limit the expansion of the arms race through the Partial Test Ban Treaty.

These treaties were only partially successful. Both states continued building massive numbers of nuclear weapons, and new technologies such as *multiple independently targetable reentry vehicles* (also known as MIRVs) limited the effectiveness of the treaties. Both superpowers retained the ability to destroy each other many times over.

Reagan and the Strategic Defense Initiative

Towards the end of Jimmy Carter's presidency, and continued strongly through the subsequent presidency of Ronald Reagan, the United States rejected disarmament and tried to restart the arms race through the production of new weapons and anti-weapons systems. The central part of this strategy was the Strategic Defense Initiative, a space based anti-ballistic missile system derided as "Star Wars" by its critics. During the second part of 1980s, the Soviet economy was teetering towards collapse and was unable to match American arms spending. Numerous negotiations by Mikhail Gorbachev attempted to come to agreements on reducing nuclear stockpiles, but the most radical were rejected by Reagan as they would also prohibit his SDI program.

Post-Cold War

With the end of the Cold War the United States, and especially Russia, cut down on nuclear weapons spending. Fewer new systems were developed and both arsenals have shrunk. But both countries still maintain stocks of nuclear missiles numbering in the thousands. In the USA, stockpile stewardship programs have taken over the role of maintaining the aging arsenal.

After the Cold War ended, a large amount of resources and money which was once spent on developing nuclear weapons in USSR was then spent on repairing the environmental damage produced by the nuclear arms race, and almost all former production sites are now major cleanup sites. In the USA, the plutonium production facility at Hanford, Washington and the plutonium pit fabrication facility at Rocky Flats, Colorado are among the most polluted sites. United States policy and strategy regarding nuclear proliferation was outlined in 1995 in the document "Essentials of Post–Cold War Deterrence".

Despite efforts made in cleaning up uranium sites, significant problems stemming from the legacy of uranium development still exist today on the Navajo Nation in the states of Utah, Colorado, New Mexico, and Arizona. Hundreds of abandoned mines have not been cleaned up and present environmental and health risks in many Navajo communities.

India and Pakistan

The South-Asian states of India and Pakistan have also engaged in a nuclear arms race. India detonated what it called a "peaceful nuclear device" in 1974 ("Smiling Buddha") much to the surprise and alarm of the world who had been giving India nuclear technology for civilian, energy producing and peaceful purposes. The test generated great concern in Pakistan, which feared that it would be at the mercy of its long-time arch rival and quickly responded by pursuing its own nuclear weapons program. In the last few decades of the 20th century, Pakistan and India began to develop nuclear-capable rockets, and Pakistan had its own covert bomb program with Chinese proliferation which extended over many years since the first Indian weapon was detonated. In 1998 India, under Atal Bihari Vajpayee government, test detonated 5 more nuclear weapons. While the international response to the detonation was muted, domestic pressure within Pakistan began to build steam and Prime Minister Mian Muhammad Nawaz Sharif ordered the test, detonated 6 nuclear war weapons in a tit-for-tat fashion and to act as a deterrent.

THE NUCLEAR ISSUE AND REGIME LEGITIMACY

The nexus between public opinion and the nuclear programme has been strengthened over time. Care has been taken to introduce changes in the directions of Pakistan's nuclear policy in such a manner as to retain public acceptance and approval. The history of the programme, which dates back to the 1960s, illustrates the domestic determinants of security policy in Pakistan.

From Partition to the first military government

A combination of hostility towards India and the need to address domestic challenges contributed to the inception of the nuclear weapon programme in the 1960s. This particular mix of internal and external factors has, in fact, existed since Pakistan's creation as an independent state. As early as 1948, Pakistani policy makers opted for anti-Indian rhetoric and the threat or use of force to advance their dual goals of regime legitimacy and external security.

By 1958, when the military took direct control of the state after a decade of indirect control in alliance with the civil bureaucracy, the role of the military as guarantor of national security had begun to bear political fruit. Although the military's political legitimacy was questioned and rejected, Pakistani decision makers proved more successful in manipulating anti-Indian sentiment, the by-product of a bitter partition and of the continued existence of territorial disputes. As a result there was general acceptance among most sections of the population of a security policy based on two assumptions: an unremitting Indian threat and a reliance on military (as opposed to diplomatic) means to counter it.

This approach suited the domestic political interests of the now- dominant armed forces. Pakistan's participation in Western security alliances, justified by the putative Indian threat, was generally accepted by the public, while the military became the beneficiary of Western economic and military assistance. Nor did the public question the emphasis on military expenditure at the cost of development. With respect to nuclear policy, Pakistan's first reactor started up in 1965, but the weapon option was not yet an important activity. India's nuclear ambitions were condemned, but key officials disclosed their intention to counter a potential Indian nuclear threat with a similar capability. Thus, General Ayub Khan's politically ambitious Foreign Minister, Zulfikar Ali Bhutto, could declare in January 1965 that if India developed an atomic bomb Pakistan would also have to because there was no conventional alternative.

In the wake of the Indo-Pakistani War of 1965, Pakistani policy makers faced new and more serious domestic challenges. The miscalculations of the military regime, combined with heightened public expectations, led to widespread opposition to authoritarian rule.

In the regime's attempts to divert domestic attention away from an unpopular cease-fire in the West wing of the country and disillusionment with the prospects of a stable and secure East Pakistan, anti-Indian propaganda reached new heights in the officially controlled print media.

Despite the intention to develop a nuclear option, the military's main priority was the resumption of security links with the USA and access to US arms, disrupted during the 1965 war. The 1970s were to lead to a change in nuclear policy as decision makers faced new inter- linked internal and external challenges.

The civilian government after the 1971 war

Following its defeat in the 1971 Indo-Pakistani War and the independence of Bangladesh, the Pakistani military opted for a strategic withdrawal from politics, handing over power to civilian hands.

Under President, later Prime Minister, Zulfikar Ali Bhutto, the new government faced the onerous tasks of restoring domestic legitimacy and providing a new sense of identity to the truncated state. At the same time, conscious of the military's resentment at their loss of power and prestige, the civilian leadership had to ensure that the interests and goals of the armed forces were given priority in policy making.

In the domestic realm, the PPP Government relied on the tried and tested approach of using the external threat to foster internal unity, exploiting anti-Indian sentiment and suspicions, which also served to legitimize a gradual military build-up in both the conventional and the nuclear realms.

The nuclear aspect became more important following the Indian nuclear test in 1974. The Bhutto Government embarked in earnest on an ambitious nuclear programme aimed at providing Pakistan with an equivalent nuclear standing, and nuclear policy was justified on the ground of the Indian threat to receptive internal audiences.

Although the programme clearly had a weapon orientation, the Pakistani authorities insisted that it was peaceful in nature as they attempted to acquire the necessary technology and hardware from external sources, including a French nuclear reprocessing plant.

Pakistan also attempted simultaneously to justify its nuclear pro- gramme and discredit its Indian adversary by proposing a nuclear weapon-free zone for South Asia, an offer which was promptly rejected by India.

Although official offers of regional disarmament and their rejection by India reinforced Pakistani public perceptions of the Indian threat, they did little to reassure the USA of Pakistan's peaceful nuclear intentions.

The return to military rule after the 1977 coup

The nuclear programme became even more of a symbol of Pakistan's national prestige and sovereignty when the French rescinded the nuclear reprocessing deal under US pressure.

Following the military coup which brought General Zia ul-Haq to power in 1977 and led to Bhutto's execution, nuclear policy still proved to be a successful tool in providing a degree of legitimacy to an unpopular military regime, since it projected itself as the guardian of Pakistan's national security and sovereignty.

Although domestic legitimacy continued to elude the Zia regime throughout its 11 years, there were no significant internal divisions on the issue of the nuclear weapon programme. While the successful use of the government-controlled broadcast media and the co-optation of the academic community helped in creating a domestic consensus on the issue, the regime's role in Afghanistan during the second cold war helped it to acquire external legitimacy and substantial economic and military support.

Deliberate US inattention helped Pakistani decision makers in their clandestine quest to acquire an independent ability to produce fissile material, which was achieved by the mid-1980s. When Under-Secretary of State James Buckley was questioned by the Senate Government Affairs Committee on Pakistan's nuclear programme, he said that he had been 'assured by Pakistani ministers and by the President himself that it was not the intention of the Pakistani government to develop nuclear weapons', stating even more categorically on another occasion, 'I fully accept the statement of President Zia that Pakistan has no intention of manufacturing nuclear weapons or acquiring nuclear weapons'.

A State Department memorandum in 1983, however, disclosed that Pakistan had shifted from 'procurement of weapon components themselves to procurement of machinery necessary for their manufacture'. Certain of Western economic and military assistance, the military regime continued to expand and consolidate Pakistan's nuclear capabilities.

Nor were any attempts made to resolve tensions with India, exacerbated by the tendency, on both sides, to exploit internal tensions.15 As relations continued to decline, war was narrowly averted in 1985 and 1987.

These crises were, however, used in the internal Pakistani context to justify the directions of both security and domestic policies, including the forcible repression of dissent in the province of Sindh.

In a deteriorating regional climate, Pakistan's achievements in the nuclear field were also used to buttress the legitimacy of the military regime. Although ambiguity remained Pakistan's nuclear policy, high-profile figures within the nuclear establishment revealed that Pakistan had acquired the ability to produce weapon-grade uranium, joining the select club of nuclear-capable countries. Abdul Qadeer Khan, head of Pakistan's uranium enrichment programme, admitted that Pakistan had a nuclear capability in an interview with a visiting Indian journalist, Kuldip Nayar, in March 1987, an interview which could only have been held with the military regime's approval and connivance.

Thus the nuclear programme was presented to domestic audiences not only as the ultimate means of ensuring Pakistani security against aggressive Indian intentions, but also as a symbol of national prestige and sovereignty. Zia stated, for instance, 'We are among the five countries in the world who know and practice this technology', that is, the production of reactor-grade enriched uranium; while Khan, in an interview with a widely read Urdu-language daily, *Nawa-i-Waqt,* declared that 'Pakistan had broken the western countries' monopoly on the enrichment of uranium'.

Conscious, however, of the need to divert international attention from the rapid progress of the nuclear weapon programme, Pakistani policy makers offered proposal after proposal for regional nuclear disarmament to an unresponsive Indian establishment. India's rejection of Pakistan's diplomatic offensive was then used to undermine Indian credibility in international forums and to strengthen the domes- tic consensus in favour of Pakistan's nuclear capability.

TENDENCIES IN THE GLOBAL DEFENCE INDUSTRY

The global defence industry has undergone profound changes in recent years. Changes in demand for military weapons and equipment, the allocation of resources for national security, national and international security priorities especially by major states, among others, have affected the defence industry in many ways. While the Cold War era witnessed a massive military build-up by many countries, thus fuelling demand for this lucrative sector, the immediate post-Cold War period witnessed just an opposite scenario. Demand for military equipment went down during the late 1980s and early 1990s. Budgetary allocations for security sectors fell. Military downsizing occurred. In just a period of half-a-decade, roughly from 1987 to the early 1990s, the defence industry witnessed a different scenario and shrank considerably. It had to shift priorities to adjust to the new environment. In brief, since the end of the Cold War, the defence industry has faced numerous challenges from all quarters. Most of the decline in the volume of arms production took place during the early and mid-1990s. During this time, significant down-sizing, rationalisation and diversification (primarily into dual-use and civilian production) were witnessed in the defence-industrial sector.

Mergers and acquisitions during the 1990s resulted in the creation of a few giant companies like Boeing, Lockheed Martin, British Aerospace, Northrop Grumman, EADS, and others. This also resulted in many smaller companies either having to merge with big ones or having to shift their priorities toward civilian production, thus leaving the defence sector. Defence industries of major countries like the United States and of Western Europe were affected most during this period although countries like Russia, Israel, South Africa, Brazil, India, and others were also affected. Arms reductions during the 1990s were extensive and fetched a sizeable 'peace dividend'.

It was desirable that such a decade of disarmament should have been extended. However, as evidence suggests, indicators of disarmament and conversion now show stagnation; in many cases even a reverse trend toward a strengthening of military postures are witnessed. A decade of cuts in military expenditure ended in 1998/99 when it went up again. The upward trend in military expenditure is likely to continue in future. The 11 September 2001 terrorist attacks in the United States are likely to result in a major shift in defence-industrial developments because of their impact on security requirements at national and international levels. But this is not to suggest that the upward trend in military expenditure was a product of such an unfortunate event.

This trend had already started in the late 1990s, primarily because of increased military spending by countries like the United States and regions like the Middle East and South and East Asia. In this changed scenario, the defence industry seems to gear up to meet new challenges. As procurement budgets have started to swell again and are likely to stay that way, new opportunities are expected for the defence industry. In fighting terrorism, additional defence programmes initiated by countries like the United States will most likely change the structure of the defence industry. While it is expected that giant weapons producers, especially in the United States, are likely to benefit most from the on-going 'War on Terror', national defence industries elsewhere are also likely to reorient themselves to meet future challenges. In brief, the global defence industry, after a period of significant downsizing and rationalisation, is likely to enter into a phase of renewed attention. Demand for smart weapons, increased emphasis on military technology including investment in R&D, growing demand for aerospace and cutting-edge technology products, are all likely to boost defence-industrial activities in many parts of the world.

Trends of India's Defence Industry

Trends in global defence industry have impinged India in many ways. India's defence industry has witnessed significant changes since the end of the Cold War. In the 1990s, changes in both institutional and policy spheres became more prominent. The most far reaching change that has occurred in recent years in India's defence-industrial sector is related to its opening up to the market. Long protected as a closed sector, India's defence industry has now opened up for private participation. As if this was not enough, it is also showing enough willingness to become an exporter and dares to venture into the competitive global arms market. How far it will succeed in its objectives is examined elsewhere, but changes are certainly a product of and response to the contemporary changes in the global industrial defence scenario. At the same time, it is also showing willingness to diversify its range of products, which not only include modern weapons systems but also technologies for wide and popular civilian uses. The Indian defence-industrial sector targets the national, and even global, civilian market to sell its products, especially in the fields of civilian space, medical, and electronics. Thus conversion through diversification has been witnessed in many areas of defence production in India.

India's defence industry has come a long way from being at the lowest end of the production spectrum, catering to the maintenance and repair and overhaul of imported weapons, to a stage where it can boast of designing and developing a range of state-of-the-art weapons systems. Half a decade of defence-industrial experience in India shows that while it started from scratch, it has been able not only to learn and absorb various stages of production intricacies but also produce complex systems that are primarily an indigenous activities. Another important factor is that the Indian defence industry has produced various weapons systems under licenses acquired from various foreign sources.

Although the first Prime Minister of India, Jawaharlal Nehru, believed in 'self sufficiency' in arms production, which became a policy mantra for subsequent years, it had to be supplemented by what is roughly called 'self-reliance in defence'. Self-reliance does not preclude accessing external sources for technology and systems, or external help in any stage of the production cycle. It is the degree of dependency on external sources that is tested in the case of India's quest for self-reliance. India opted to choose an incremental path, in which it was necessary to continue to meet urgent requirements through imports while striving hard on achieving indigenous capabilities in defence production. Both policies continued till the late 1980s and many of the components of both still continue till today. The 1990s witnessed a series of far-reaching initiatives in the field of national security, of which defence industry was a critical component.

The creation of six Special Task Forces to reform major aspects of national defence coordination and management, under the Chairmanship of the then Defence Minister in 1994 may effectively be considered as the first major step after a long time to initiate and implement much-desired reforms in the defence-industrial sector. This was followed by a series of intensive interactions between various organs of the armed forces, government departments and institutions like the Confederation of Indian Industries (CII). The 'Army-Industry Partnership', a partnership between CII and the Indian Army to get acquainted with each other's needs and to facilitate channels of communication between the armed forces and the private industry, was a result of this process and, in turn, led to other cooperative initiatives. Events like India's nuclear tests in mid-1998 and the Kargil conflict in mid-1999 provided grounds for an intense debate on various aspects of India's national security. Also, as a by-product of the current disinvestment programme, which is primarily aimed toward lessening or wiping out government control and responsibilities in state-owned public enterprises in India, the debate on a reform of the defence industry got a major boost as demands for a privatisation of and private participation in this hitherto closed sector grew more in tune with the changing times.

In January 2001, the Government of India initiated a series of major initiatives that, among others, included Foreign Direct Investment (FDI) up to about 26 percent and full private participation in certain sectors in the defence industry. This policy indeed marks a critical departure from the past. Followed by this, the Group of Ministers (GoM) Report on 'Reforming the National Security System' was made public in early 2001. This laid stress on reforms in all-encompassing aspects of national security, of which changes sought in higher defence management emphasised the need to create specific institutions like the Defence Acquisitions Board to adapt and facilitate changing needs of the defence industry.

While these far-reaching institutional and policy-oriented changes have been underway for quite some time especially since the early 1990s, the demand for private participation has assumed significance in recent years. In such a scenario, analyses of India's defence-industrial sector and policies have become critically important to understand the complex web of linkages that determine national policies in the defence-industrial sector. This, in turn, needs a closer look into the past performance of the defence industry, lessons learnt and a peep into the likely future course.

Research Objectives

The objectives are primarily four-fold. First, we will examine critical aspects of defence-industrial policies adopted by India in the past and link those to performance. It will examine the factors that have influenced India's defence production and their co-relationship with policies and decision-making in this sector. Second, we will examine the main trends during the 1990s, during which major policy changes occurred. It will critically examine the impact of such policy changes. Third, we will examine the contemporary scenario. Fourth and last, it will look into future problems and prospects. The last two are essential in understanding the intricacies involved in India's defence-industrial strategies and are expected to give some clues related to the future course of action in this sector.

Some of the major queries that will be examined here are: Why a quest for self-reliance in the past? Has the policy of self-reliance paid off? If not, what are the options for the future? Why the changes in defence-industrial policies during the 1990s? Are the objectives achievable? What are likely options for the future? Does it have scope for more diversion, thus leading to conversion through the increase in civilian production, in future? We will invariably try to find answers to these queries, although not necessarily in the same order.

Methods and Sources

We will follow a general descriptive-analytical approach. The scope is limited somewhat to policy analyses due to constraints in the availability of information. This is because India's defence industry has long been a 'closed' sector and thus been under exclusive government control. It is only in recent times that it has opened up, thus leading to an availability of information in a low to medium scale. We will also follow a historical method whereby it will emphasise linkages at policy-and decision-making levels to performance, and this is important in understanding the nature of development that this sector has undergone for the past half-a-century. Available data on specifics will be evaluated. Emphasis will be on an evaluation and interpretation of data from primary (especially government) sources. In brief, the overall approach will be descriptive and analytical.

Literature on the subject is scarce. At international level, the study of India's defence industry has attracted very little attention. The same is true at national level. Barring a few books, written by scholars like K. Subrahmanyam, Air Marshal Samir Sen, Major General Pratap Narain, Chris Smith, WPS Sidhu, and others, substantial work is not evident on this subject. Occasional research papers by G. Balachandran, Rahul Roy-Choudhury, Ajay Singh and others have also focused on limited themes. Secondary and tertiary sources are scarce. Primary sources, however, constitute the most important component of this study. Annual Reports (published by the Ministry of Defence, Government of India), Annual Reports of major Defence Public Sector Units (published by respective organisations), periodic reports published by the Comptroller and Auditor General of India, Parliament Secretariat and similar other reports constitute primary sources for this endeavour. Select interviews with senior government officers, analysts and industry-watchers have been taken into account.

HUMANITY MILITARY EXPENSES TRENDS

In bearing in mind the trends in military expenses it is important to treat the published data with care, especially when looking at developing countries. There are numerous problems with the data: definitions, coverage, accuracy etc which make it particularly difficult to use figures for comparison across country, or to aggregate to larger groups. There is also growing evidence that important amounts of security expenses do not enter the accounts or budgets of developing countries. This can be simply because of the different conventions or attempts to "massage" the figures using mechanisms such as double -bookkeeping, extra budgetary accounts, highly aggregated budget categories, military assistance, and foreign exchange manipulation (Ball, 1984). Scheetz (1991) illustrates the degree to which the official figures may differ from those of interest to the researcher. In a detailed analysis of defence expenses in Latin America, he constructed series for military spending directly from the government accounting agencies in charge of public sector budget outlays, so capturing some of what had been excluded from the defence budget figures. He also made attempts to find secret (off budget) accounts used to acquire arms, for example in Chile. The result is figures which are considerably larger than those published by international organisations, but which Scheetz still considered to be conservative estimates. Such problems are also reflected in the fact that different data sources, SIPRI, ACDA, IISS, IMF and World Bank, can give markedly different numbers. The most extreme case was Argentina in 1982 where the IISS military expenses figure and that published by the IMF differed by 1034%.

Such differences are chiefly important for cross section analyses of countries, but not so much for time series data. If looking over time, the concern is with the changes rather than the absolute or relative values of variables and as long as the definitions do not change significantly and systematically one can be relatively confident of the analysis. Also, in most cases researchers are left with only the published sources to use and these are at least the products of attempts to achieve consistency. Even if data are comparable, the use of the exchange rate to put them into a common currency is not without its problems, as it will not reflect the different relative prices of the categories of military expenses and the different compositions across countries. Heston and Atena (1983) provide data for a cross section of countries which have been adjusted to take account of these problems, but in most cases researchers focus upon standardised data such as the share of military expenses in GDP or GNP. Developing countries may also differ in the way in which the treat or define military related aid, the fungibility of aid, and the way in which arms sales are financed.

Bearing these data problems in mind the most striking features of the world military expenses trends is the domination of the superpower arms race, with NATO and WTO accounting for 78% of world expenses in 1981 and superpower involvement in local conflicts leading to higher expenses in other countries. Between 1960 and 1987 military expenses by developing countries grew three times as fast as those of the industrial countries, with very little concern shown internationally. Superpower military and military related aid and their direct involvement in conflicts, the search for export markets by the major arms producers and a number of regional conflicts and instabilities fuelled this growth. Porter (1989) suggested that there were four "stylised facts" of the contemporary development process up to 1980:

1. Military Expenses had risen as a fraction of GDP.
2. Capital cost component was rising relative to operational component.

3. The proportion of the developing countries' population in the armed forces was rising.
4. Military wages were rising relative to civilian.

Unfortunately for him, when these stylised facts were published things were already changing. As Figure 1 shows the military burden for the developing countries peaked in the mid seventies, then declined and rose again peaking in 1982-3. It then declined to 1989, before rising briefly 1989-90 and then continuing the downward trend. Figure 2 shows world military expenses to have peaked in constant prices in 1987 and then to have declined continuously. The pattern for the developing country differs with the peak occurring in 1982 and with the brief increase in the early 1990s. The overall picture for developing countries does hide some regional differences. Figure 3 shows that real military expenses has continued on an increasing trend in South Asia, while declining in Africa and South America. The high growth rates of the South Asian economies has meant, however, that their military burden has not increased as shown in Figure 4. In the Middle East real military expenses peaked in 1982-3, fell to 1989 and then rose again briefly as shown in figure 5. The rise in military expenses, both in constant prices and as a share of GNP, in the developing world in the early 1990s was in fact is almost entirely the result of this increases in the Middle East. Table A1 provides the source data for the Figures.

In the recent UNDP Report an estimate was made of the savings from the cuts in military expenses that have been made and are likely to be made. This allows the computation of a cumulative peace dividend as presented in Table 1. They estimate that the cumulative "peace dividend" to 1987-94 has been 933 billion dollars of which only 126 billion has been in the developing countries (although weighting by their share of world military spending makes similar to the developed economies). Clearly the earlier cuts are also the easiest but there is still considerable potential for further cuts. Assuming an annual reduction of 3%, they estimate a further saving of 459 billion by 2000 with 73 billion in the developing countries. While there may be considerable potential for cuts in military expenses in developing countries, the questions we now have to ask are what are the likely effects of such cuts and if they are positive, what are the preconditions required to make the most of the opportunity presented, both for the individual countries and for the international community? In general the answers to such questions will be contingent on the theoretical understanding of the process of economic growth and it is to these issue we now turn.

DETERMINANTS OF MILITARY EXPENSES

There are two broad groups of empirical studies in the literature on the determinants of military spending. First, the arms race models developed from Richardson's (1960) seminal work, which presented arms increase in an action-reaction framework. These models have been developed in a number of ways but there are still many problems with them, both in general and in the specific application to developing countries. They are clearly more suited to analyse situations in which countries are in conflict, such as India-Pakistan and are therefore of limited applicability. But more importantly they have failed to perform well empirically.

Second, there are those studies which focus upon the economic, political and military determinants of military spending. These vary across disciplines, with international relations, political science, sociology, and economics all contributing studies within the focus of their disciplines. The most satisfactory empirical analyses have tended to take a comprehensive approach, combining all of the plausible economic, political and military influences and operationalising as many of them as possible. In many studies the unit of analysis varies from attempts to include all countries to case studies of individual countries. In addition, various techniques are used to analyse the data, including correlation analysis, factor and discriminant analysis, and econometric analysis.

Econometric analysis of the determinants of military spending requires some theoretical framework to allow a specification of causality, functional form, relevant variables and the testing of implied restrictions. A formal model also allows hypotheses can be well defined and tested, assumptions become explicit, and the number of parameters needed can be reduced through tests of restrictions. This approach is most consistently applied within a neoclassical framework using a model of the state as a rational actor maximising social welfare subject to a resource constraints. The social welfare function can be determined by the state, based on individual preferences, or based on some voting rule such as the median voter. Military expenses is then determined by balancing its opportunity cost and the security benefits it provides. Smith (1980) and Hewitt's (1991) public choice study are examples of this approach. Gonzalez and Mehay (1990) use a formal theory of bureaucracy.

There are also case studies which are less formal in approach but which nevertheless make important contributions. At their best they can bring together a considerable amount of historical and institutional information to complement regression analysis and can be aware of the limitations of their estimates. No matter how formal the approach, in analyzing developing countries the specific nature of these countries have to be taken into account. Indeed, such factors lead to serious questions being raised about the computational ability and rationality of actors assumed in formal neoclassical models (eg Park, 1994). In many countries military expenses is often independent of economic conditions and generated mainly by the internal logic of the state. The overall economic surroundings may provide a constraint on military burdens over time, but the importance of the strategic factors, security and threat perceptions, both internal and external, has to be recognised. In estimating demand functions the income variables need to be specified and these political and strategic effects quantified.

GDP per capita is often used to reflect the income effect. Higher income is likely to lead to higher military spending, which may or may not translate into a higher military burden. Also, higher income can lead to structural changes, inequalities and hence conflict requiring higher military spending to maintain internal control. The share of total government expenses in GDP is used to account for the fact that the military will likely benefit from high government expenses per se (McKinlay, 1989). The effect of incorporation of a country into the world economy is measured by the share of trade (exports plus imports in GDP) (Rosh, 1988). In addition, there are attempts to model the dynamics of the government spending process. Allowing for inertia due to some hangover from previous expenses, commitments to programmes , or simply a ratchet effect as in Peacock and Wiseman (1967). This can be incorporated by estimating a dynamic model where the lagged dependent variable will pick up such effects. There are also many attempts to introduce political factors within the countries. The type of government can effect military spending, with military governments most likely to be higher spenders, though there is unlikely to be a simple dichotomy between military and non military governments. The situation in developing countries is a bit different than in developed countries as there is less likely to be arms production. There will, however, still be a 'military industrial complex' with vested interests in maintaining or increasing military spending, comprising the civil servants, industrialists, officials, and workers involved with arms imports.

The results of the studies are mixed but do tend to suggest that in developing countries economic conditions are not the most important determinant of military burden. Studies have found clear differences in the different types of countries and their types of governments, to the extent that some argue that the determinants are country specific and not amenable to generalisation. This is disputed by a recent contribution by Hewitt (1991) who finds for a wide sample of countries evidence of economic and financial determinants which are common to the sample.

DISARMAMENT AND GROWTH

As we have seen, the evidence of the empirical work on military spending in developing countries suggests that it is determined mainly by strategic factors, with the superpowers playing an important role in escalating conflicts. It is also clear that military spending does not have the positive effect on economic development suggested by Benoit's initial study. This suggests that changes in the strategic surroundings for developing countries can allow a reduction in military expenses and that it will not have a negative effect on economic growth in the long run. Whether it has a positive impact will depend upon the effects of changes in military expenses on the economy and the policies taken to ease problems of adjustment. As Hartley (1993) argues disarmament needs to be seen as an investment process with short run costs but with the potential for long run benefits. As with any investment sound planning is required and there are risks.

Individual developing countries will also have their own particular problems which may limit the potential for cuts. There will be political problems caused by ongoing civil and regional wars; highly militarised security webs; military regimes; the use of the military for internal repression; ethnic/religious conflicts. Ongoing disputes can mean that decreases in military expenses may be destabilising and actually undermine the process of disarmament. The international community has to find some way to deal with such problems. This will need new approaches to security; the provision of effective international mediation; the promotion of non military solutions to conflicts; the support of democratisation processes.

Institutional structures within developing countries will provide opposition to cuts. While few developing countries have an arms industry of any magnitude, they do have a form of "Military Industrial Complex" that will resist any reductions in military spending. There are bureaucrats/politicians; salesmen/importers; corporate interests, private and state; workers/managers all benefiting from the import of weapons and the maintenance of a strong military group. Their power and resistance is helped by foreign companies with their hard selling techniques and the well known corruption surrounding the arms trade (Ball, 1988). Some groups include those who will lose out even if the civil sector grows, while others will only be effected by the short run economic costs of adjustment. As we have noted in the short run unemployment may result from demobilisation and reduced numbers of related civilian workers and indirect employment effects. There may be a decline in corporations/companies, involved in arms production/importation. There are also likely to be effects on local communities dependent on bases or factories.

Cuts in military spending will cause different problems depending on whether the country has an arms industry or not.

It may also depend on what form that industry takes. Many developing countries have small arms and munitions production facilities but some have major industrial sector eg Brazil, Chile, Israel, South Africa, Egypt. The effects of cuts in military expenses will be contingent on nature of government and the policy responses. The main effects are likely to be:

- reducing demand in the economy. Which could lead to reduced output and unemployment, though resources will also be freed for alternative uses.
- demobilisation. Which may lead to unemployment and may be destabilising.
- reducing the role of the army in the non military sector. Which may mean that any training, infrastructure, national cohesion that this may have provided will need to be replaced.
- reducing imports of arms. Which will free scarce foreign exchange but will also lead to a reduction of employment of bureaucrats and of workers involved in the trade.

All of these will have an impact on the corporate sector and could lead to the closure of facilities, the demise of companies, and further unemployment. To overcome such problems require some supply response, some alternative use of released resources, otherwise there will be adjustment problems. Taking a "hands off" approach and leaving the adjustments to "market forces" could be costly as the experience of the UK shows.

If there is an arms industry then these problems can be compounded. An arms industry can of course vary from simple munitions production eg Nigeria and Sudan to weapons systems production, Egypt, Brazil, Chile and South Africa (Katz 1986, Anthony 1993). With a significant arms industry the strength of the MIC will be greater and so will the opposition to cuts. There will also be greater problems of structural adjustment, in moving from arms production to other civil production, especially as the linkages of defence companies in some countries can be very important. If the use of scarce skilled/technological resources by the military has contributed to the underdevelopment of the private sector then disarmament could increase the difficulty of responding to alternative demands if provided. Even if released, the transfer of skilled workers is not straightforward because of skill differences across sectors. An export drive is also unlikely to work given the increasing competitiveness of the world market, although this is the route a number of countries seem to be taking.

Structural adjustments are always easier in a growing economy but could be rather difficult when the WB and the IMF are forcing "austerity" programmes. In the past the WB/IMF structural adjustment packages required cuts in public expenses with averse effects on inequality an unemployment often leading to political tensions and social instability. The spread of low level violence can lead to pressure to increase military expenses, especially if it includes the police and paramilitaries. Military expenses has often been the last to be cut in austerity packages, especially if it was tied to aid given previously. Even though the WB and IMF are now requiring client countries to reduce military expenses, this is still part of a general policy of reducing total government spending and this limits the possibility of governments being able to reallocate military expenses savings to other uses to provide the supply responses discussed above.

While developing policy proposals is beyond the scope of this paper, it is clear from the survey that if disarmament is to be successful in developing countries it will be necessary for the international community to provide support. Firstly, regional conflicts will need to be defused, the arms trade controlled, and moves to democracy encouraged and demanded, a task made easier by the end of the Cold War. Secondly, some form of economic assistance will be required to aid the development of developing countries and to provide alternatives to military production, to allow them to attain "economic security" rather than military security. The role of aid and foreign investment remains controversial but it is clear that to achieve disarmament and development will require international coordination on an unprecedented scale. This is a challenge for the United Nations which might prove the ultimate test of its credibility.

As a starting point for a comparison of the empirical studies a survey of the methodological and theoretical issues was undertaken. There are a number of schools of thought -neoclassical, Keynesian, institutionalist and Marxist- but only one, the underconsumptionist has military spending as an integral part of the theory. There is, however, no consensus in these general theories on the impact of military spending on economic growth. In fact much of the empirical work has focused on Keynesian and neoclassical models and when attempts are made to operationalise the general theories, outlining the channels through which military spending can effect growth, the question of whether or not it is positive is seen to be an empirical one.

It is important to recognise the interdependence of the demand and supply side and to consider the determinants of military spending. The results of the empirical studies are mixed but do tend to suggest that in developing countries economic conditions are not the most important determinant of military burden. Studies have found clear differences in the different types of countries and their types of governments, to the extent that some argue that the determinants are country specific and not amenable to generalisation, though this is disputed.

The survey of the empirical analyses of the economic effects of military spending, mainly within the Keynesian framework, suggested that military expenses has at best no effect on growth but is likely to have a negative impact, certainly there is no evidence of a positive effect. Most of the studies finding positive effects (often insignificant ones) adopted a single equation estimation approach. At best they are derived from an explicit underlying theoretical model and at worst are purely atheoretical. Some studies have investigated the statistical causality of military spending and economic growth but with no dominant result. Studies which have attempted to develop simultaneous models to allow for a variety of indirect effects have tended to find that military spending has a negative impact on growth. Overall, these results suggest that disarmament need not be costly and does indeed provide an opportunity for improved economic performance. There are still problems, however, in moving to lower levels of military spending and policies of conversion are required at a national and international level, including assistance from the developed world.

In an inflential study Smith and Smith (1980) suggested that: "If analysis suggests a weak causal relation between high military spending and unmet basic needs, and implies that there is no automatic mechanism, no 'hidden hand', to direct resources released by disarmament towards development, then attention must be given to the forms of political and social intervention required to direct resources to the desired end. In other words, if there is a relationship between disarmament and development, it may be one that has to be constructed politically, not one that is pre-given by economic forces."

NUCLEAR WEAPONS PROGRAMME

The end of World War II marked a revolution in world affairs - the recasting of nations and relations between nations, and the emergence of a new technology which fundamentally changed the role of warfare. Within the span of two years and two months, from 1945 to 1947, three critical events occurred whose reverberations have brought the threat of nuclear war in South Asia seemingly daily to the front pages of newspapers everywhere. The three events were - in chronological order - the establishment of the United Nations on 26 June 1945; the dramatic demonstration of the destruction of which even crude nuclear weapons are capable in August 1945; and the calamitous partition of British India into the modern states of India and Pakistan at midnight on 14-15 August 1947.

It is clear to everyone that the legacy of partition is a key driving force behind the nuclear standoff that now exists between India and Pakistan. Partition split apart a region that had been united for millenia amid communal massacres on a scale never before seen, leaving in its wake the unresolved issue of contested Kashmir - a Muslim-majority region held by Hindu-majority India. The skirmishing that has continued now for over fifty years, punctuated by outbreaks of full-scale war (in 1947, 1965, and 1971), have given both nations ample motivation to develop potent weapons to gain advantage over — or restore balance with — the other. Another motivation for India's acquisition of nuclear weapons, less often considered in the West, is the potential threat and regional challenge presented by the nuclear-armed state of China, which faces India along much of its northern border. Disputes covering 80,000 square kilometers of this border region exist:

- China currently occupies the Aksai Chin plateau adjacent to Ladakh in Kashmir;
- India occupies the North-East Frontier Agency claimed by China.

These territorial disputes, a legacy of British rule, erupted into the Sino-Indian War on 20 October 1962, when China launched a massive attack on India to which India was powerless to respond. India had relied for years on a warm relationship with the Soviet Union as a counterweight to China, but with the USSR facing down the United States at the same moment in the Cuban Missile Crisis, India was shocked to find the Politburo suddenly switching to support China in an effort to bolster its own position. PM Nehru was forced to appeal to the U.S. for help. U.S. naval air forces arrived off the coast, but before the USAF could deploy to India, China halted its attack on 21 November and partially withdrew. China continues to hold the Aksai Chin region captured in the initial advance. The legacy of this incident was the discovery that the Soviet Union was an unreliable ally, and the deep resolve not to be at a similar disadvantage with respect to China in the future.

Finally, an even less well known factor is a deep-seated drive to achieve international influence commensurate with India's size, and its importance throughout history as one of the world's principle civilizations. At the founding of the United Nations in 1945 the composition of the UN Security Council, the world's most influential and powerful international body, was fixed and has never changed from that time. By an accident of history India was not an independent state at that moment, and its only hope for representation at the conference was the Churchill administration, then in its closing days, which vehemently opposed India's national aspirations. As a result China - with a similar geographic size, population, and state of economic development - was given a seat on Security Council, but India was not. Nuclear weapons did not exist at the time the Security Council composition was debated, but over time the five Council members all acquired nuclear, then thermonuclear, arms. With the signing of the Nuclear Non-Proliferation treaty in 1970, and the replacement on the Council of the non-nuclear Taipei Chinese government with the nuclear armed government in Beijing shortly thereafter, the de facto principle that Security Council permanent members and the "nuclear club" were one and the same was firmly established.

The crucial importance of the desire for recognition of India as a world power in driving forward the nuclear weapons program, even overshadowing considerations of military necessity and deterrence is underscored by remarks by former weapons program leader Raj Ramanna: "There was never a discussion among us over whether we shouldn't make the bomb. How to do it was more important. For us it was a matter of prestige that would justify our ancient past. The question of deterrence came much later. Also, as Indian scientists we were keen to show our Western counterparts, who thought little of us those days, that we too could do it."

Thus it should be no surprise that India, now tied for third place among the world's largest economies (with Germany), and soon to become the most populous nation on Earth, has concluded that to be given its due in world affairs, it must become a member of the nuclear club as well.

What is notable however is how the world's largest democracy developed such capabilities. The decisions were made by a handful of people, with virtually no input or oversight by the public or the legislature. India's nuclear weapons program from its outset has answered only to the Prime Minister's office, and only the Prime Minister and a select few of his or her appointees have ever had any say in its development and acquisition.

Origin of India's Nuclear Weapon Program

India's indigenous efforts in nuclear science and technology were established remarkably early. The first step was taken by Dr. Homi Jehangir Bhabha in March 1944 when he submitted a proposal to the Sir Dorab Tata Trust (established in honor of Bhabha's own uncle, Sir Dorab Tata) to found a nuclear research institute, over three years before independence and a year before the first nuclear weapon test. This led to the creation of the Tata Institute of Fundamental Research (TIFR) on 19 December 1945 with Bhabha as its first Director. The new government of India passed the Atomic Energy Act, on 15 April 1948, leading to the establishment of the Indian Atomic Energy Commission (IAEC) not quite one year after independence. At that time Prime Minister Pandit Jawaharlal Nehru declared: We must develop this atomic energy quite apart from war - indeed I think we must develop it for the purpose of using it for peaceful purposes.... Of course, if we are compelled as a nation to use it for other purposes, possibly no pious sentiments of any of us will stop the nation from using it that way."

This note of ambivalence in Nehru's speech foreshadowed his policies on nuclear research for the next decade. Nehru took a prominent role in international politics, founding the Non-Aligned Movement, and advocating nuclear disarmament. However, he refused to foreclose India's nuclear option while other nations maintained nuclear arsenals and supported programs designed to bolster India's weapons potential. In 1954 the Indian nuclear program began to move in a direction that would eventually lead to establishment of nuclear weapons capability. On 3 January 1954 the IAEC decided to set up a new facility - the Atomic Energy Establishment, Trombay (AEET), later to become the "Indian Los Alamos". On 3 August 1954 the Department of Atomic Energy (DAE) was created with Dr. Bhabha as Secretary. This department answered directly to the Prime Minister and has continued to do so down to the present day.

The program grew swiftly. The atomic energy budget increased 12-fold from 1954 to 1956. By 1958 the DAE consumed one third of India's research budget. By 1959 AEET employed over one thousand scientists and engineers. In 1955 construction began on India's first reactor, the 1 MW Apsara research reactor, with British assistance. And in September 1955, after more than a year of negotiation, Canada agreed to supply India with a powerful research reactor - the 40 MW Canada-India Reactor (CIR). Under the Eisenhower Administration's "Atoms for Peace" program the

US agreed to supply 21 tons of heavy water for this reactor in Februrary 1956, and the reactor was dubbed the Canada-India Reactor, U.S. or CIRUS (now commonly written as Cirus).

The acquisition of Cirus was a watershed event in nuclear proliferation. Although the sale was made with the understanding that the reactor would only be used for peaceful purposes (the heavy water contract at least made this explicit), it occurred before any international policies were in place to regulate such technology transfers and no provision for inspections were made. And in fact India was careful to ensure that no effective regulation would accompany the reactor. India refusing to accept fuel from Canada for the reactor and set up a program to manufacture the natural uranium fuel for Cirus indigeneously so as to keep complete control of the plutonium produced there. This program, led by metallurgist Brahm Prakash, succeeded in developing the techniques for producing the precisely manufactured, high purity material demanded by the reactor.

The reactor was a design ideal for producing weapons-grade plutonium, and was also extraordinarily large for research purposes, being capable of manufacturing enough plutonium for one to two bombs a year. The acquisition of Cirus was specifically intended by India to provide herself with a weapons option and this reactor produced the plutonium used in India's first nuclear test in 1974; provided the design prototype for India's more powerful Dhruva plutonium production "research" reactor; and is directly responsible for producing nearly half of the weapons grade plutonium currently believed to be in India's stockpile. The sale further set a precedent for similar technology transfers which greatly assisted Israel in obtaining its own plutonium production reactor from France shortly thereafter. The Atomic Energy Establishment, Trombay was formally inaugurated by PM Nehru on 20 January 1957. It acquired its present name — Bhabha Atomic Research Centre (BARC) — on 12 January 1967 when PM Indira Gandhi renamed it in memory of Dr. Bhabha who died in an airplane crash on 24 January 1966.

Apsara, fueled by enriched uranium from the UK, went critical on 4 August 1957, becoming the first operating reactor in Asia outside of the Soviet Union (though only days ahead of Japan's first reactor). Cirus achieved criticality at BARC on 10 July 1960.

As a nation India has always placed a premium on self-sufficiency. It is, in fact, the most self-sufficient large economy in the world and does not import any nuclear fuel. [The traditionally closed nature of economy though accounts for the import/export based Chinese economy far outstripping its growth from the late seventies to the early nineties.] Due to its vast domestic resources of thorium (a potential fuel for breeder reactors) but limited supplies of uranium, from the start of its nuclear program India has always placed strong emphasis on the development of breeder reactor fuel cycles. Breeder reactors require highly concentrated fissionable material for reactor fuel: either highly enriched uranium or plutonium. This provided a peaceful rationale for developing a plutonium separation capability, but the principal impetus for the India's first fuel reprocessing plant was to obtain a nuclear option.

In July 1958 PM Nehru authorized project Phoenix to build a plant with a capacity of 20 tonnes of fuel a year - sized to match the production capacity of Cirus. The plant was based on the U.S. developed Purex process and an American firm, Vitro International prepared the plans for it. Construction of the plutonium plant began at Trombay on 27 March 1961 and was commissioned in mid-1964.

India's civilian nuclear program was also established during this period. Discussions with American firms to construct India's first nuclear power plants at Tarapur were held in 1960-61. An interesting incident sheds light on Nehru's amd Bhabha's thinking at that time. In 1960 Kenneth Nichols, a former U.S. Army engineer who played significant roles in the Manhattan Project, represented Westinghouse in discussions on power plant construction. In a meeting with Nehru and Bhabha, Nichols relates that Nehru turned to Bhabha and asked:

"Can you develop an atomic bomb?" Bhabha assured him that he could and in reply to Nehru's next question about time, he estimated that he would need about a year to do it.... He concluded by saying to Bhabha "Well, don't do it until I tell you to."

NUCLEAR DELIVERY SYSTEMS

Development continued on India's nuclear delivery systems - on 11 April 1999 India conducted a successful 14 minute test flight of the 2,500 kilometer Agni-II missile. "The entire process of achieving a minimum deterrent has been completed," Vajpayee announced following the test. "We are satisfied that we are now fully capable of defending our borders," he added. Pakistan responded with an eight-minute test flight of the Ghauri II three days later.

The promise of the Lahore Declaration proved to be stillborn. On 5 May 1999 two Indian army patrols in the snowy Yaldor area in Kargil, a border region next to Kashmir, were surprised to encounter a group of armed men, apparently from Pakistani Kashmir (known in India as "Pakistan-occupied Kashmir" or POK; in Pakistan they are called the Northern Areas or NA). This was the first contact with an infiltration operation from Pakistan to seize the mountain peaks inside India as an escalation of the long-standing Kashmir conflict, which would be become known as the Kargil War.

The "line of control", or LoC, between India and Pakistan runs across some of the harshest, most rugged, and highest territory in the world and consequently much of it consists of "unheld areas", territory so inhospitable that both sides abandon it during the brutal winters. It was because India had suspended patrol operations in the winter that made it possible for infiltrators to set up camp without being detected. The patrols that encountered them were the first of the season. Such areas had been opportunities for adventurousness in the past, as when the Siachen glacier was suddenly occupied by armed forces many years ago - becoming the highest and coldest battlefield on Earth. But this was the first time Pakistan had ever tried to exploit this particular region.It appears the infiltration operation was already underway during the signing of the Lahore Declaration The larger of the two patrol parties went to check on the strangers, and found itself in an ambush and lost four soldiers. Firing continued for nearly a week before aerial surveillance on 12 May revealed to the army realized that the incursion was far more serious than it had assumed.

Around 500 heavily armed guerillas had occupied at least 35 well-fortified positions atop the ridges facing Dras, Kargil, Batalik and the Mushko valley. Cover fire was being provided by the Pakistani artillery, which had begun a systematic bombardment of National Highway 1A that connects Leh to Srinagar in the Dras-Kargil region.

Within days the Indian army moved nearly 30,000 troops into the Kargil-Dras area along with special forces dropped on the high ridges by helicopter, and the battle was on in earnest; "Operation Vijay" (victory) to recapture the heights was launched in late May. Pakistan initially claimed not to be involved with the infiltration effort, a remarkable attempt at dissociation considering that the infiltrators were very well equipped and supplied, came from territory controlled by the Pakistani military, and were clearly in direct contact with the Pakistanis from which they were receiving direct artillery fire support. Eventually the continued direct involvement of regular Pakistani forces made the pretense an embarrassment for Pakistan, which dropped the attempt at evasion.

Over the next several weeks India outmaneuvered Pakistan both on the battlefield and in international diplomacy. Heavy Pakistani fire directed by the infiltrators from their commanding positions made the situation very difficult for India, but Pakistani positions on the Indian side were progressively captured or cut off from support as the superior weight of Indian forces made itself felt. By promising not to cross the LoC itself, India garnered nearly universal international support - and especially active Amercian support - for its position, while at the same time by mobilizing its forces along the entire Pakistani border it signalled that India was prepared to escalate and use its full military strength if necessary to prevent a Pakistani victory. The objective of this operation seems to have been to try to obtain a limited gain on the ground - revising the LoC several kilometers in Pakistan's favour. The LoC has after all always been defined in de facto terms - it has no recognized status, it simply marks the effective zones of control of the two nations. The operation was calculated to circumvent India's military superiority - by picking the most difficult terrain possible for India's operations, and achieving the initial gain through stealth alone. Pakistan evidently hoped that international pressure would halt the conflict before India succeeded in driving the guerillas back.

By mid June the tide was turning, and by mid July the Kargil incursion had turned into a rout for Pakistan, both militarily and diplomatically. Pakistani forces retreated behind the LoC, and Pakistan suffered another severe blow to its international credibility, and in turn boosted India's prestige. After the end of the war Pakistani Prime Minister Nawaz Sharif asserted that the operation had been instigated without his knowledge - a claim, which whether true or not, was unfortunately all too plausible in Pakistan, with its tradition of the military operating free from civilian control.

The total depth of penetration across the LoC was no more than eight or nine kilometres at most. As intended by Pakistan, the operations for retaking the occupied areas were very difficult for India and this short, sharp war resulted in 474 killed and 1109 wounded on the Indian side (as of July 26, 1999).

A crucial but at the time unreported consequence of the Kargil War, tied in with the Indian mobilization along the Pakistani border, was the apparent deployment of at least five nuclear armed missiles. "Four nuclear armed Prithvis and one Agni were deployed for retaliatory strikes" according to Dr. Sanjay Badri-Maharaj, author of *The Armageddon Factor* (Indian Express, 18 June 2000). This would have been a preproduction model of the Agni-II, the first deployable Agni version. Sharif's demurral became even more plausible three months later when a showdown occurred between PM Sharif and army chief Gen. Pervez Musharraf on 13 October 1999. Acting while Musharraf was out of the country, Sharif fired him, but hours later Musharraf returned and overthrew Sharif in a coup (later to put Sharif on trial for his life).

Following the aggressive, destabilizing, and ill-conceived military operation of Kargil, the military coup in Pakistan did absolutely nothing to reassure India or the world regarding Pakistan's soundness and circumspection. The result was naturally even deeper isolation for Pakistan, on top of the sanctions that followed the 1998 tests, and the Kargil adventure.

Overt hostilities along the border continued to persist after the conclusion of the Kargil War. On 10 August 1999 an Indian fighter jet shot down a slow-moving Pakistani reconnaissance plane, killing all 16 aboard. The Indians said the plane had strayed across the border, though most of the wreckage landed in Pakistan. On 17 August 1999, India took the major - though belated step - toward formalizing its declared status as a nuclear power by issuing a six-page document detailing a proposed doctrine governing its nuclear arsenal, entitled the "Draft Report of National Security Advisory Board on Indian Nuclear Doctrine". The report, which was prepared by a government-appointed advisory board, was made public Tuesday by National Security Advisor Brajesh Mishra.

The essential points of this doctrine were that India asserted a right to possess nuclear weapons, and would pursue a policy of credible "minimum" nuclear deterrence and use nuclear weapons only to retaliate against a first strike. According to the draft, "Any nuclear attack on India and its forces shall result in punitive retaliation with nuclear weapons to inflict damage unacceptable to the aggressor." "India's peacetime posture aims at convincing any potential aggressor that any threat of use of nuclear weapons against India shall invoke measures to counter the threat," the draft said. It further stated that India would not use nuclear weapons against a state that does not have them or is not aligned with a nuclear-armed power, and that nuclear weapons would be tightly controlled and launched only with the authorization of the prime minister, or a designated successor.

The draft said the size, components, deployment and employment of nuclear forces would be decided in light of the strategic environment, economic imperatives and the needs of national security. But it took an expansive view of the concept of "minimum deterrence", recommending an arsenal that is able to deliver a nuclear blast from "a triad of aircraft, mobile land-based missiles and sea-based assets," one that can respond to an attack "in the shortest possible time" and employs a space-based early warning system. To raise the threshold for the outbreak of military conflict, India also would maintain highly effective conventional warfare capabilities, the draft document said.

The draft did not mention the Comprehensive Test Ban Treaty (CTBT) but it criticized the Nuclear Nonproliferation Treaty, saying it legitimized the possession of nuclear weapons by states that already had them. The official U.S. State Department reaction given by Spokesman James P. Rubin was that India was "moving in the wrong direction" by trying to create a credible nuclear deterrence. Rubin said "We think it would be unwise to move in the direction of developing a nuclear deterrent and encouraging the other country to develop a nuclear deterrent and thereby creating an action-reaction cycle that will increase the risks to both countries."

China also condemned the document; and Pakistan, which 15 months ago matched India's nuclear tests with its own, said it would soon be matching India's doctrine with a published doctrine of its own. Unlike from the U.S., the initial reaction from Europe was cautious. France welcomed the draft doctrine as a logical consequence of the decision to develop nuclear weapons.

The situation was cogently summarized by Tanvir Ahmad Khan in the Pakistani newspaper *The Dawn* on 24 August 1999: The present draft is a landmark for three major reasons.

- First, it gathers together in a forceful single document elements that had surfaced disparately and with a certain air of tentativeness since the tests.
- Secondly, it relegates to history half-way concepts like existential deterrence and recessed deterrence that had been debated in both India and Pakistan. In doing so, it delivers a mighty blow to efforts aiming at freezing Indian and Pakistani capability at a non-weaponized level.
- Third, the nuclear doctrine as set forth in the text has hardly any meaning unless the weapons are manufactured and actually deployed in large numbers, and a sizable reserve of warheads and delivery vehicles is permanently maintained.

Tanvir Khan also observed that "the draft published at the moment does not add any transparency to the Indian targeting policy. Nor does it specify Pakistan or China as the principal zones of targeting." He also made some interesting assertions about Indian strategic literature: Some analysts define the objective as the destruction of Pakistan as a social and economic entity. The targets considered in the relevant Indian literature include six to ten Pakistani metropolitan centres, four hydroelectric and thermal power stations, flooding of Punjab, obliteration of Pakistani railway system with attacks on Gujrat, Bahawalpur, Hyderabad and Dera Ghazi Khan, and disruption of all sea communications with nuclear attacks on Karachi and Gwadar. It has been calculated that a total of seventeen nuclear strikes will achieve all the objectives. If Pakistan also draws up a similar list of countervalue targets, breakdown of deterrence and the ensuing nuclear exchange would mark the end of a civilization. Although a the time of its announcement, it was expected that the government in place following the elections in the autumn of 1999 would enact the draft doctrine formally, by early 2001 no action had been taken and the draft remained a proposal without official weight, except to the extent it reflected the thinking of Indian government officialdom.

In May 2000 the Atomic Energy Regulatory Board (AERB) which has been set up on 15 November 1983 by order of the President of India to exercise regulatory and safety functions for atomic energy in India was split off from the Bhabha Atomic Research Centre (BARC). According too an unnamed senior official of the Dept. of Atomic Energy (DAE) quoted by *Aviation Week & Space Technology* (19 June 2000), this split indicated that nuclear warheads for India's armed forces had entered series production. The separation "means the weaponization program at BARC is completed," explained the official. "It is a clear assertion that BARC does not want the AERB to look into its weaponization program." Instead, BARC will have an internal safety committee, which was set up by BARC Director, Anil Kakodkar. The order for the split issued by Atomic Energy Commission (AEC) Chairman, Rajgopalan Chidambaram stated, "The regulatory and safety mechanism of BARC and its functions, hitherto exercised by the AERB, will henceforth be exercised through an internal safety committee structure to be constituted by the BARC director....

This is being done so as to ensure safety of the strategic nuclear program." Chidambaram added that the regulatory body is "always transparent" and has frequent interactions with the public. He said that BARC's internal committee will ensure compliance "wherever applicable" with the principles of good safety management as given in safety standards developed by the AERB. Despite the assertion of 'transparency' Chidambaram, speaking to a UNI reporter declined to give any details of the new committee saying that it was of strategic importance and details could not be revealed.

The DAE official said, "Most weapon laboratories have their internal checks systems, the Lawrence Livermore [Laboratories] in the U.S. being an example." However, he omitted to mention that in the U.S. the Department of Energy maintains independent oversight with the Defense Nuclear Facility Safety Board (DNFSB) which even includes reviewers outside of the DOE. S. Rajagopal, an expert on nuclear affairs and a professor of the Bangalore-based National Institute of Advanced Studies, observed that this decision effectively reclassified BARC as a nuclear weapons laboratory. "This in turn will eliminate the need to place it under the International Atomic Energy Agency (IAEA) safeguards programme," he said.

Chidambaram's eight years in office as Chairman of the Atomic Energy Commission ended on 30 November 2000 when he was replaced by Dr. Anil Kakodkar today took charge as AEC Chairman, and as Secretary to the Government of India, Department of Atomic Energy in a brief ceremony held at Anushakti Bhavan, CSM Marg, Mumbai. Kakodkar This continued the tradition since Vikram Sarabhai's death in 1971 of having the top official in Atomic Energy be a leader of India's nuclear weapon program. As BARC director, Kakodkar had been the principal scientist involved in the May 1998 nuclear tests.

8

Cyber Arms Race

STUXNET SHIFTS THE CYBER ARMS RACE UP A GEAR

In the 1980s, information was mostly still analogue. It was stored on paper, in binders, on shelves and in safes. Today, of course, almost all information is digital.

It's created and stored on computers and transmitted over computer networks. From a security viewpoint, this means that secret information can now potentially be reached from anywhere in the world; you no longer have to physically be where the information is.

This means that espionage has also gone digital - and while we've seen several cases of nation-state espionage done with backdoors and trojans, we've seen only one documented case of a nation-state doing cyber sabotage with malware. That case is Stuxnet.

During my years in this industry I've seen multiple mysteries, but few of them have been as interesting as the case of Stuxnet.

F-Secure Labs estimates that it took more than 10 man-years of work to develop Stuxnet. Related attacks like Duqu and Flame might have taken even more.

Stuxnet had a "kill date" of 24 June 2012, which means the worm has now stopped spreading. But that has little significance, as the operation had already been active for years and reached most of its targets already by 2010.

Deniability

Stuxnet is a good example of the thinking behind these new kinds of offensive attacks: If you want to disrupt the secret nuclear programme of a foreign nation, what can you do?

Well, you have a couple of options. You can try international pressure and boycotts. But if that doesn't work, then what? You can try a conventional military attack and bomb their facilities. However, attribution back to you as an attacker is a problem. So is the fact that you can attack only the facilities you know about.

Using a digital attack like Stuxnet has several advantages. Especially, it provides deniability.

Continue reading the main story

"Start Quote

Maybe we'll eventually see cyber disarmament programs"

Stuxnet was obviously a game changer. But what does it mean in the long term? I think we are now seeing the very first steps of a new arms race: The cyber arms race.

Just like modern hi-tech research revolutionised military operations over the last 50 years, we are going to see a new revolution, focusing on information operations and cyber warfare. This revolution is underway and it's happening right now.

We haven't seen real online warfare yet, of course. This is because thankfully we haven't lately seen wars between technically advanced nations. But any future crisis is likely to have a cyber component as well.

Attack capabilities

It's important to understand that cyber warfare does not necessarily have anything to do with the internet. Many of the more devastating cyberattacks can not be launched remotely, as the most critical networks are not connected to the public network.

Think along the lines of a special forces unit going deep into enemy territory with embedded geeks in the team, to dig up fibre-optic cable to be able to reach the systems that were supposed to be unreachable.

The main point of any arms race is to let your adversaries know about your capabilities so they don't even think about starting a fight. We're not yet at this stage in the cyber arms race. Almost all of the development in this area is secret and classified.

However, eventually it will become as public as any other defence technology. Maybe we'll eventually see public cyberwar exercises where a country will demonstrate their attack capabilities. Maybe we'll eventually see cyber disarmament programmes.

Defending against military strength malware is a real challenge for the computer security industry.

Furthermore, the security industry is not global - it's highly focused in just a handful of countries. The rest of the world relies on foreign security labs to provide their everyday digital security for them. For example, there are only around 10 virus labs in all of Europe, and the vast majority of the countries have no labs of their own.

On the internet, borders don't really matter. But in time of crisis, they do.

THE NEW CYBER ARMS RACE

Banks of computers, hard drives humming on desktops, are tied into an electronic filtering system that monitors billions of bits of information flowing into dozens of federal agencies each second. At any given moment, an analyst can pop up information on a wall of five massive television screens that almost makes this feel like Cowboys Stadium in Arlington, Texas, rather than a bland office building in Arlington, Va.

The overriding purpose of all of it: to help prevent what could lead to the next world war. Specifically, the "Einstein II" system, as it is called, is intended to detect a large cyberattack against the US. The first signs of such an "electronic Pearl Harbour" might include a power failure across a vast portion of the nation's electric grid. It might be the crash of a vital military computer network. It could be a sudden poison gas release at a chemical plant or an explosion at an oil refinery.

Whatever it is, the scores of analysts staffing this new multimillion-dollar "watch and warn" centre would, presumably, be able to see it and respond, says Mr. McGurk, the facility director. The National Cybersecurity and Communications Integration Centre (NCCIC, pronounced en-kick) is one of the crown jewels of the Department of Homeland Security (DHS). It is linked to four other key watch centres run by the FBI, the Department of Defence (DOD), and the National Security Agency (NSA) that monitor military and overseas computer networks.

They are monuments to what is rapidly becoming a new global arms race. In the future, wars will not just be fought by soldiers with guns or with planes that drop bombs. They will also be fought with the click of a mouse a half a world away that unleashes carefully weaponized computer programs that disrupt or destroy critical industries like utilities, transportation, communications, and energy. Such attacks could also disable military networks that control the movement of troops, the path of jet fighters, the command and control of warships.

"The next time we want to go to war, maybe we wouldn't even need to bomb a country," says Liam O'Murchu, manager of operations for Symantec Security Response, a Mountain View, Calif., computer security firm. "We could just, you know, turn off its power."

In this detached new warfare, soldiers wouldn't be killing other soldiers on the field of battle. But it doesn't mean there might not be casualties. Knocking out the power alone in a large section of the US could sow chaos. What if there were no heat in New England in January? No refrigeration for food? The leak of a radiation plume or chemical gas in an urban area? A sudden malfunction of the stock market? A disrupted air traffic control system?

These are the darkest scenarios, of course — the kind that people spin to sell books and pump up budgets for new cyberwar technology. Interviews with dozens of cyberconflict experts indicate that this kind of strategic, large-scale digital warfare — while possible — is not the most likely to happen. Instead, some see a prolonged period of aggressive cyberespionage, sabotage, and low-level attacks that damage electronic networks. As one recent study done for the Organization for Economic Cooperation and

Development put it: "It is unlikely that there will ever be a true cyberwar."

Yet others say that conclusion might be too conservative. The fact is, no one knows for sure where digital weaponry is heading. The cyber arms race is still in its infancy, and once a cybershot is fired, it's hard to predict where the fusillade might end. In the seconds or minutes it might take staffers at the NCCIC to detect an attack, it could have already spread to US water supplies, railway networks, and other vital industries. How does the US military respond — or even know whom to retaliate against? If it does hit back, how does it prevent cyberweapons from spreading damage electronically to other nations around the world?

Policy experts are just beginning to ask some of these questions as the cyberweapons buildup begins. And make no mistake, it is beginning. By one estimate, more than 100 nations are now amassing cybermilitary capabilities. This doesn't just mean erecting electronic defenses. It also means developing "offensive" weapons.

Shrouded in secrecy, the development of these weaponized new software programs is being done outside public view and with little debate about their impact on existing international treaties and on conventional theories of war, like deterrence, that have governed nations for decades.

"Here's the problem — it's 1946 in cyber," says James Mulvenon, a founding member of the Cyber Conflict Studies Association, a nonprofit group in Washington. "So we have these potent new weapons, but we don't have all the conceptual and doctrinal thinking that supports those weapons or any kind of deterrence. Worse, it's not just the US and Soviets that have the weapons — it's millions and millions of people around the world that have these weapons."

In the new cyber world order, the conventional big powers won't be the only ones carrying the cannons. Virtually any nation — or terrorist group or activist organization — with enough money and technical know-how will be able to develop or purchase software programs that could disrupt distant computer networks.

And the US, because it's so wired, is more vulnerable than most big powers to this new form of warfare. It's the price the country may one day pay for being an advanced and open society. "If the nation went to war today, in a cyberwar, we would lose," Mike McConnell, director of national intelligence from 2007 to 2009, told a US Senate committee a year ago. "We're the most vulnerable. We're the most connected. We have the most to lose."

Still, none of this means people should immediately run for a digital fallout shelter. Many analysts think the cyberwar threat is overblown, and the US is developing sophisticated defenses, such as the digital ramparts here in Arlington. The question is: Will it be enough, or will it all amount to a Maginot line?

Alamogordo Redux

The cyber equivalent of the dropping of the atom bomb on Hiroshima came last fall. That's when the world found out about Stuxnet, the software program that wasn't just another annoying virus. It was a sophisticated digital superweapon. Unlike typical malicious software — Trojans and viruses that lurk hidden in a computer to, say, steal a bank account password or some proprietary corporate information — Stuxnet was designed to inflict damage in the real world. In this case it was apparently intended to destroy machines critical to Iran's nuclear ambitions.

The marauding software was introduced into Iranian computers in five locations sometime in 2009, probably, experts believe, by an infected "thumb drive," a portable memory stick, inserted into the network by unwitting Russian engineers who were working on the Iranian nuclear facility. Once inside the system, analysts say, Stuxnet sought out its target, the computer-controlled nuclear centrifuge system, and sabotaged the machinery. Experts believe, in the end, the software may have damaged up to 1,000 of the plant's centrifuges. It did so without any human help — without anyone clicking a mouse or guiding it electronically.

Since its emergence, Stuxnet has demonstrated that cyberattacks will not remain just banal attempts to delete or steal information inside computers or on the Internet. It showed that a cyberweapon can destroy actual plants and equipment — strategically important equipment. It is a "game changer," McGurk told Congress last fall.

Experts believe that Stuxnet was developed by a nation with a top-notch covert cyberweapons team, probably at a cost of millions of dollars. But now that elements of its software code — its electronic blueprint — are available on the Internet, it could be downloaded and reverse-engineered by organized crime groups, cyberweapons dealers, so-called "hactivist" organizations, rogue nations, and terrorists. The hactivist group Anonymous recently touted that it had acquired a copy of the Stuxnet code. Individual tinkerers are getting it, too.

"What Stuxnet represents is a future in which people with the funds will be able to buy a sophisticated attack like this on the black market," says Ralph Langner, a German cyber-security researcher and Stuxnet expert. "Everyone can have their own cyberweapon." He adds that Stuxnet could be modified by someone who isn't even a control-systems expert into a "digital dirty bomb" that could damage or destroy virtually any industrial operating system it targets. Amr Thabet, an engineering student at the University of Alexandria in Egypt, typifies how easy it is to access the new world of cyberweaponry. During recent mass street protests in his country, he found time to post on his blog a portion of the Stuxnet cyberweapon he had reverse-engineered. The blog drew the attention of cybersecurity experts, who were unhappy, but not surprised, by what he had done.

"This kid's work makes Stuxnet a lot more accessible and portable to other computer architectures," says Bob Radvanovsky, an industrial control-systems expert at Infracritical, a Chicago-based computer security organization. "It's something a number of people are doing for intellectual exercise — or for malicious purposes. It's not a good trend. If a college student is trying to dabble with this, who else on the dark nets with more nefarious intentions might be [as well]?"

In an e-mail interview, Mr. Thabet said he did it largely for the thrill. He noted that he spent two months deconstructing a small but crucial part of the code after he saw all the attention surrounding the discovery of Stuxnet last fall. "It's the first time I see a malware becomes like a gun or like a weapon close a whole company in few days," he writes in broken English. "You can say

[Stuxnet] makes the malware a harder challenge and more dangerous. That's maybe what inspire me."

The 'War' Has ... Already Begun?

Definitions of what constitute a "cyberattack" or "cyberwar" vary, but experts roughly agree the US is now immersed in a continuous series of cyberconflicts. These are with state and nonstate actors, from Russia and China to criminal gangs and online protest groups.

"Are we in a cyberwar now?" asks John Bumgarner, research director at the US Cyber Consequences Unit, a Washington-based think tank, who once was a cyberwarrior with the US Army. "No, not yet. Are we being targeted and our nation's networks attacked and infiltrated by nations that may be our adversaries in the future? Yes."

Melissa Hathaway, former acting senior director for cyberspace at the National Security Council, says the threat is less a military one by nation-states and more about the need to protect US intellectual property from spies and organized crime groups.

"We are currently in an economic cyberwar," Ms. Hathaway says. "It is costing our corporations their innovation, costing Americans their jobs, and making us a country economically weaker over the long term. I don't see it emerging as a military conflict, but as an economic war in which malware and our own digital infrastructure is being used to steal our future."

Others agree that a strategic cyberwar isn't likely right now. But they do see the potential for escalation beyond the theft of the latest blueprints for an electric car or jet-fighter engine, particularly as the technology of digital warfare advances and becomes a more strategic imperative.

"We in the US tend to think of war and peace as an on-off toggle switch — either at full-scale war or enjoying peace," says Joel Brenner, former head of counterintelligence under the US Director of National Intelligence. "The reality is different. We are now in a constant state of conflict among nations that rarely gets to open warfare.... What we have to get used to is that even countries like China, with which we are certainly not at war, are in intensive cyberconflict with us." While he agrees the notion of big-scale cyberwarfare has been over-hyped, he says attacks that move beyond aggressive espionage to strikes at, or sabotage of, industrial processes and military systems "will become a routine reality."

Anything You Can Do, We Can Do Better

The attacks were coordinated but relatively unsophisticated: In the spring of 2007, hackers blocked the websites of the Estonian government and clogged the country's Internet network. At one point, bank cards were immobilized. Later, in 2008, similar cyberstrikes preceded the Russian invasion of Georgia. Moscow denied any involvement in the attacks, but Estonia, among others, suspected Russia.

Whoever it was may not be as important as what it's done: touched off a mini cyber arms race, accelerated by the Stuxnet revelation.

Germany and Britain announced new cybermilitary programs in January. In December, Estonia and Iran unveiled cybermilitias to help defend against digital attack. They join at least 20 nations that now have advanced cyberwar programs, according to McAfee, a Santa Clara, Calif., computer security firm. Yet more than 100 countries have at least some cyberconflict prowess, and multiple nations "have the capability to conduct sustained, high-end cyberattacks against the US," according to a new report by the Cyber Conflict Studies Association.

McAfee identifies a handful of countries moving from a defensive to a more offensive posture — including the US, China, Russia, France, and Israel. Experts like Mr. Langner say the US is the world's cyber superpower, with weapons believed to be able to debilitate or destroy targeted computer networks and industrial plants and equipment linked to them. Indeed, China widely assumes that their nation's computer systems have been "thoroughly compromised" by the US, according to Dr. Mulvenon of the Cyber Conflict Studies Association, even as the Chinese penetrate deeper into US industrial and military networks.

As well armed as the US is, however, its defenses are porous. The US may have the mightiest military in the world, but it is also the most computerized — everything from smart bombs to avionics to warship controls — making it unusually vulnerable to cyberassault.

The DOD's communication system includes some 15,000 computer networks and 7 million computing devices. According to the Pentagon, unknown attackers try to breach its systems 6 million times a day. More than a few attempts have succeeded.

Hackers are believed to have stolen key elements of the F-35 jet fighter a few years ago from a defence contractor. In 2008, infiltrators used thumb drives to infect the DOD's classified electronic network, resulting in what Deputy Defence Secretary William Lynn later called the "most significant breach of US military computers ever."

Unlike many of its potential adversaries, the Pentagon is heavily reliant on computer networks. Over the past two decades, US industry, along with the military and federal agencies, have linked some networks and elements of the nation's infrastructure — power plants, air traffic control systems, rail lines — to the notoriously insecure Internet. It makes it easier, faster, and cheaper to communicate and conduct business — but at a cost. Almost all electrical power used by US military bases, for instance, comes from commercial utilities, and the power grid is a key target of adversaries. "We're pretty vulnerable today," says a former US national security official. "Our defence is superporous against anything sophisticated."

Countries that are less wired are less vulnerable, which represents another danger. Some analysts even suggest that a small power like North Korea could do serious damage to the US in a cyberattack while sustaining relatively little itself. In a report presented at a NATO conference, former NSA expert Charlie Miller estimated that Pyongyang would need only about 600 cyber experts, three years, and $50 million to overtake and defeat America in a digital war.

"One of North Korea's biggest advantages is that it has hardly any Internet-connected infrastructure to target," he says. "On the other hand, the US has tons of vulnerabilities a country like North Korea could exploit."

I Spy, The Sequel

The elite group of hackers sit at an oval bank of computers in a second-floor office on the wind-swept plains of Idaho. Their mission: infiltrate the computer network of Acme Products, an American industrial plant. They immediately begin probing for ways around the company's cyberdefenses and fire walls. Within minutes, they tap into the plant's electronic controls, sabotaging the manufacturing process.

"They're already inside our system," howls an Acme worker, looking at his unresponsive computer after only 20 minutes. "They've got control of the lights. We can't even control our own lights!"

Less than a half-hour later, a plastic vat is overflowing, spraying liquid into an industrial sink. The company's attempts to retake control of the system prove futile. Is the leak a toxic chemical? Something radioactive?

Fortunately, in this case it is water, and the company itself is fictitious. This is simply an exercise by members of the DHS's Industrial Control System-Computer Emergency Readiness Team (ICS-CERT), simulating an attack and defence of a company.

The message to emerge from the war game is unmistakably clear: Industrial America isn't well prepared for the new era of cyberwar, either.

"We conduct these training classes to alert industry to what's really going on and educate them as to vulnerabilities they may not have thought of," says a senior manager at the Idaho National Laboratory (INL) in Idaho Falls, where the readiness team is located.

Down the street, in another warehouselike building, high walls and locked doors shroud rooms where commercial vendors bring their industrial-control software to be probed for weaknesses by the cyber teams.

Despite all the efforts here, experts say gaping holes exist in America's commercial electronic defenses. One reason is the vast number of people and organizations trying to penetrate the networks of key industries. Some people liken the intensity of the spying to the height of the postwar rivalry between the US and the Soviet Union – only the snooping now isn't just by a few countries.

"I personally believe we're in the middle of a kind of cyber cold war," says a senior industrial control systems security expert at INL. "Over the past year our team has visited 30 to 40 companies in critical infrastructure industries – looking for threats on their [networks and industrial-control] systems – to see the level of penetration. In every case, teams of professionals were already there, embedded on every system."

If only part of this infiltration turned out to be corporate espionage, that would be bad enough. But there's a more insidious threat lurking underneath. In his book "Cyber War," Richard Clarke, former counterterrorism chief with the National Security Council, writes that foreign nations are "preparing the battlefield" in key US industries and military networks, in part by creating "trapdoors" in electronic industrial-control systems.

These trapdoors, in the form of nearly invisible software "rootkits," are designed to give the attacker access and control over industries' computer networks, which could later be used to disrupt or destroy operations – for instance, of the US power grid. "These hackers are invading the grid's control systems right now where it's easiest, getting themselves in position where they could control things if they wanted to," says the senior cybersecurity expert. "But they're not controlling them yet."

Michael Assante, a former Navy cyberwarfare specialist and INL industrial-security expert, sees calculated hacking taking place as well. "I agree we have a lot of cyberespionage going on and a lot of preparation of the battlefield," he says in an interview at his home on a butte overlooking Idaho's Snake River Valley. "There's no question the grid is vulnerable."

The Genie Is Out Of The Hard Drive

Despite their dangers, cyberweapons hold clear appeal to the US and other nations. For one thing, they don't involve shooting people or inflicting casualties in a conventional sense. If fewer people die from bombs and bullets as a result of surreptitious software programs, nations may be more inclined to use them to try to deal with intractable problems. Cyberweapons may also be far cheaper than many conventional weapons.

No doubt these are among the reasons President Obama has accelerated the development of US cybersecurity efforts, building on programs begun late in the tenure of President George W. Bush. In 2009, when announcing the new position of cybersecurity coordinator, Mr. Obama called digital infrastructure a "strategic national asset." Then, last spring, the Pentagon unveiled its joint US Cyber Command to accelerate and consolidate its digital warfare capabilities – including the ability to strike preemptively. Cyberspace was added to sea, air, land, and space as the fifth domain in which the US seeks "dominance."

"Given the dominance of offense in cyberspace, US defenses need to be dynamic," wrote Mr. Lynn in Foreign Affairs magazine. "Milliseconds can make a difference, so the US military must respond to attacks as they happen or even before they arrive."

Yet the digital war buildup could have far-reaching – and unexpected – consequences. Cyberweapons are hardly clinical or benign. They can infect systems globally in minutes that were not the intended target. Experts say Stuxnet, a self-propagating "worm," corrupted more than 100,000 Windows-based computers worldwide. Its damage could have been far more widespread if the digital warhead had been written to activate on any industrial-control system it found instead of just the one it targeted in Iran.

Because strikes and counterstrikes can happen in seconds, conflicts could quickly escalate outside the world of computers. What, for instance, would the US do if an adversary knocked out a power plant – would it retaliate with digital soldiers or real ones? NATO and other organizations are already weighing whether to respond militarily against nations that launch or host cyberattacks against member states.

"The US cybersecurity strategy since 2003 has stated that we're not just going to respond to cyberattacks with cyber," says Greg Rattray, a former director of cybersecurity for the National Security Council. "If somebody cripples the US electric grid, a nuclear power plant, or starts to kill people with cyberattacks, we have reserved the right to retaliate by the means we deem appropriate." Yet figuring out whom to retaliate against is far more complicated in a cyberwar than a conventional war. It's not just a matter of seeing who dropped the bombs. The Internet and the foggy world of cyberspace provide ample opportunity for anonymity.

The US and other countries are working on technical systems that would allow them to reverse-engineer attacks, detecting identifying elements among tiny packets of information that bounce among servers worldwide.

Yet even if cybersleuths can trace the source of a strike to an individual computer, it might be located in the US. Foreign governments could send elite hackers into other countries to infiltrate networks, making it harder to follow the electronic trail.

"Access is the key thing," says Dr. Brenner, the former counterintelligence chief. "If we ever get to real hostilities, all these attacks are going to be launched from within the US...."

All this makes it difficult to apply conventional doctrines of war, such as deterrence and first-strike capability, to the new era of cyberconflict. Does the US retaliate if it's unsure of who the enemy is? Can there be deterrence if retaliation is uncertain? There are more mundane questions, too: When does aggressive espionage cross a threshold and constitute an "attack"?

"We live in a glass house so we better be careful about throwing rocks," says Hathaway of America's presumed prowess in offensive cyberwar and espionage tactics. "We don't have the resilience built into our infrastructure today to enter into such an escalated environment."

In the face of such ambiguity, many experts say the US needs an overarching policy that governs the use of cyberweapons.

On the plus side, multiple cyberattack technologies "greatly expand the range of options available to US policy makers as well as the policy makers of other nations...," the National Academy of Sciences concluded in a landmark 2009 study. On the other hand, "today's policy and legal framework for guiding and regulating the US use of cyberattack is ill-formed, undeveloped, and highly uncertain."

The E-maginot Line

The NCCIC staffers toiling away in their war room in Arlington do face a daunting task. The powerful Einstein II system sifts millions of attacks raining down on federal computer networks each day. The unit sends out alerts and may intervene to stop a penetration.

But can it and other federal "watch centres" really protect the country from a major cyberassault? Perhaps — if they are actually watching. The fact is, some 85 percent of the computer networks of critical US industries — water systems, stock markets, the US power grid — lie in the hands of private industry and are not monitored directly by federal agencies, McGurk acknowledges. NCCIC's mission is to safeguard government first, then private industry, if it can figure out what's happening. For the power grid, for instance, NCCIC relies on the North American Electric Reliability Corporation and individual utilities to relay information about security breaches.

Even the US military, which operates at least two large watch centres, has "no situational awareness [in cyberspace] — it's very limited," Gen. Keith Alexander, who heads the Pentagon's new US Cyber Command, admitted at a conference last June.

Still, for all the nation's vulnerabilities, people may not want to panic about the digital arms race just yet.

"Some of the greatest minds of our times were able to bottle up nuclear weapons and keep them in their silos with diplomacy," says Mr. Assante. "I think, I hope, something like that will happen with cyber. We can learn to manage the risk ... not bury our heads in the sand."

9

Economic Impact of Arms Transfers in Developing Countries

The countries which were selected for the case studies were based upon achieving as wide a sample group as possible in order to understand the impact of arms transfers upon socio-economic factors. In selecting the countries for case studies the following was taken into consideration: (1) region, (2) conflict status, (3) level of arms transfers, (4) and available data. Finally, each nation was further analyzed in order to provide a qualitative analysis to complement the quantitative data.

Colombia

Although Colombia is in the midst of a civil war, it maintains a middle level HDI, the highest out of the sample group, a close second in life expectancy and adult literacy, and the highest GDP per capita. Baring these figures in mind, out of the sample group, Colombia also spent the second least on arms imports, and the lowest per capita and percent of its GDP. The connection between low arms imports and a high HDI in relation to the sample group is visible through Colombia's statistics. Colombia had a low arms import number, the second lowest out of the entire sample grouping, and the highest HDI. However, Colombia ranked the highest in the world in kidnapping, crime per capita, and second for firearms murders. Colombia also ranked 70th in the world for health expenditures. Colombia held the 14th highest amount of the world's poor with 0.76%. Based upon these statistics, though some socio-economic factors are very weak, it appears that Colombia has balanced its military and socio-economic interests, at least more so than other nations in this study.

Egypt

Egypt is a nation which is highly militarized, ranking 11th in arms imports yet 111th in its HDI. This is quite an astounding contrast between its prioritization of arms imports over social programmes. The numbers show that Egypt invests heavily into its arms imports, but its adult literacy remains relatively low, though its life expectancy is at a moderate level for the sample group (5th). Egypt had a high level of arms imports, with a very low level of HDI. This relationship demonstrates an explicit link between high expenses on arms results in a lower standard of living. Egypt appears to have the second highest conviction rate in the world, and the fifth highest percentage income inequality for the poorest 10%. Egypt also ranked 111th in world on health expenditures. Egypt held the 33rd greatest number of poor people in the world with 0.18%. It is obvious from these statistics that Egypt's socio-economic problems are being placed behind its military interests, due to the fact that their arms imports numbers were far higher.

Eritrea

One of the strongest demonstrations of the link between arms imports and socio-economic factors comes from Eritrea. Eritrea was found to be spending the highest amount of its GDP per capita on arms imports, than any other nation. Continuous tension with Ethiopia may play a large role in this militarization. The two nations fought a war between 1998 to 2001 leading to an unstable conclusion with the 2000 Algiers Agreement. The 2000 Algiers Agreement led to a Boundary Commission ruling in favour of Eritrea, which Ethiopia rejected. This conflict has resulted in aggravation of already large socio-economic problems in both nations. Eritrea comparatively ranked in the bottom tier of the HDI rankings, with an extremely low life expectancy rate, and its adult literacy rate not being reported. Furthermore Eritrea is considered a high risk area for bacterial diarrhea, hepatitis A, malaria, and typhoid fever. It can easily be inferred from the data that socio-economic conditions are being sacrificed for the sake of Eritrea's arms imports. The conflict with Ethiopia has resulted in the heavy militarization of Eritrea. It should be noted that Eritrea spends 17.70% of it's GDP on military expenses, the highest in the world. It also had the 33rd highest HIV/AIDS rate in the world. Furthermore the BBC reports that the Eritrean government has been unable to provide food as two thirds of the population receives foreign food aid. Also, a large part of the labour force in Eritrea is composed of the army. Eritrea also remains 157th place for health expenditures.

India

India is another nation that is highly militarized, in a perpetual state of armed conflict with its neighbor Pakistan. India's HDI is extremely low, yet it is ranked first in the world in terms of arms imports. The visible prioritization of arms over social programmes is evident since its HDI rank is a dismal 126 in contrast to its first place finish in arms transfers. Both India's adult literacy and life expectancy were starkly lower than other nations.

A direct correlation can be drawn from India's socio-economic conditions and its arms imports. Perhaps a reason for this discrepancy is its state of insecurity due to long standing armed inter-state conflict and arms race with neighbouring Pakistan. India ranked 75 out of 101 countries with its average adult having 5.1 years of education. India also ranks 126 in health expenditures in the world. India appears to be another high risk nation for bacterial diarrhea, hepatitis A and E, typhoid fever, dengue fever, malaria, Japanese encephalitis, and rabies. India also holds the title of having 41.01% of the world's poor, the highest in the world. India's prioritization of arms over socio-economics is very visible.

Iran

Iran has been in a process of nuclearization, declaredly for civilian use, though contested by other nations. Notwithstanding the heavy toll the population has paid for sanctions placed upon

Iran for its pursuit of nuclear technology outside the IAEA framework, Iran ranks seventh in the world for arms imports with an astounding $1.5 billion, though that number was third last in the sample group in terms of its percentage of GDP. Though Iran held the highest GDP per capita, it ranked below Colombia and Venezuela on socio-economic factors, and a moderately low adult literacy. This analysis demonstrates that it is due to its allocation of funds that it is not achieving as high socio-economic conditions as other nations who have a lower GDP per capita (Colombia, Venezuela). Iran is the seventh leading arms importer in the world, though maintains a fairly moderate HDI rank. This discrepancy could be explained by Iran's large oil exports, the country ranks third in oil production and reserves. The large oil industry in Iran allows the government to allocate large funds towards arms imports, but also provide a significant amount towards social programming. An example of this is that it ranks third in the world for the immunization of newborns for hepatitis B. Iran ranked 96th in the world for health expenditures.

Namibia

Namibia provided for a very interesting case. Though its arms imports were not relatively high compared to other nations, 45th overall, a more nuanced analysis demonstrated a very interesting discovery. Namibia placed ninth overall for the percentage of its GDP spent upon arms imports, as well as for its per capita expenditures on arms imports. Furthermore Namibia placed 125 in its HDI ranking, the lowest out of the sample group for life expectancy. An interesting note about Namibia was that, though its overall arms import dollars were relatively low, it ranked ninth in terms of percentage of GDP spent on arms imports. This development comes from a nation which is under no immediate threat of war, and with an extremely low life expectancy. Even with this lack of emphasis on socio-economic programming, funds allocated towards arms imports were extremely high. Namibia also ranked 125th in the world in health expenditures. Namibia also has the sixth highest HIV/AIDS rate in the world at 21.30%, in addition to the 50th most poor people in the world with 0.06%, even with its small country size of just over two million.

Pakistan

In a constant arms race with India, Pakistan holds sixth place in terms of arms imports, yet a ranking of 134 for HDI. In terms of per capita and GDP percentage spent on arms imports, the number is moderately high. Pakistan's average adult had 3.9 years of schooling, 75th out of 101 countries. Pakistan also ranks 134th in the world for health expenditures. Pakistan is considered a high risk for several diseases including bacterial diarrhea, hepatitis A and E, typhoid fever, dengue fever, malaria, and cutaneous leishmaniasis. Pakistan is the country with the fourth largest percentage of the world's poor with 3.86%. The high level of arms imports, coupled with low HDI and high disease risk demonstrates that Pakistan's investment into arms imports comes at high socio-economic costs.

Sudan

Sudan is another nation which has invested heavily into arms imports. It should be noted that the arms import numbers are quite high considering an illicit flow of arms continues into Sudan, even despite a UN arms embargo. Even with this embargo, Sudan sits as the 10th leading arms importer, and 10th for expenditures on arms imports as percentage of its GDP. Sudan's socio-economic factors are also low, ranking second last out of the sample group for HDI, and very low in adult literacy and life expectancy.

It truly appears that arms expenditures are being prioritized over social programmes, leading to a negative impact upon socio-economic factors. Sudan is very visible in the media due to its intra-state conflicts, most notably the crisis in Darfur.

The situation in Darfur has been called a "humanitarian crisis". Even with an arms embargo in place, Sudan has managed to get a large amount of arms through its borders, as it is the 10th largest arms importer in the world. Sudan also has the 44th highest unemployment rate out of 198 countries. More striking was the fact that the average adult in Sudan had just two years of school, 96th out of 101 countries. And Sudan is ranked 141st in ranking for health expenditures. The lack of focus on socio-economic issues in favour of arms imports has had a huge negative impact upon the socio-economic factors in the nation.

Vietnam

Vietnam appeared to be at the high middle range of sample group for arms imports (27) HDI rank (109), and life expectancy. Surprisingly its adult literacy rate was very high given that the other nations with higher HDI's had lower adult literacy rates. Vietnam surprisingly invested a significant amount into arms import. Interestingly it had a high adult literacy rate.

Vietnam ranked a surprisingly high 20th in per capita GDP expenditures on arms imports, and 27th overall. This is coupled with the fact that Vietnam ranks 109th in the world in health expenditures. This coming with the fact that it is a high risk for bacterial diarrhea, hepatitis A, typhoid fever, dengue fever, malaria, Japanese encephalitis, plague, rabies, and leptospirosis. It appears that avian influenza is also becoming a risk in Vietnam. Once again the focus of Vietnam on arms import appears to have de-prioritized socio-economic issues, especially health.

Venezuela

Hugo Chavez's Venezuela is in a rapid process of militarization as well. Though it ranks the lowest out of the sample group in terms of arms imports, another study says that it secured $1.9 billion in arms transfer agreements in 2005 alone (fifth in the world). Venezuela had the second lowest arms imports, along with the second highest HDI rank out of the sample group. Out of the non-conflict ridden nations, Venezuela fared the best, with the highest life expectancy and adult literacy. This should demonstrate a correlation between arms import numbers and socio-economic factors. Venezuela ranked 72nd in the world in health expenditures, and 69th in arms imports. This, similar to Colombia, is a demonstration of the capability to balance arms interests with socio-economic concerns, at least within the sample group. Venezuela came in 22nd largest amount of the world's poor with 0.51%. Though Venezuela fared better than all but Colombia on HDI factors, it was nevertheless below medians for the world.

IMPACT OF SMALL ARMS PROLIFERATION

The persistence and the complication of wars in Africa are

partially due to small arms proliferation. The consequences of small arms on African people due to international conflicts within Africa, rebel group activities, mercenary groups, and armed gang activities have yet to be fully measured. The International Action Network on Small Arms, Saferworld, and Oxfam International put it in perspective when they reported that armed conflict cost Africa $18 billion each year and about US$300 billion between 1990-2005. During this period, 23 African nations experienced war: Algeria, Angola, Burundi, Central Africa Republic, Chad, Democratic Republic of Congo (DRC), Republic of Congo, Cote d'Ivoire, Djibouti, Eritrea, Ethiopia, Ghana, Guinea, Guinea-Bissau, Liberia, Niger, Nigeria, Rwanda, Senegal, Sierra Leone, South Africa, Sudan, and Uganda.

Although proliferation of small arms generates a lot of money for those who manufacture and trade them, African people pay a heavy price due to a lack of accountability or international regulations to address the abuses those products cause. According to the Global Facilitation Network Security Sector Reform, nations such as France, Russia, China, UK and USA – the five permanent members of the UN Security Council – together account for 88 percent of the world's conventional arms exports. These exports contribute regularly to gross abuses of human rights in Africa and elsewhere. Some of these are legal arms sales to irresponsible governments who use them to oppress the people. Other supplies are made available to rebel groups by some countries in an effort to overthrow dictatorial regimes which in many cases become worse or as bad as the previous regime. The United States and France, for example, assisted Chadian President Idriss Deby in removing his predecessor, Hissene Habre, from power. Deby then became another dictator who still has not stabilized his country.

Is violence the only tool we have to bring about change? Whoever said "who wants peace, prepares for war" was wrong in this case. Violence is not the answer to the root causes and triggers of instability in Africa. Nonviolence still stands in the forefront as a means of bringing about true peace. While the root causes of violence in Africa vary, it is unquestionable that small arms are a major challenge to security. The United Nations Security Council's report on small arms, S/2008/258, expresses it well by saying that "[T]he dividing lines between underdevelopment, instability, fragility, crisis, conflict and war are increasingly blurred; the small arms issue is therefore intertwined with the security, development, and human rights preconditions for sustainable peace. Present-day conflict prevention, conflict resolution, and peacebuilding require multidimensional interventions."

In fact, more than ever before, strong measures and appropriate attention must be given to this issue. The United Nation's General Assembly resolution (A/C.1/63/L.39*) on the arms trade treaty aims to establish common international standards for the import, export and transfer of conventional arms. It states that the absence of these standards is "one of the contributory factors to conflict, the displacement of people, crime and terrorism, thereby undermining peace, reconciliation, safety, security, stability and sustainable social and economic development." In addition to finding a solution to the proliferation of small arms, manufacturers and traders of small weapons should bear partial responsibility for the abuses and crimes that are committed as a consequence of use of these arms. Among nations that are culpable, let us single out the United States, as Africa Faith and Justice Network's mission is to advocate for just and fair U.S.-Africa relations. The same way U.S military policies in Africa have promoted dictatorship rather than democracy, the presence of American made weapons on the African continent has hurt the African people more than it has helped. The U.S. is aware that some of their legally transferred weapons contribute to feeding the illegal arms market. It was U.S. made weapons that supported the rebel groups RENAMO in Mozambique, UNITA in Angola, RPF in Rwanda and CNDP in the Democratic Republic of the Congo (DRC). In the UN experts' report on the crisis in the DRC, S/2008/773, paragraph 28 connects the origin of military uniforms shipment destined to the rebel group CNDP from the United States in these terms: "In October 2008, Rwandan security services seized a shipment of uniforms destined for CNDP at Kanombe airport in Kigali. ... The shipment reportedly originated in Boston, Massachusetts, United States." Although this shipment contained uniquely military uniforms, it does not rule out the possibility that weapons were shipped from the U.S destined to CNDP.

Political instability in Africa continues to create more demand for small arms. Manufacturers of weapons know best the link between politics and weapons markets and are therefore often linked to these political instabilities to take advantage of the weapons business it creates.

For example, former Congresswoman Ms. Cynthia McKinney of Georgia, in her opening remarks before the Subcommittee on International Operations and Human Rights of the Committee on International Relations of the US House of Representatives on May 17th, 2001, stated that " [W]hat we do know is that the U.S. Special Forces and U.S funded private military companies have been arming and training Rwandan and Ugandan troops to deadly effect. The U.S. taxpayer should be directly assisting the military efforts of Rwanda and Uganda, the aggressors in this tragic conflict and who are confirmed by Amnesty International and Human Rights Watch as the authors of terrible atrocities against Congolese civilians. Our efforts in Africa have amounted to nothing more than bankrolling belligerent and mass murders." War creates a demand for weapons. This is why manufacturers and traders are opposed to international standards for small arms trade.

In addition to the illegal arms sales network, there is a link between the legal and the illegal trade that consists of illegally selling legally obtained arms. This is the core of the problem of small arms proliferation which violators are not interested in solving. As of September 26, 2008, the United States of America, France, Russia, and permanent members of the UN Security Council had not signed the protocol against the illicit Manufacturing of and Trafficking in Firearms, Their Parts and Components and Ammunition, a supplement to the United Nations convention against Transnational Organized Crimes. Africa Faith and Justice Network, in its advocacy effort to the US government for peace and stability in Africa, calls upon President Obama's administration to take a leadership role on this long overdue issue. We recommend that the U.S. signs the international Arms Trade Treaty by the United Nations, passes legislation to hold violators accountable, and reforms its arms production and export policy. Such legislation should include ways to track down U.S. weapons wherever they are used to prevent illegal arms trade from the U.S. to Africa and elsewhere.

THE SOCIAL AND ECONOMIC IMPACT OF SMALL ARMS IN WARRING NATIONS

Small arms trade plays a prominent role in the economies of nations at war, and particularly in intrastate conflicts. The availability of small arms makes war possible, and their continuing availability fuels the protraction of war. War economies require continuing violence for sustenance. In many protracted civil wars, the availability of weapons exceeds that of soldiers, leading to the mushrooming prevalence of child-soldier "recruitment" by kidnapping (Sudan, Uganda, Sierra Leone, Sri Lanka, and elsewhere).

Thus, the small arms market helps to drive the diverse disabling economic and social effects of war. Wars fed by small arms supply divert economic investment and energy from normal productivity, and suck up resources otherwise available for domestic services and infrastructure (education, health care, social welfare, and productivity-related infrastructure like roads, energy provision, and water supply). "War interrupts, and indeed reverses, economic development." War destroys physical and social capital, and erodes what Sen calls the "capacities" and "entitlements" of people's lives.

Small arms warfare is intimately connected to poverty and arrested economic development in conflict-affected areas. Agriculture suffers both from the loss of opportunity to work in fields and from the weapons themselves, especially land mines. Looting and the ruination of croplands are common tactics. Commerce suffers as well; necessary safety, reliable transportation, and open communication become extremely difficult in areas infused with small arms. Industry and international trade suffer for all these reasons, plus the increased risks of loss to combatants. The stability of government and policy, required for the smooth function of economies, suffers in the presence of active violence. When war concludes, conflict-damaged societies must then face the economic burdens of both weapons disarmament and disposal and the education and employment of habituated combatants. The ready availability of small arms enables conflict economies of robbery and looting, extortion systems, and kidnapping. Lives lost to small arms violence are a major economic loss to societies torn by conflict, with long-reaching adverse effects on the economic function of families and communities. Small arms violence results in major dislocations of refugees and internally-displaced persons, who are rendered both severely needy and unable to be productive. And the supply of small arms stimulates drug-running and other smuggling economies. Finally, when active warfare abates, the presence of abundant small arms and abundant ex-soldiers fosters the escalation of crime rates and the development of organized crime that has been a virtually constant sequel to recent wars.

Even the ability of outside humanitarian donors to ease the suffering of people in conflict-infected regions risks being hijacked for economic gain by warring groups empowered by small arms. In many situations, armed independent gangs or unofficial militias derive significant funding from regular looting or "taxation" of humanitarian aid providers.

The Case of Sudan

The individual case of the complex, protracted intrastate war in Sudan clearly exemplifies the terrible hazards of the global small arms market. In Sudan, the genocidal campaign of the Sudanese (Muslim) government against native Muslims living in the newly-discovered oil field lands of Darfur has been actively pursued through government-assisted militias, primarily the Janjawid. The Janjawid are able to carry out their program of mass terror, murder and intentional starvation by virtue of their wealth of small arms provisions — Kalashnikov AK47 assault rifles, rocket-propelled grenades, and jeep-mounted machine guns — despite the UN adoption in 2001 of Article 16 of the UN International Law Commission's Articles on Responsibility of States for Internationally Wrongful Acts. The agreement is binding on *all* states, and forbids any assistance of another state in the commission of "any internationally wrongful act." The Janjawid's atrocities clearly surpass international definition as "Internationally Wrongful Acts," and the Sudan government's claims to be uninvolved and opposed to the arbitrary and indiscriminate killing, "disappearances," systemic rapes, and torture fly in the face of heavily documented evidence of the government's supply of and government troop participation in the atrocities. In 1994, the European Union joined in an arms embargo against all non-governmental entities in Sudan in order to "promote lasting peace and reconciliation within Sudan," but the world weapons industry has continued to sell arms to the Sudanese government without restriction. Given the clear evidence of the Sudan government's programmatic support of and participation in the Darfur genocide and crimes against humanity, any sale of arms to Sudan violates Article 16 of the UN International Law Commission. Every nation fully understands this, yet the world community of weapons exporters have continued to feed small arms into Sudan, fueling the Darfur genocide. In March, 2004, The UN Security Council voted 13-0-2 to demand that Sudan disarm its paramilitary militias, but issued its demand without teeth. Further, small arms shipments to other East African countries from the USA and Germany, among others, is certain to bolster Sudan's stockpile of weapons. It is estimated that 85% of the personal assault weapons in Africa originate in the five countries of the UN Security Council: the USA, the UK, Russia, China, and France.

Finally, only two weeks ago, the UN Security Council approved a total weapons embargo, targeted economic sanctions against atrocity perpetrators, a 10,000-person peacekeeping force, and an International Criminal Court investigation and prosecution of criminals against humanity in Sudan. Principal exporters of small arms to Sudan appear to be Iran, China, France, Saudi Arabia, Switzerland, and the UK (this tally excludes further volumes of arms sales in terms of fighter jets, helicopters, etc.). The fact that UN Security Council nations have stakes in the illegal arms supply of the Janjawid/Sudanese government genocide in Darfur (and China's strong oil-supply relationship with the Sudanese government) helps explain the Security Council's failure to act to stop the war. In November 2004, Amnesty International revealed densely documented details of the uncontrolled arms exports that have fueled massive human rights abuses in Sudan, including the killing, rape, torture and displacement of more than a million civilians since the Darfur conflict escalated in February 2003 after the discovery of Darfur oil deposits.

The inability (or unwillingness) of the Swiss, paragons of organization, to regulate their own export of weapons demonstrates the degree to which the weapons market is out of control. After being told by the Geneva-based Graduate Institute of International Studies that Swiss small arms exports to Sudan totaled more than $4 million in 2002, the Swiss Finance Ministry promised that Switzerland would review its weapons exports. The Swiss government records reveal less than *$4,000* worth of handgun exports to Sudan, to be used "for use as personal protection or sporting purposes." "Such trade would not have been approved by us," stated Ottmar Wyss, responsible for export control. "Either there is illegal export trade going on, or the numbers are wrong." Reason and experience suggest that the wrong numbers are those of Mr. Wyss.

The Sudanese government estimates that "two to three million" landmines cover 32 % of the country; the original exporters of the landmines were Russia, China, the UK, Iraq, Iran, the USA, and a list of others.

While Sudan's population is impoverished and has been victimized by its two decades of civil war, and although Sudan is one of the 38 "Heavily Indebted Poor Countries" eligible for favourable borrowing terms, Sudan is also sitting on major oil reserves — a resource pool that could possibly deliver economic stability and domestic freedoms to the people of Sudan. Instead, oil production is bankrolling the government's pursuit of genocide against its own people, through the purchase of small arms and other weapons, a political economic decision founded on abuse of one part of its population for the benefit of a relative few. The main foreign direct investors in Sudan are companies from China, Malaysia, and India.

GIVING STATES IN AFRICA A RUN FOR THEIR MONEY: ECONOMIC IMPACT OF ILLICIT TRADE

Armed conflicts facilitated by illicit trade of small arms not only lead to direct costs such as medical costs, military expenditure, the destruction of infrastructure, and the care for displaced people – which divert money from more productive uses – but has far more impinging consequences. The indirect costs indicate that each nation has a huge price to pay. The economy of a nation comes to almost a standstill, especially industries like tourism which are capable of contributing heavily to a country's gross domestic product (GDP). The country suffers from inflation, debt, and reduced investment, while people suffer from unemployment, lack of public services, and trauma. To top it all, the loss of life is one that cannot be priced nor neglected. The millions who lose their lives at the behest of such conflicts supported by illicit arms only worsen the situation.

The absence of a global regulatory framework resulted in at least US$ 2.2 billion worth of arms and ammunition being imported by countries under arms embargoes between 2000 and 2010. Africa loses around US$ 18 billion per year due to wars, civil wars and insurgencies. On average, armed conflict shrinks an African nation's economy by 15%. A civil war in one country reduces the growth rate of neighbouring countries by around 0.9%; thus the combined growth loss to neighbours can exceed the loss to the country itself. Effects become more marked as the conflict intensity increases.

Between 1990 and 2007, around US$ 300 billion have been lost by Algeria, Angola, Burundi, Central African Republic, Chad, Democratic Republic of the Congo (DRC), Republic of Congo, Côte d'Ivoire, Djibouti, Eritrea, Ethiopia, Ghana, Guinea, Guinea-Bissau, Liberia, Niger, Nigeria, Rwanda, Senegal, Sierra Leone, South Africa, Sudan and Uganda combined as a result of armed conflict. This was nearly the same as the total amount of Official Development Assistance that the continent received during this time. The World Bank estimates that the economic cost of lost production due to conflict ranges from 2% to 3% of GDP.

The Small Arms Survey estimates that small arms have resulted in hundreds of thousands of deaths and millions of injuries each year. They are further responsible for 60% to 90% of total conflict deaths. In the few African countries where reliable data is available, small arms are a leading cause of unnatural deaths. For example, up until the late 2000s, small arms were the principal cause of unnatural deaths (close to 30% of the total), more than road accident fatalities, in South Africa.

In a study conducted by Oxfam and IANSA, researchers Stewart and Fitzgerald studied nine African conflicts from 1970 to 1995; the average loss as percentage of GDP was 10.5% per annum. This was expected to be an under-estimate due to lack of data for four countries.

Some countries in Africa have already made significant efforts to prevent irresponsible transfers of weapons. In particular, two instruments have created new regional standards for arms control in a whole range of areas, including robust controls on international arms transfers. Firstly, the 2004 *Nairobi Protocol for the Prevention, Control and Reduction of Small Arms and Light Weapons* applies to countries in the Great Lakes region and the Horn of Africa. Under its aegis, at least 6 out of 11 African member states reviewed their standards and procedures for the management and security of stockpiles between 2001 and 2005. The Nairobi Protocol has led to the development of best practice guidelines on stockpile management. Secondly, in 2006, the *Economic Community of West African States (ECOWAS) Convention on Small Arms and Light Weapons, their Ammunition, and other Related Materials* was yet another initiative that aimed at establishing principles and norms on small arms and light weapons. It aims at prohibiting the possession, use, and sale of light weapons by civilians; encouraging licensing systems including the following criteria: minimum age; no criminal record or subject of a morality investigation; proof of a legitimate reason to possess, carry, or use; proof of safety training and competency training; proof of safe storage and separate storage of ammunition. It also requires a limit on the number of weapons a licence may cover; a waiting period of at least 21 days; expiration dates on licences and periodic reviews; seizure laws and revocation of licences for contraventions of possession laws; and adequate sanctions and penalties for illicit possession and use.

Though these acts and norms were implemented, their validity and impact remained questionable for quite some time. It soon became clear that national or even regional regulations are insufficient to prevent arms from reaching the hands of abusers. What was indeed required was international regulations.

Hence, in December 2006, 153 countries agreed to start developing an Arms Trade Treaty (ATT). A United Nations Group of Governmental Experts (GCE) began their work in January 2008 and presented their recommendations to the General Assembly in October 2008. The ATT is a potential multilateral treaty that would regulate the international trade in conventional weapons. The treaty was negotiated at a global conference under the auspices of the United Nations from 2–27 July 2012 in New York, but no consensus has been reached yet.

Since 1991, at least eight regional agreements covering more than 110 countries have touched on elements of civilian possession – typically in the context of armed violence prevention or efforts to address illicit trafficking and manufacturing. These agreements are either intended to be incorporated into participating states' national law, to guide the adoption of legislation meeting minimum requirements, or to set broad standards and norms. Four of the eight agreements are legally binding which are the*European Weapons Directive*, the *Firearms Protocol of the Southern African Development Community,*the Nairobi Protocol, and the Convention of the Economic Community of West African States.

African governments are also seeking changes at national level. Between 2001 and 2005, at least 10 African countries revised their laws and procedures on export controls; nine did so in relation to import controls and five on transit controls.

With difficulty in creating and establishing laws as well as measuring the efficacy of these laws, it is evident that the conventions, treaties and agreements, whether statutory or otherwise, have not borne fruit so far, however, with the increased involvement of many African nations; a lot of change can be expected in the near future.

Conclusion

Though efforts have been made at regional, national and international levels, there is however still a lot of room for improvement. Policy makers over the years have suggested various steps which if implemented in a phased manner could lead to a more regulated small arms market. Apart from strengthening our existing laws and regulations, it has now also become imperative to consider regulating the activities of small arms brokers, improving effectiveness of transfer controls, destroying surplus arms, implementing a common system for marking and tracing weapons, etc.

Illicit trade of small arms is a problem that has existed for a long time but has been brought to light only in the past decade. It is of utmost importance to acknowledge the gravity of the current situation and come up with solutions with the help of political will and the commitment of states.

Africa has been tagged as the abode for failed nations for far too long, but as a continent it shows potential to be the land of hope and promise. It still has to rid itself of social and economic evils such as illicit trade of small arms, and although Africa has a long way to go, it has already begun walking the talk and there remains hope that as long as nations and organisations collaborate and choose to contribute for each other's betterment, there lies a bright future for Africa.

Bibliography

Alan S. *War, Economy and Society, 1939-1945.* Berkeley: University of California Press, 1977.

Allison, Graham: *Nuclear Terrorism: The Ultimate Preventable Catastrophe,* New York: Times Books, 2004.

Backman, Jules. *War and Defense Economics.* New York: Rinehart, 1952.

Bhatia, Shyam: *India's Nuclear Bomb,* Ghaziabad: Vikas Publishing House, 1979.

Greider, William. *Fortress America: The American Military and the Consequences of Peace.* New York, 1998.

Gurr, T.: *Minorities at Risk: A Global View of Ethno-political Conflicts,* United States Institute of Peace Press, Washington D.C, 1993.

Harkavy, Robert E. *The Arms Trade and International Systems.* Cambridge, Mass., 1975.

Harold G. *U.S. Economy in World War II.* New York: Columbia University Press, 1985.

Hasan-Askari Rizvi: *Nuclear Terrorism and South Asia,* Albuquerque, NM: Sandia National Laboratories, February 2003.

James L. *The Economic Impact of the Cold War: Sources and Readings.* New York, 1970.

Krause, Keith. *Arms and the State: Patterns of Military Production and Trade.* Cambridge, U.K., 1992.

Laurance, Edward J. *The International Arms Trade.* New York, 1992.

Nininger, Robert D. *Minerals for Atomic Energy.* New York: D. Van Nostrand Company, Inc., 1954.

Pierre, Andrew J. *The Global Politics of Arms Sales.* Princeton, N.J., 1982.

Rhodes, Richard, *The Making of the Atomic Bomb,* New York: Simon and Schuster, 1988.

Robert E. Harkavy: *Arms Transfers in the Modern World.* New York, 1979.

Robert H. *The Navy and Industrial Mobilization in World War II.* Princeton, N.J., 1951.

Schroeer, Dietrich, *Science, Technology, and the Nuclear Arms Race*, Ontario: John Wiley & Sons, 1984.

Sivard, R L.: *World Military and Social Expenditures,* World Priorities, Washington D.C, 1993.

Smith, C.: *The Diffusion of Small Arms and Light Weapons in Pakistan and Northern India,* Centre for Defence Studies, Brassey's, London, 1993.

Thayer, George. *The War Business.* New York, 1969.

Van de Goor, L.L.P.: *Conflict and Development: The Causes of Conflict in Developing Countries,* The Netherlands Institute of International Relations, The Hague, 1994.

Zwoll, Wayne van. *America's Great Gunmakers.* South Hackensack, N.J., 1992.

Index

❑❑❑